DOLCE ITALIANO

DESSERTS FROM THE BABBO KITCHEN

DOLCE ITALIANO

DESSERTS FROM THE BABBO KITCHEN

by Gina DePalma

FOREWORD BY MARIO BATALI

PHOTOGRAPHS BY GENTL & HYERS/EDGE

W. W. Norton & Company

NEW YORK LONDON

For information about permission to reproduce selections
from this book, write to Permissions,
W. W. Norton & Company, Inc.,
500 Fifth Avenue, New York, NY 10110

For information about special discounts for bulk purchases,
please contact W. W. Norton Special Sales at
specialsales@wwnorton.com or 800-233-4830

Manufacturing by Courier Westford
Book design by Chalkley Calderwood
Production manager: Julia Druskin

Library of Congress Cataloging-in-Publication Data

DePalma, Gina.
Dolce italiano : desserts from the Babbo kitchen / by Gina DePalma.
p. cm.
Includes index.
ISBN 978-0-393-06100-0 (hardcover)
1. Cookery, Italian. I. Title.
TX723.G6294 2004
641.8'60945—dc22

2007027546

W. W. Norton & Company, Inc.
500 Fifth Avenue, New York, N.Y. 10110
www.wwnorton.com

W. W. Norton & Company Ltd.
Castle House, 75/76 Wells Street, W1T 3QT

1 2 3 4 5 6 7 8 9 0

For my mother, Evelyn,
and in loving memory of my father, Nunzio,
WITH ADMIRATION, THANKS, AND ALL MY LOVE

CONTENTS

ACKNOWLEDGMENTS

There have been many times in the course of the past two years when the task of writing this book seemed close to impossible, but none more so than this attempt at expressing my gratitude to the seemingly countless number of people who have had a hand in helping me to conceive and complete *Dolce Italiano*.

Sometime back in 2004, I can't remember exactly when, I huddled under an awning in the pouring rain with Mario Batali. My mood matched the bleak weather as I confessed to him that I felt restless; I didn't know what the next step in my career and life should be. He didn't even pause a second before he smiled and told me that I was going to write a book. I thought he was nuts. As usual, his confidence and genuine, infectious enthusiasm soon had me considering that I could actually do just that, or at least give it a try. From that day forward, Mario's faith in this project has been unshakable, especially on the days when I didn't believe in myself very much. For that, and so many other gifts, I can never express enough thanks. Joseph Bastianich graces me every day with his generosity, his knowledge, his honesty and an unfailing faith in my abilities. Together, Mario and Joe have been my employers, my mentors, and my friends. I am so lucky to be a member of their restaurant family.

Not long after that rainy day, I found myself sitting across a table from Anthony Gardner, who is quite simply the best agent in the whole wide world. He has been my constant companion on this, the trippiest of trips, and I would have been utterly lost without him. My brilliant editor, Maria Guarnaschelli, has guided me, word by word, with a loving and sure hand, and this book is everything I wanted it to be and more because of her. I also offer my sincere thanks to the entire team at Norton, and the monstrous effort they put into making it perfect, especially to Sarah Rothbard, who calmed my raw nerves and always had the right answer for every question I tossed her way.

The days we spent shooting the splendid photographs for this book were among the happiest of my professional career. Being in the presence of the creative force that is Gentl & Hyers was a thrilling experience I will treasure forever. I also want to thank my good friend Susan DeMirjian, whose talents produced the beautiful map of my beloved Italia included herein.

My colleagues at Babbo, and its offspring, have nourished me both creatively and personally for nearly a decade. I send special thanks and love to my staff; each person who has stood next to me in our tiny corner of the Babbo kitchen has contributed to our collective success. I especially want to thank Salvador Hernandez, Melissa Funk, Ashley O'Neal, Cameron Wallace, Brian Levy, Mayes Lozada-Noye, Simeon Manber, Mona Meng, Esti Rothstein, Annie Sparks-Dempster, Sigrid Benedetti, Nick Anderer, Jessica Lambert, and Amanda Moniz. I also wish to thank Elisa Sarno, Frank Langello, Andy and Patty Nusser, Mark Ladner, Chris Fischer, Yoshi Yamada, Derek Rowe, Bruce Logue, Tony Liu, Memo Trevino, and John Eisenhart. Watching these great chefs do what they do has been an endless source of pure inspiration.

Colum Sheehan's contribution to this book was a dream come true for me. I am in awe of him, and his entire staff of wine professionals. Colum, David Lynch, and Luca Pasquinelli have generously shared their encyclopedic knowledge of wine with me, and tried in vain to teach me how to look cool while swirling. I will get there some day, I promise.

Wait, there's more. Thanks and love to all my brothers and sisters in the Batali/Bastianich clan, current and fomer, especially Jim Logan, John Mainieri, Kevin Galligan, Caroline McHale Marshall, John Giorno, Levi Jones, Ken Weller, Ramiro Butron, Jesus Salgado, Alex Obando, Simone Shubuck, L. R. Laggy, Thomas Foster, Adam Reiner, Morgan and Karina Pruitt, Alfredo Ruiz, Nancy Selzer, Martin Gobbee, Patrick Tarpey, Ryan Tarpey, Chris Crocetti, Jeremy Noye, Michael Montalto, David Massoni, Kamal Ahmed, Teresa Legrottaglie, and Sunah.

An extra-large measure of gratitude to Pamela Lewy and her predecessors, Sarah LaGrotteria and Laurie Woolever, for their assured application of first aid and uplifting encouragement.

Thanks to my dear friends Paul Grimes, Andrew Carmellini, Karen Page and Andrew Dornenburg, Johnny Iuzzini, Jonathan and Gabrielle Rubenstein, Lou and Sal DiPalo, Lisa Ainbinder, Rosario Procino, German and Leah Casati, Robert Weakley, Phil Rosenthal, and Monica Ahearn. They never failed to ask about this book in every conversation with me, and on the days when it wasn't going so well, it meant everything.

My best friends in the world have been so wonderfully patient with my prolonged periods of absence from their daily lives. For always being there even when I wasn't, I thank Donna Rinehart, Nicole Novakoski, Johnathan Mark Nelson, Steve Bielarkski and Ben Prayz, Nancy Contrastano, Kristin and Michael Ariola, Tim Carosi, Mike Riley, Virginia Coyne, Rosemary Merino, Jason Brown, Roxanne Fontana and Mat Trieber, David Court and Lynette Caturano.

Thanks and love to Owen McCarthy, Ben Toro, Joel Cannon, and John Melville for implanting their music directly into my heart, and to Amy, Chris, Rich, and Steve for so many years of pure, mind-blowing musical joy, and for always letting me visit them on the road.

To Diana Strinati Baur and Michael Baur, thank you for wisdom, friendship, and love. May we share many future Piemontese sunsets and glasses of wine together with Max.

Frank Dabell and Jay Weissberg, you reside in my heart each and every day. Thank you for taking me under your wings.

And finally, to my huge, loving, proudly Italian family, you have withstood my crazy life as a restaurant chef for far too many years. Uncle John, Mom, Chris, and Maria, I love you. More than anything.

FOREWORD BY MARIO BATALI

Gina DePalma is one smart cookie. When I first met her in a professional situation, she was the very first person I scheduled for an interview for the then nascent Babbo. We had met briefly years before at my first New York City restaurant, which had kind of become a place for cooks and chefs to dine, and she had early on understood the no-nonsense aesthetic and spare style of food that I valued. She came highly recommended by her entire team at Danny Meyer's Gramercy Tavern and was a little jumpy at the start of the interview, but very smart and quite poetic. As we spoke for an hour about desserts in general, her passion for the whole world of food was obvious and her birthright knowledge and love of Italian dining habits, quirks, and delightful idiosyncracies became clear; most important, her zest for life and constant quest for perfection came to life, as vibrant and excited as a character in one of her family stories.

I was immediately impressed with her résumé but even more wowed by her clarity and her literary speaking style. She was clearly up to the task of creating an entire dessert and pastry program for what I hoped would be a three-star restaurant in a city awash with good to average Italian restaurants, none of which, other than Felidia and San Domenico, had a true dessert program beyond tiramisu and hot zabaglione that I could get my head around or enjoy.

The following pages represent Gina's voyage from being a great pastry chef in a tiny kitchen (filled with everything you would not want in a pastry kitchen) to becoming a nationally significant expert and source of information on all things Italian, from chestnut honey to Zibibbo grapes, from Piedmontese cheeses to Sardinian cookie crumbs, from late-harvest Genovese olive oil to the Friulian coffee cake culture. Gina runs not only the Babbo pastry world but also the Babbo cheese world and the Babbo coffee world. Holiday specialty items are one of her many pets, and every single Italian specialty item for any level of holy day has been not only recognized but perfected in her tiny pastry kingdom. Gina is integral to the development of the constantly evolving Babbo kitchen recipe and service bible and writes every month on the Babbo website about topics far and wide, in a constant search to improve an already great restaurant.

From a nearly criminal situation, with lack of space to store products, lack of burners to cook on, tiny ovens, a room often as warm as 118 degrees, and a walk-in fridge shared with the entire savory kitchen, Gina is able miraculously to produce one tasty treat after another. It defies nature that we have *gelato*, creamy and intensely flavored, that is better than Italian *gelato*. Hot *bomboloni* come out of the 12-square-foot area at the same time as perfect *panna cotta*, and 2 six-tops worth of predesserts designed just for tasting menus all fly out of the Babbo kitchen as if on a rocket. An ongoing cookie program to provide the little bites to end a meal meets a whole new summer of love every June when the local strawberries finally come in, ideal for the annual strawberry variation.

In her mind, Gina is not perfect. She tortures herself each and every season to come up with this year's apple or quince or pineapple or cherry dessert. She is in the Union Square Greenmarket at least three days a week, early enough to keep Jean-Georges' rough-looking henchman from taking everything. She denies herself the simple pleasure of repeating items annually for the simple reason that they were superb last year. She struggles with her own perfectionism even when I beg her to leave something on the menu or bring it back. She is addicted to rock and roll, she loves the Eternal City as much as the *Grande Mela*, and she is a diehard Black Crowes fan. But Gina's real passion is sweet love and all its potential on the plate night after night at Babbo in Greenwich Village in Manhattan.

This book can be used in a thousand ways. Obviously, that cooks will peruse it for information, inspirational food porn, and the occasional dessert recipe when entertaining is the primary intention of Gina's esteemed editor and publisher. It might also serve as a nice gift for all the Italophiles you know, to remind them of the magnificence of Italian culture, both gastronomically and culturally. I will use this book in both of these ways. But I will also use it in a slightly different way, having read and reread chapters looking for errors—I will use it as pure inspiration. Never have I seen such a focused book express in such a focused voice so much of what I want and need to know about my tempestuous love affair with everything Italian. This must be the first book like this that I have ever found, and to top it off, Gina works with me and I get to start it off with a foreword! It just continues for me—I am the luckiest chef in the world, proud and honored to work with the defining light in Italian culture and desserts, Gina D from NYC.

VINI DA MEDITAZIONE AND THE ART OF PENSIVE SIPPING, BY COLUM SHEEHAN, WINE DIRECTOR OF BABBO

Just as Italy offers a greater variety of dry wines than anywhere else in the world, the same can be said for its dessert wines, from the light and fresh *moscati* and *brachetti* of Piemonte to the rich and concentrated *Passiti di Pantelleria*. Italy's dessert wines run the full gamut from lightly to full-on sweet, and also include wines that blur the lines conventionally drawn between sweet and dry, like *vin santi* and the curiously sweet yet tannic *Sagrantino Passito di Montefalco* of Umbria.

The tradition of desserts is perhaps not as deep in Italy as in other countries, since Italy struggled with poverty for much of its history and sugar was somewhat of a luxury for many centuries. Yet throughout these leaner years, the vines continued to thrive and the Italians made wine with their fruit. It is for this reason that Italians often refer to their sweet wines as *"vino da meditazione"* rather than *"vino da dessert"* or *"vino dolce."* The fact that these wines evolved free of a dessert culture has enabled the characteristic wide variety of styles.

In today's Italy, desserts are more prolific and more affordable. Dining out in restaurants is also more common. The pairing of these sweeter wines with desserts has therefore worked its way into the dining culture. It is, however, truly remarkable how pairings change from region to region, as *campanilismo*—faithfulness to one's hometown bell tower, best translated as regional pride—still rules. The most illustrative example of this is what is paired with chocolate in Italy's different regions. In Piemonte, *Brachetto d'Acqui*'s slight sparkle, fresh acidity, and berry scent is preferred, working as a complement to the flavor of chocolate. In central Italy, *Vin santo*'s nutty intensity balances chocolate's richness. In Puglia and elsewhere in the south, wines made from the rare *aleatico* grape behave much like the *brachetto*, yet are sweeter and without fizz. I have yet to meet a Piemontese who prefers his chocolate with a *vin santo* or an *aleatico* wine, and the Pugliesi would more than likely scoff at the notion of the lightly alcoholic *brachetto* with the deep flavor of chocolate, yet they all make sense in one way or another.

Sweeter wines are most safely paired with drier pastries. A classic example that has even made it overseas is the pairing of Tuscan *biscotti* with *vin santo*. In Friuli the sweet yet slightly tannic *Ramandolo* is pleasant with the *Gubana* cake on page 264. The Veronesi sip a *Recioto di Soave* with their *Pandoro* (page 258). Again, a Veronese would probably find the suggestion of a *Ramandolo* with his *Pandoro* absurd, but the truth is that it pairs just as well. In all of these cases the dryness of the pastry is the perfect foil for the sweeter wine. At Babbo, when attempting to match dessert wines with Gina's dishes, I let myself be guided by this basic principle and expand on it: find a wine sweeter than the dessert itself that produces a beautiful melding of flavors.

Like Italian wines, both Gina's and Mario's cooking often cross the boundary between sweet and savory. This enables us to pair sweeter wines with savory dishes and drier wines with slightly sweet desserts. One evening, I made a classic pairing of a brightly acidic *Vin Santo di Chianti Classico* with Mario's Goose Liver Ravioli, finished in a brown butter and balsamic sauce. For the dessert course, Gina added a savory touch of shaved Pecorino Toscano to a lightly sweet pear *crostata*. We matched this with a beautifully aged 1985 Gaia & Rey *Langhe* Chardonnay from the famed *Gaja* winery in Piemonte. The first pairing was classical, and fail-safe, but the fortunate guests at the dinner who experienced the second were so floored by it, they talked more about it than the magnificent *Barbareschi* from the same producer that were served earlier in the meal.

But even today dessert wines are not matched up with the splendid variety of Italian cheeses as often as they might be. Gina selects the assortment of cheeses featured on Babbo's cheese board, and is as passionate about them as she is about her desserts. Diners still often feel that red wine is most appropriate with cheese, yet crisp whites and dessert wines are many times the better choice. Very rich and intense cheeses like Taleggio and gorgonzola prefer the powerful flavor of dessert wines. While our selection is constantly evolving, I am, at the time of this writing, having a lot of fun pairing more aromatic dessert wines with a stunning *Bleu del Moncenisio* that Gina has recently sourced.

While the subject of the dessert wines of Italy is too vast to completely cover in these pages, a few are worth mentioning that are available in our market for your "experimentation."

Moscato d'Asti and *Brachetto d'Acqui*, made respectively from white and red grapes, can be found in the green market as table grapes (Gina often uses fresh *moscato* grapes in her desserts). As delicious as they are to eat, a brief fermentation in tanks that seal in the carbon dioxide yields wines with a slight sparkle, while leaving enough residual sugar so that they work well with desserts and are still delicious on their own. They are like puppies or kittens—you can't resist them!

Recioto della Valpolicella is made in a similar fashion to the more famous *Amarone della Valpolicella*, but with less fermentation so as to leave more sweetness. It is often referred to as the port wine of Italy, but I must disagree, as the alcohol is not nearly as intense and the wine is therefore much less sweet. Similarly, ***Recioto di Soave*** is made from the dried grapes of Soave as a white dessert wine.

Picolit is a rare Friulian varietal that makes small quantities of what many believe to be Italy's greatest dessert wine. This sentiment is of course most strongly held by the Friulians. I remember tasting a wonderful *Picolit* in the company of the producer and commenting that the wine is Italy's answer to the Sauternes of France. He rapidly informed me that Sauternes is France's answer to *Picolit*. It is a white grape that produces exquisite and elegant wines with a subtle tannin but wonderful complexity.

Ramandolo, made from the *verduzzo* grape, is also becoming harder to find, but the wine is terrific. Less versatile because of higher tannin (very unusual in a dessert wine), I think of it as a true *Vino da Meditazione*.

Italy's central regions, especially Tuscany, are dominated by **Vin Santo**. Many restaurants offer a complimentary *vin santo* with cookies, but unfortunately, if they're giving it away it is more than likely an industrial imitation. The genuine article is slowly fermented over a period of four or more years in tiny barrels in an attic with no control over the temperature. The extreme variation in temperature, from the heat of summer to the cool of winter, oxidizes the wine, leaving it with a compelling hazelnut perfume and varying degrees of sweetness. The curious name translates as "holy wine." Legend has it that it comes from a meeting between the bishops of the Greek and Roman churches in Florence. A Greek bishop, upon tasting the wine, declared that it was the wine of Xantos, a tiny isle where a similar wine was made.

No discussion of dessert wines is complete without mentioning those of Sicily. The historic presence of the Saracens in medieval times has established Sicily as king of the Italian dessert scene. Sicilian dessert wines are too good to miss. **Passito di Pantelleria** is from Sicily's tiny island off the coast of Tunisia. On Pantelleria, the two main crops are capers and the *Zibibbo* grape, which is said to be the strain of muscat grape known as Muscat Alexandria elsewhere. The grapes are harvested and left to dry in the sun until intensely sweet, crushed, then fermented at a controlled temperature, yielding one of my personal favorite dessert wines. Should you ever have the opportunity to sample the *Khamma* or *Martingana* vineyards of Salvatore Murana, it is most proper to first drop onto one knee. They are pure ambrosia. More readily available is the *Ben Rye* from the *Donnafugata* winery, as well as the *Bukkuram* from Marco de Bartoli. From the tiny Lipari Islands to the north of Sicily comes **Malvasia delle Lipari,** another wine from dried grapes, which, while not quite as rich as the Pantelleria wines, I find has slightly livelier acidity and pleasant freshness.

As I say, there are many more, so feel free to explore. Dessert wines are always worth the hunt. At Babbo we are constantly unearthing new discoveries. As I always say about wine: the more you know, the more you know you don't know.

DOLCE ITALIANO

DESSERTS FROM THE BABBO KITCHEN

Italia

Switzerland

Austria

Hungary

Trentino-
Alto Adige

Friuli-
Venezia
Giulia

Slovenia

Valle
d'Aosta

Lombardia

Torino

Milano

Veneto

Venezia

Croatia

Piemonte

Emilia-Romagna

Bosnia-

Liguria

Bologna

Herzegovina

France

Firenze

Ligurian Sea

Toscana

Le
Marche

Umbria

Adriatic Sea

Corsica

Abruzzo

Roma
Lazio

Molise

Puglia

Campagna

Napoli

Sardegna

Basilicata

Tyrrhenian Sea

Calabria

Mediterranean Sea

Palermo

Sicilia

0   50   100   kilometers

0   50   100 miles

Ionian Sea

Tunisia

INTRODUCTION

It is just past two o'clock in the morning, and I am awake in my tiny bedroom in Brooklyn. A group of late-night revelers has just exited from the subway and are loudly engaged in a drunken debate on the sidewalk. Cars on Flatbush Avenue steadily whiz by, despite the hour. But it is not the vocal capabilities of my neighbors or the idling engine of a utility truck conveniently parked under my window that has caused my eyes to fly wide open so deep in the night. I was dreaming, in vivid detail, about a lemon tart. I actually fell asleep thinking about a lemon tart. The first hint of a craving crept into my head and spread to my stomach just before bedtime. Sensing the impending self-torture, I tried to put the tart out of my mind with a full hour of sitcoms and a couple of graham crackers. Wide awake, I now pound my pillow and try to rationalize the situation. Perhaps it is time to put a lemon tart on my dessert menu at Babbo; some of my best menu brainstorming happens in odd places during off hours. My job awaits me in the morning, but I know that this moment has nothing to do with work. It is simple: I want a slice of *crostata di limone*, at once both tart and sweet on my tongue, creamy and fragrant in my mouth, with a substantial yet tender crust of *pasta frolla* that just melts. I am actually *yearning* for it, along with a shot of smooth, dark espresso, no sugar, to offset the sweet-tart sensation I would be experiencing if I were sitting in a café in Rome rather than lying in my bed in Brooklyn. I groan and roll over, and my now-awakened cats glare at me indignantly.

Dessert has this power over some of us. I say "us" because I consider people who are passionate about all things sweet to be among a select group of highly developed individuals, otherwise known as my brethren. Within that group exists a particular Italianate sect: we buy only cannoli that will be filled to order, we have tales of waiting in an endless line at Balducci's to purchase that last-minute *panforte di Siena* for Christmas Eve dinner, and we can be jolted awake from a sound sleep by the phantoms of *dolci* past. *Gelato* is a form of worship. A Neapolitan pastry shop, whether on Via Santa Lucia in Naples or Bleecker Street in Greenwich Village, is our idea of heaven, and the quest for the ultimate ricotta cheesecake may rival that for the Holy Grail. We have waded through a formidable tide of pastry classics: the giants of Swiss and Austrian tradition, nouvelle French fantasies of spun sugar and artfully arranged *tuiles*, and American standards such as mom's apple pie and Toll House cookies. I find it hard to argue with anything sweet, and I carry my own long list of dessert favorites that are anything but Italian. But it is the simplicity of *biscotti* randomly spiked with anise seed, alongside a glass of *vin santo*, that stirs my senses and holds me captive.

My journey from a somewhat sane person to a dessert-obsessed insomniac began in my childhood and has continued through my tenure as the pastry chef of Babbo Ristorante and Enoteca in New York City, where I have been blessedly free to develop and nurture my love of Italian desserts for the past nine years. The fact that I am a pastry chef today stuns me when I stop to think about it. In my family, desserts never took center stage, to the dismay of my siblings and me. My mother spent much of her childhood in a small town in the southern Italian region of Calabria. To her, the ideal dessert was quintessentially Italian: a perfect piece of fruit. A ripe fig or a bunch of plump grapes happily satisfied her sweet tooth. I remember her silently slicing a ripe, juicy cantaloupe and distributing it around the dinner table with an air of reverence and finality that suggested we could not fathom a better finish to a meal. My brother, sister, and I clung to the hope that she would suddenly jump up from the table and pull a carton of ice cream out of the freezer, but in the end we knew better. As long as fruit existed, our chances of getting a nightly cookie were pretty slim.

It took me many years to understand my mother's obsession with fresh fruit. Italian produce, whether it is found in a tiny *frutta e verdura,* or produce shop, in a small town or the large weekly open-air markets in a big city, is decidedly better than what you find in the average American supermarket. Fruit is not waxed, nor does it bear the indignity of a numbered sticker smacked onto it. Italian apples at a local market may appear drab to American eyes, but they offer deeply intense flavor; peaches are sold ripe and ready to eat; berries are little, yet heady with enticing fragrance. Italian produce is sold and purchased with the understanding that it will be consumed quickly; shoppers buy no more than what they need for the next day or two. It comes as no surprise, then, that refrigerators in the average Italian home are small in comparison to the monster-sized appliances favored in America. When I pick up a peach that feels like a cannonball at my local supermarket, I am dismayed.

Fresh figs, plums, and cherries; unsullied eggs, milk, and cream; velvety mascarpone; creamy ricotta from the milk of cows, sheep, and buffalo; extra-virgin olive oil; local honey; fragrant almonds, rich pine nuts, perfect hazelnuts, walnuts, and chestnuts; juicy lemons, clementines, and blood oranges. . . . Armed with superb ingredients, I find that recipes come together effortlessly. For me, this is the core principle of the Italian baking experience. Italian home baking follows the same rules as the rest of Italian cooking: use what is local, use what is available, and use ingredients to their fullest potential. The term "seasonality" has become a cliché in the ever-spinning cosmos of professional cooking; too often it is a trendy, convenient way of stating the obvious. Efficient use of what the surrounding landscape provides is common to every world cuisine, even American cooking. Italy does not own this concept.

What distinguishes Italian desserts in my mind—and my heart—is the particularly vivid sense of history, religion, culture, and locale that accompanies them. There seems to be a story, a quirky name, or a celebration for nearly everything Italians eat, and I find this sense of time and place in food absolutely mesmerizing. I love the spooky drama of the crunchy, dry cookies known as *ossi dei morti*, or "bones of the dead"; it is hard to munch on one without thinking twice. In Tuscany, the favorite local plum is known as *coscia di monaca,* which translates to the slightly kinky "nun's thighs," a concept that never fails to make me giggle, since I survived years of Catholic school tyranny. I am quite fond of the story of *minni di Sant'Agata,* or "Saint Agatha's breasts," in honor of the virgin saint, martyred by having her breasts slashed off by Roman guards. Saint Agatha is often pictured carrying a plate on which her breasts lie, symbols of her torture and sacrifice. The pastries, plump mounds of custard encased in sweet dough, are finished with a cherry "nipple" on top. As wacky as these sweets may seem to Americans, they are consumed with reverence and gratitude on Saint Agatha's feast day in the Sicilian city of Catania, where she is the patron and guardian. Eating them on that day becomes a form of participation in the continual weaving of a long thread through the tapestry of time.

Families have the same sense of time and tradition—especially mine. Our family kitchen always marched to the drumbeat of the changing seasons. Shortly after I was born, we moved from New York to the suburbs of northern Virginia. My mother struggled to maintain her food traditions, formed during her childhood in Italy and her coming-of-age in the Italian neighborhoods of the Bronx. Shopping in her new home state proved a strange and unnerving experience. The only place to buy food was at big, homogeneous supermarkets, a stark contrast to the small, family-run shops and markets she was accustomed to in her old neighborhood. Mom made some attempt to conform to her new environment, but her habits were still glaringly different from those of the other suburban mothers. She shopped for food nearly every day rather than making those big weekly trips that involved cartloads of groceries.

There was no choice but to patronize the dreaded supermarkets, yet she still found a way to make her own sense of them. She was convinced that Safeway had better fish than A&P, and the best produce was to be found at Giant on Thursdays. Mom often asked to speak directly with the butcher or the fishmonger, to the obvious annoyance of the counter person, who was trying to keep the line moving quickly. As I fidgeted beside her and guarded our shopping cart, I knew that my mother was a fish out of water, the unusual little Italian lady who was always asking for things that were not already on display in the cold case, like pigs' knuckles or calf's brains or chicken feet. She never seemed very happy in the produce aisle, sighing to herself as she picked her way through vegetables and fruit already trapped in plastic bags. There was a resonating sense that she knew she was settling for less than she deserved. A large bowl of fruits in various stages of ripening always sat on our kitchen counter; we were not to touch them lest we interrupt the process, which she monitored daily, feeling and pressing and turning her treasures.

I remember feeling an odd mixture of pride and embarrassment when it came to my mother and her seeming obsession with food. On any given day, our house was either the place where all of our neighborhood playmates wanted to eat (we had pasta most Saturday nights) or the place where everyone was afraid to eat anything (the weekday menu might include lentil soup with escarole followed by fried smelts or a huge frittata made with chicken livers and onions). The one thing that remained constant was her reverence for the ritual of the family gathering at the table for the evening meal, especially after my father's sudden death, when I was not yet six years old.

A considerable amount of closet space in our cramped apartment was devoted to a makeshift storage area for the truly important food items, which came several times a year by mail or were delivered in person by our most special visitor. My maternal grandmother traveled from New York to Fairfax, Virginia, at least once a year and stayed for a few magical weeks. At the airport I would strain my eyes gazing down the long corridors until I saw her emerge from the gate. A tiny, roundish figure, always impeccably dressed, she slowly made her way toward us as she carefully maneuvered her bags. There was only one time-worn suitcase with her few bits of clothing. The rest was an assortment of cardboard boxes tied with string and lovely hand-sewn bags filled to capacity with the items vital to the survival of our family: a tremendous chunk of Parmigiano-Reggiano, large square cans of extra-virgin olive oil, homemade *salumi* and *capicola*, dried figs stuffed with walnuts and baked in honey, my favorite crunchy black-pepper *taralli*, imported dried pastas, several large loaves of Italian bread from Arthur Avenue in the Bronx. If we were very lucky, there might even be a box of Italian pastries to have for dessert that night. I used to imagine that in the event of a catastrophe, my grandmother could keep her fellow plane passengers alive for weeks while they awaited rescue.

Once Nonni was settled in, there was plenty of work to do; the following weeks were a flurry of food-related activities. There were sheets of fresh pasta to be made, cut, and frozen. A special order from the butcher at Safeway provided pounds of pork and fat to be made into sausages, which were dried and stored in olive oil. Peaches were canned, berries were made into jams and jellies, cherries were plunged into brandy, green tomatoes and onions were pickled, and eggplant was made into *caponata*. By the time Nonni left, our hall closet was transformed into a powerhouse of a pantry, filled with glass jars and recycled espresso cans sealed with tinfoil and rubber bands.

My older brother and sister were only mildly interested in these kitchen activities, but I was a shy child, and I much preferred the company of my mother and grandmother to that of other children, as I listened to them speak Italian and assisted them as much as they would allow. By the time I was eight I could use a small knife with some proficiency, I knew how to hold a sausage casing as filling was extruded into it, my fingers could clean berries and pit cherries in a most efficient and least wasteful way, and I could carefully measure ingredients according to the old, yellowed recipe cards my mother kept in one of her cupboards. Nonni showed me how to make a well with flour and salt and then to crack eggs gingerly into the center for her pasta dough. I would step aside and watch as she kneaded the dough and then rolled it out, using a tremendous, thick dowel that was almost as tall as I was. She was in her early seventies by then, and could still cut the paper-thin sheets into perfect *tagliatelle* with a pair of kitchen shears, her hands never wavering from the straight line in her mind.

I don't know if I could have written this cookbook without the examples of my mother and grandmother; their influence on me as a chef was that profound. Before I even entertained the thought of cooking for a living, they taught me to understand the importance of food in the daily life of a family. The time I spent at their sides helping prepare dinner was time I spent learning about the wonders of food: to cook it properly, to be thankful for its quality, to be mindful of where it came from, and to prepare it with respect for tradition. I also learned what I could accomplish, even as young child. Mom taught me to follow a recipe's directions carefully, and I was rewarded with the excitement of seeing and tasting the results. Cooking with my mother when I was a child was not a special occasion, it was a daily part of life, and it was the most loving way for her to connect with me. I knew from a very early age exactly who I was and where I came from. I am Italian, and the foods Nonni, Mom, and I prepared together and shared at the family table formed my cultural heritage as well as my personal history. Learning about food helps children develop healthy habits. Knowing that a peach grows on a tree and a potato grows in the ground makes eating these foods an exercise in learning as well as in tasting. The more children find out about food, the less they fear it, and the better their chances are of following a healthy diet for the rest of their lives. Becoming disconnected from food is what makes us so willing to accept less flavor and less quality. Food becomes something we hardly think about and therefore cannot fully enjoy.

Although I did not realize it at the time, those days with my mother and grandmother were shaping me into a chef. As I grew older and experienced the standard rites of passage of American teenagers, my relationship with food waxed and waned. My mother returned to New York and I enrolled in college, where junk food became the usual diet and my mother's ritualistic meals became a monthly treat when I visited. My initial dream after graduation was to become a lawyer, but the more I tried to shake the memories of my food-saturated upbringing, the more they rattled around in my head. I supplemented my weekly income from a nine-to-five job with a progression of weekend stints as a cook and caterer, always telling myself that it was simply a way to earn some extra cash while I saved up for law school. But after a few years I found myself at the proverbial fork in the road; I had narrowed down my next step in life to two choices, graduate school or culinary school. In a move that surprised no one in my family, I chose the rigorous, itinerant life of a chef.

My foray into the world of sweets was something of an accident. I had already spent several years cooking professionally, and I had neither trained in pastry nor had any exposure to over-the-top confectionery techniques. When I did bake, I saw it as a diversion, a change of pace, and a way to create things that made my friends and family smile. I found myself flipping through the dessert section of every cookbook I owned, I put myself in charge of every birthday cake possible, and Sunday mornings seemed always to involve bread dough or muffins. I drifted to the sweet side of the kitchen because as much as I loved to cook, I discovered that I loved baking more. As a chef, I had learned the importance of technique and organization, but baking became what I did to truly extend my heart. Dessert was the course that was always genuine and joyful, and creating it somehow brought me a sense of comfort and peace.

During my first few years of pastry apprenticeship, I flirted relentlessly with the notion of fancy little desserts, but I could never quite bring myself to make a commitment. They represented the exact opposite of my mother's spartan sense of sweets and never fully made sense to me. In the end, it seemed that they could not supply the instinctive pleasure that comes with a scrumptious piece of cake or a splendid fruit tart. I functioned on the edge of the professional pastry solar system, constantly learning but always being more a spectator than a true participant. I was lucky enough to land jobs at some of the best restaurants in New York. A *stagiaire* position at Chanterelle was followed by over two years at Gramercy Tavern, which ended when I was offered my first job as a full-fledged pastry chef, at the Cub Room. It was during this stint that I met Mario Batali, and though I wasn't fully aware of it at the time, I was once again at a crossroads of pivotal importance in my life, both personally and professionally.

Mario was planning to open a new restaurant that would undoubtedly hit the New York dining scene like a resounding hand-smack on a leg of prosciutto. Our first formal meeting took place in March 1998, on a quiet Sunday afternoon. We talked in the crowded basement of his first restaurant, Po, amid shelves lined with olive oil and dried pasta. Mario laid his vision of Babbo before me with his trademark combination of passion and knowledge. As far as the desserts were concerned, my ingredients were not to be manipulated beyond recognition; nor would the garnish confound the presentation. I would not be expected to spin sugar, construct intricate frameworks of *tuiles* and chocolate, or make ten perfect circles of raspberry coulis on a plate. It was a concept of dessert that was entirely familiar to me. Italian cuisine was heating up in New York, blossoming into a true contender on the local dining scene. People were clamoring to grasp something that was already within me, something that I had never really thought about twice before that day. I walked away from that meeting into a surprise late-spring snow shower, feeling positively charged.

A few months later, as the opening date of Babbo approached and construction was near completion, the team of chefs assembled to have our first look at our new home. Babbo is housed in the former site of the venerable Coach House Restaurant near historic Washington Square, and space would be tight. The heart of the operation would be no exception. All the preparation and cooking would take place in one small kitchen, and the pastry area, located a few feet from the hot line, was the size of two large cutting boards fitted on top of a low-boy refrigerator—a shock to the sensibilities of any pastry chef. The size of my so-called pastry kitchen would most definitely dictate the direction of my menu. It did not take long for me to realize that my repertoire of desserts must be not only delicious but absolutely straightforward and unfussy. The only approach, I decided, would be to think of my professional kitchen as just slightly more advanced than a humble home kitchen, and to allow a combination of my angst and my imagination to take it from there.

So it has been within the confines of my tiny kitchen space that the pastry program at Babbo has evolved. There have been numerous tortured cries of "Why me?" and moments when I have valiantly wrestled with a crisis of confidence. But in looking back at my body of work from the vantage point of a prospective author, I have realized that the limitations of space and equipment at Babbo have been my biggest assets as a pastry chef. Those very limitations, which I initially perceived as obstacles, forced me to think in terms of ingredients rather than obsessing about technique. And it has been the wealth of local and imported ingredients, so delightfully and constantly available in New York City, that has provided me with constant inspiration.

By focusing on the quest for the ultimate use of the best possible ingredients, my creative process has developed into a very specific set of steps. I never begin by thinking of how a dessert will look. Instead, I imagine what flavors I hope will take center stage, what textures will play off one another. First I take a quick walk to the bountiful greenmarket at Union Square, to check in with my favorite farmers and see what produce is in peak season at that moment. Are Concord grapes from upstate New York ready? Can I get perfect blueberries from New Jersey? I also call my purveyors. Is this a good time to buy sheep's-milk ricotta imported from Campania? Can I get my favorite hazelnuts from Piedmont? Next I grab a *doppio* espresso and a crunchy *biscotto*, sit in a quiet corner of the empty restaurant, and try to figure out the best way to let the ingredient of the moment shine. Should I bake a cake, whip up a *semifreddo*, or perhaps fry a fritter? The answers usually come after some tinkering on my allotted 17 inches of workspace, crammed next to my assistant and muttering to myself. In the end I wind up going with whatever it may be that I am craving at the crucial moment. Am I in the mood for roasted chestnuts, dying for a drizzle of honey, or itching to have just a bite of chocolate? This is the best part of being a pastry chef—you eventually make what you dream about, or in my case, what wakes you up.

It is always my goal to create desserts that just make sense. I feel very strongly and quite personally that dessert should not be an object of whimsy or nonsense. Whether I am planning a dessert for my menu at Babbo or for a family gathering, I try to make sure that it will fit in comfortably with the rest of the meal and be a wonderful final punctuation mark for the courses preceding it. Many traditional Italian desserts, with their tendency toward simplicity and freshness, accomplish this with perfection. To me, they always seem to occupy their intended space rather than overwhelm or overstate. Take, for example, my very favorite Italian dessert, *panna cotta*. Fresh cream, either plain or subtly flavored, is thickened—today with gelatin, but historically through cooking, hence the translation, "cooked cream." Often served plain or dressed up with fruit or chocolate, *panna cotta* calls for the barest minimum of ingredients and the simplest of preparations, used to make something that is nonetheless supremely satisfying.

One of my favorite Italian proverbs is *"Il meglio è nemico del bel bene,"* loosely translated as "The perfect is the enemy of the good"—a comforting bit of wisdom for anyone facing a few hours in the kitchen. I have always thought that perfection is something that should remain on the horizon, just beyond our grasp, because once you reach perfection, there is nowhere else to go. Keep this in mind as you wind your way through these recipes. Baking and cooking are processes, and they should be experienced, and I hope enjoyed, as a whole. Pastry has an undeserved reputation for being scientific, confusing, and intimidating. It need not be, though science and formula, at times necessary, can still be ultimately enjoyable. The pleasure of baking derives from the simplest of details—the orderly arrangement of ingredients, the visual and tactile feast as the steps are followed, the gush of excitement as the cooking progresses. The result, perfect or not, is just part of the journey. Italians are warm and friendly but not gratuitous with their praise; *"Perfetto!"* is not a compliment bestowed lightly. I am as just as happy to hear a purr of *"Buonissimo,"* followed by a wide smile. Very good is a fine thing indeed.

LEARNING ITALIAN

The cuisine of Italy is my passion, and I hope that readers of this book will be inspired to learn more about the history, culture, and traditions of this beautiful country. At Babbo we never shy away from our desire to share our passion and knowledge with our customers, and it is in that spirit that I have chosen to provide the Italian as well as the English names for many of the recipes. If there is no direct English translation, I prefer to let the Italian name stand alone, rather than invent a translation that is inaccurate or inappropriate or simply makes no sense.

As a self-confessed mapaholic, I have included a map (page 2) and a listing of Italy's twenty wonderfully distinctive regions, along with information about some of the European Union's designations for specific foods and products.

THE REGIONS

I find it most helpful to have a map and a list of Italy's regions handy whenever I am developing a particular recipe, since Italian cooking is actually a collection of the particular cuisines of these regions. The country's topography has shaped the cooking as much as any other factor has, and a firm grasp of the names and location of the regions will help you connect more fully with the recipes in this book, which span the country's length and breadth. In cases where the English name differs from the Italian, the English is included in parentheses.

PIEMONTE (PIEDMONT)	MARCHE
VALLE D'AOSTA	LAZIO
LOMBARDIA (LOMBARDY)	ABRUZZO
TRENTINO–ALTO ADIGE	MOLISE
VENETO	PUGLIA
FRIULI–VENEZIA GIULIA	CAMPAGNA (CAMPANIA)
LIGURIA	BASILICATA
EMILIA-ROMAGNA	CALABRIA
TOSCANA (TUSCANY)	SARDEGNA (SARDINIA)
UMBRIA	SICILIA (SICILY)

DOP AND IGP

Throughout this book you will see the letters DOP and IGP in relation to certain agricultural foodstuffs, cheeses, and other traditional Italian foods. Learning the meaning of these initials is integral to truly understanding the connection between the foods and the history of Italy and the cultural reality that still thrives today.

DOP stands for *Denominazione d'Origine Protetta,* or "Protected Designation of Origin." Italian foods and products labeled DOP originate in a specific geographical place, most likely a town or a very limited regional area, and possess unique characteristics or qualities that are directly linked to that place. These special qualities are the result of specific environmental conditions, both natural and human, and all elements of production are limited to that location. *Ficondindia dell'Etna,* or prickly pears from Sicily, and *Pecorino Toscano*, sheep's-milk cheese from Tuscany, are examples of DOP products.

IGP stands for *Indicazione Geografica Protetta,* or "Protected Geographical Indication," and carries essentially the same spirit as the DOP designation, but the criteria are less stringent. Although an IGP product must have a distinct reputation that is connected to a specific geographical place, only one phase of production must occur within the designated area of protection. *Nocciole di Piemonte,* or hazelnuts from Piedmont, and *Mela Val di Non,* apples from the Val di Non, are examples of IGP products.

Both DOP and IGP classifications are comprehensive, encompassing the geographical, environmental, and historical characteristics of the foods and products that receive them. They were established in 1992 with the creation of the European Union, replacing similar labels previously applied by the Italian government. New products receive the coveted designations only after an exhaustive application and review process, and producers must maintain rigorous standards of production to keep them.

According to the Italian Trade Commission, Italy has more culinary specialties than any other nation in the European Union. Currently, over twenty-one hundred products are candidates for either DOP or IGP protection, including almost four hundred types of cheeses and an array of fruits and vegetables, grains, legumes, mushrooms, truffles, honey, herbs, spices, condiments and preserves, wine and fruit vinegars, olive oils, meat products, breads, pastas, and of course pastries and sweets. What these labels guarantee is *autenticità,* or authenticity, a quality that is becoming increasingly elusive in today's fast-food world.

SOURCES AND A SUGGESTED READING LIST

I would have never been able to complete this book without the wealth of information in two books by Carol Field, *The Italian Baker* and *Celebrating Italy*. The pages of my copies are dog-eared and smudged from countless hours of poring over them in the years before I embarked on writing this book. For historical perspective, *The Food of Italy*, by Waverly Root, is invaluable. I cannot say enough about *Italian Cuisine: A Cultural History*, by Alberto Capatti and Massimo Montanari, a fascinating historical work of astounding detail. *The Italian Food Guide: The Ultimate Guide to the Regional Foods of Italy,* published by the Touring Club of Italy, belongs on the shelf of everyone who loves to travel and eat in Italy.

Cheese Primer, by Steven Jenkins, was the first, and I think still the best, book on cheese that I own, and it continues to expand my knowledge of the cheese-making process. *Italian Cheese: Two Hundred and Ninety-Three Traditional Types*, published by the editors of Slow Food International, is required reading for anyone who wants to learn about Italy's finest and least-known cheeses. The title of Ari Weinzweig's *Zingerman's Guide to Good Eating: How to Choose the Best Bread, Cheeses, Olive Oil, Pasta, Chocolate, and Much More* says it all—thank goodness! Joe Wolff has written *Café Life Rome* and *Café Life Florence*, two wonderful books about cafés, *gelaterie*, and pastry shops, their characters and culture, in two of Italy's most beloved cities. *Gelato!*, by Pamela Sheldon Johns, is a wonderful book that demystifies the process of making artisanal *gelato*. And for inspiration, *Bitter Almonds: Recollections and Recipes from a Sicilian Girlhood,* by Maria Grammatico and Mary Taylor Simeti, will fill your heart, as it did mine.

TEN ITALIAN INGREDIENTS YOU SHOULD KNOW

One of the hallmarks of Italian desserts is that their inherent simplicity allows the quality of the ingredients to shine, whether it is the finest cheeses, the ripest fruits, or some local specialty. Here in the United States, the search for excellent ingredients can be a bit trickier, especially when navigating the aisles of your local grocery store. I find that the average supermarket contains many more abominations than treasures. Of course, being a chef in New York City means that I am pretty spoiled, with imported Italian products arriving weekly at my doorstep from a number of fine merchants and distributors. The bounty of produce at my fingertips from upstate New York, Long Island, New Jersey, and Pennsylvania is a blessing, and my trips to the legendary farmers' market in Union Square are truly the highlight of my week.

But it is possible to find wonderful ingredients elsewhere in the United States too. These days, most major cities and suburban areas have at least one gourmet specialty store, and many sponsor daily or weekly farmer's markets. Even better are the local merchants who specialize in fresh and imported Italian products, usually found wherever there are large pockets of Italian Americans in the community. But the truth is, finding the best ingredients in the United States isn't as easy as it should be. Too often Americans suffer from a willingness to accept mediocrity in our food supply. I am guilty of lecturing innocent bystanders about the importance of finding the best seasonal ingredients, and I am pretty sure that I am not the only chef who does it. I hope these people realize that my intentions are good. As overused and obvious as the cliché may be, there is still a need to state it again and again. Until American cooks take premium foods for granted, as Italian cooks do, the quest for excellent ingredients must continue. Italians do not settle for anything but the best when it comes to buying their ingredients, and Americans should not settle either.

But first we must back up for a moment. Before you decide where to do your shopping, you need to acquaint yourself with the goods. Knowing why you need the right ingredients and understanding their role in the glorious desserts you create are essential. To that end, I have compiled this list of ten Italian ingredients you need to know and have in your pantry. It includes some of my very favorite ingredients to work with, the building blocks of my dessert repertoire. I honestly don't think I could survive in my corner of the Babbo kitchen if any one of these items was missing. Even if you are only slightly familiar with Italian cooking, take comfort in the fact that this list will not appear entirely foreign. So read on, and shop fearlessly.

RICOTTA

If pressed to name the single Italian product that fills me with the most comfort and joy, it would be ethereal fresh ricotta, at once light yet luxurious, delicate, sweet, and buttery. Ricotta, which literally translates to "recooked," is not actually a cheese but rather a by-product of the cheese-making process. It is made from whey, the milky liquid that is drained away from other cooked cheeses, such as mozzarella and provolone. The transformation occurs when the whey is heated to a specific temperature and the casein, or milk protein, coagulates to form tiny curds. Ricotta is also commonly made from a combination of whey and milk, to create a richer, creamier result.

Traditionally, ricotta is a basket cheese, which means that the curds are scooped up and placed in a round basket so that any unwanted liquid can slowly drain away. It is more likely that you will see fresh ricotta in what is referred to as a cone, a tall white tin filled to capacity with a dome of ricotta sitting on top. The entire cone usually weighs about three pounds; if you don't need that much, your cheesemonger should be willing to weigh out whatever portion you want.

In Italy it is common to find ricotta that is made from the milk of sheep or buffalo; both varieties are quite different from American ricotta, which is almost always made from a combination of cow's milk and whey. Italian ricotta is usually drier and firmer than American ricotta, but the texture varies from region to region. Sheep's-milk ricotta has a tangy, assertive flavor; buffalo's-milk ricotta is delicate and light. Both are more perishable than cow's-milk ricotta; this is especially true of the sheep's-milk variety. I have substituted both for cow's-milk ricotta in sweet and savory recipes with great success, but my favorite way to enjoy them is to eat them as a table cheese. Honey is a spectacular accompaniment, as are fresh berries and sliced pears.

I am lucky to be able to get terrific fresh cow's-milk ricotta right here in New York City. By fresh, I mean ricotta that is made locally or by small, regional dairies rather than by larger national companies, which distribute to supermarkets and may use stabilizers to improve shelf life. DiPalo Dairy, a corner of heaven located on a narrow street that skirts Little Italy and Chinatown, offers a huge selection of the finest Italian cheeses and other imported Italian products. Its fresh ricotta is made daily with the greatest care. DiPalo is also a source for fresh ricottas made from sheep's milk and buffalo's milk, which are flown in from Italy weekly when available.

At Babbo, I also use the Calabro family's award-winning fresh cow's-milk ricotta, which is found in most gourmet food emporiums and cheese shops in the New York metropolitan area. The Calabro cheese company, in East Haven, Connecticut, has been making ricotta and other Italian cheeses for over a century. Its creamy, sweet, and delicate ricotta is sold in the New York area as well as in parts of New England and Pennsylvania, and it recently expanded its distribution to Florida, Texas, Ohio, Wisconsin, and Colorado.

Look for fresh ricotta in a cheese shop or in a store that specializes in fresh Italian products. Always use it within three days of purchase; if an orange film develops on the surface, you have kept it too long. If you cannot find fresh ricotta in your area, you can certainly use ricotta from the supermarket for the recipes in this book with good results. I do recommend that you only use whole-milk ricotta, however. Ricotta is not exceedingly high in fat, so there is little need to substitute the skim or part-skim variety, and the payoff in flavor and texture is significant.

MASCARPONE

If fresh ricotta is ethereal, then mascarpone must be luxurious. I have heard it described as the Italian version of cream cheese, but no comparison does it justice. Most cooks associate mascarpone with their first attempt at making the ubiquitous tiramisu, but it is worthy of wider appreciation.

The original mascarpone comes from Lombardy and Emilia-Romagna and can be either double- or triple-cream. Technically speaking, mascarpone isn't actually a cheese, as no rennet or starter is used, nor do any curds form. A bit of citric acid is added to cream, which gently coaxes the moisture from it, yielding a dense, creamy product. The texture is velvety-smooth and rich, similar to that of soft butter; the color is the palest ivory. It is difficult for me to describe the flavor adequately. It is not at all tangy, like American cream cheese; the taste is light and very sweet, not in a sugary sense, but dairy-sweet, like the freshest cream. I like to think that it comes from the happiest of cows, a statement not far from the truth. The cows of Lombardy are said to graze on grasses dotted with herbs and wildflowers, which contribute to the delicately perfumed flavor of mascarpone.

Because mascarpone is incredibly rich, it can be used to embellish any recipe that calls for heavy cream or sour cream. It can be a little tricky to work with because of its high butterfat content; overbeating mascarpone will cause it to break, or appear curdled. I like to use it in *budini*, or puddings, to enrich whipped cream, in cake fillings, or simply on its own, with fresh fruit. You will not find a better partner for tiny wild strawberries or succulent ripe peaches.

Traditionally, mascarpone was made in the fall and winter and consumed quickly thereafter, but today it is made year-round in Italy and widely exported to the United States. It pays to shop around and taste a few different brands to find the one that makes you swoon, and stick with it whenever possible. I happen to adore mascarpone from the Vermont Butter & Cheese Company, even more than certain Italian brands. It is carried by some major supermarkets and many gourmet stores and well worth seeking out. As with ricotta, mascarpone should be used quickly after being purchased, within three or four days. It too will develop an orange film on the surface if kept too long; your mantra should be buy fresh, use fresh.

HONEY

Honey is too easily taken for granted. It sits on a shelf in the pantry or a kitchen cupboard, maybe confined within a tubby plastic bear, and is used only for the occasional cup of tea or peanut butter and banana sandwich. Yet honey was the first source of sweetness in Italian cuisine, originating with the early Romans, who began introducing sweet, sour, and bitter flavor components to their foods. The practice was revived during the Renaissance, when Italy looked back to ancient Rome for inspiration in both cooking and art. Sugar was not widely used until the thirteenth century, entering through the port of Venice in the north and through Arab-occupied Sicily in the south. Gradually the use of sugar evolved along economic lines; as cane sugar became the primary sweetener for the elite, honey remained more accessible to the masses. It is no wonder, then, that honey remained a traditional and favored staple of home cooks.

Honey, like olive oil, is used in every region of Italy from the top to the bottom of the boot. Not surprisingly, Italians take their honey seriously—so seriously, in fact, that they have developed stringent labeling regulations, similar to those for cheeses and olive oil. The type of honey is determined by origin or by the specific blossom or nectar used to make it, and by the method of extraction, such as whether pieces of honeycomb are present and whether heat or pressure is used to extract the honey. Labels may also note the geographical area where the honey was produced and whether any special processes were used to preserve or alter the consistency.

Tuscany, Sicily, Sardinia, and Piedmont produce some of Italy's finest honey. Among the numerous varieties you will find are acacia, chestnut, sage, thyme, lavender, eucalyptus, orange, lemon and lime blossom, and sunflower. Sulla honey is made from crimson clover, and my personal favorite is *millifiore,* or honey from "a thousand flowers," which speaks for itself. Corbezzolo honey is another exotic favorite, far less sweet than most, with a bitter, almost mentholated flavor. It comes from the blossom of the arbutus, a rare shrub with fruit like strawberries found only in the untamed areas of Sardinia and the Maremma region of Tuscany.

Many small Italian producers offer their honey only in small quantities, and sadly, these jars do not often make their way to American shelves. A few imported Italian honeys are available in specialty stores and from online sources (see pages 285–87). Il Forteto is a Tuscan farm cooperative that makes fine honey as well as numerous other good Italian products and some fantastic cheeses. I have reliably found their acacia, *millifiore,* and chestnut honeys at Italian specialty stores in New York City.

Even better news is that the United States has its own treasure trove of local honey varieties. I am particularly fond of bamboo honey, which I sometimes see at the Union Square greenmarket via an apiary from upstate New York. I also love tupelo honey from Florida, which I first received as a gift from a proud Floridian friend. Most farmers' markets have a honey stand or two, and it is definitely worth investigating what local varieties can be found in your area. I encourage you buy them when you see them and experiment with abandon. Some honeys are naturally prone to crystallization but can be easily heated to bring them back to life. Storing honey for too long, however, will result in an unpleasant, musty, or even rancid odor. In a dusty cabinet, this can happen within six months to a year, in which case you must start your collection anew. Try to buy your honey in quantities that you can comfortably use up within two to three months.

EXTRA-VIRGIN OLIVE OIL

You may find it a bit strange to find a discussion of olive oil in a dessert cookbook. Perhaps so, except that this is an Italian dessert book. And olive oil is . . . well, *everything* in Italy. Olive oil is used in Italian sweets because olive oil is part of the history of Italy. In a country with more than fifty million olive trees, some dating back a staggering five thousand years, it is no wonder that olive oil is omnipresent. From a pastry standpoint, it is not unusual to find olive oil in recipes for cakes, tart dough, cookies, breads, and fritters. Of course, it is by no means the only fat used in Italian pastry. Butter and lard still play predominant roles, especially in the north. Weather has a bit to do with some of these traditions; before the advent of refrigeration, it was difficult to keep dairy products in the ever-sweltering southern regions, and butter was not widely available. In economic terms, butter also represented an opulence reserved for the ruling classes, much like cane sugar. Olives were indigenous, easy to procure, and easy to press, which meant that olive oil was easy to use in everything, including sweets.

It is important to remember two things when it comes to olive oil in desserts. First, you must wrap your mind around the fact that *Italians like the flavor of olive oil*. They like the way it perfumes the flavor of a cookie or cake. It is as desired an effect as the taste of butter in the best French pastry. Second, you must always seek out a high-quality olive oil to use for cooking, whether for sweet or for savory food. Olive oil is subject to a distinct hierarchy, and navigating your way through the labyrinth of grades and types is no easy feat. It begins with the quality of the olives themselves and moves on to how they are pressed to obtain the oil. At the top of the quality ladder is extra-virgin, first cold-pressed oil. The term "extra-virgin" is a specific designation reserved for oils that contain no more than one percent oleic acid. A lower percentage of oleic acid translates directly to superior flavor, since oleic acid causes oxidation of the oil. When lesser quality olives are pressed, sometimes along with the residues of the first pressing, the resulting oil will contain higher amounts of oleic acid and must be labeled "virgin." Cold-pressing refers to an extraction method in which the olives are pressed between granite or stainless steel millstones, producing very low levels of heat from friction. Cold-pressed oils taste better than oils extracted with heat, which causes the flavor to deteriorate.

Factors beyond the pressing also determine the flavor and quality of olive oil—the variety of the trees, the soil, the air, the method of harvest, and the time of year you purchase and consume it, to name a few. The bottom line is that extra-virgin oil will have significantly more flavor and aroma, while poor oil will merely be greasy. It is not necessary to use the most expensive extra-virgin oil in cake batters, cookies, or tart dough. The oil's grassy, peppery qualities are somewhat lost in the midst of other pastry ingredients. Nor should you choose an inferior, cheap olive oil, which contributes no taste to the final product. The best bet is to taste, taste, taste, ultimately allowing the flavor of the oil to make the decision for you. It should be fruity, peppery, and a little grassy; olive oil should never be greasy and fall flat on your tongue. The recipes will offer you clues as well; if olive oil is a central ingredient, a better-flavored oil will lend its special qualities to the flavor of the finished dessert.

When it comes to selecting an olive oil, a dizzying number of options are available. Remember, it is most important that the oil tastes great. From Italy, look for oils from Tuscany, Puglia, Liguria, Campania, or Sicily. At Babbo, in addition to using an array of Italian olive oils, we are especially fond of DaVero Dry Creek Estate extra-virgin olive oil, from Sonoma County, California, produced from olive trees transplanted from Lucca, in the Tuscan countryside. DaVero's excellent website is full of information about the process of making olive oil and includes an online store for ordering oils.

LEMONS AND ORANGES

A friendly salesman delivers wonderful vanilla beans from Madagascar to Babbo weekly, but he is always disappointed that I don't buy nearly as many beans as my fellow pastry chefs in town. I feel bad, because I think he takes my small orders rather personally, unaware that I grate far more lemon and orange zest into my recipes than he can imagine. Admittedly, lemons and oranges are not solely Italian ingredients. But they are abundant and important crops in Italy and are venerated sources of flavor in Italian pastry recipes. Whether it is the fruit itself, the juice, or the zest, grated and candied, you will find citrus fruits everywhere in Italian sweets.

Lemons are cultivated in several Italian regions, but the finest and most distinctive fruits come from the Sorrento Peninsula, overlooking the Bay of Naples, and along the Amalfi coast, facing the Tyrrhenian Sea, both in Campania. Sorrento lemons were first cultivated in the first century, and lemons were widely grown in Amalfi by the early eleventh century. During the fifteenth century, vitamin C–laden citrus fruits were proven effective against scurvy and the export of lemons expanded greatly.

Limone costa d'Amalfi, or lemons from the Amalfi coast, are known locally as *sfusato amalfitano.* They are grown on narrow, steep terraces overlooking the Tyrrhenian Sea, providing important ecological protection against the erosion of the coastline. In the springtime, the scent of blossoming lemon trees wafts through the air of the surrounding towns of Ravello, Positano, and Maiori. Amalfi lemons have pointed ends, with a pale yellow rind that is redolent with fragrant oil and an abundance of acidic juice with very few seeds. They are harvested a few times a year, the peak picking taking place from March through early summer.

Limone di Sorrento, or lemons from Sorrento, are also blessed with exceptional aroma and flavor. The trees' branches often extend over ten feet and are coaxed to climb upward on chestnut-wood trellises. Straw mats are stretched over the trellises to protect them from threatening weather conditions and encourage even ripening of the fruit. Sorrento lemons are oval and long and have a medium-thick, aromatic skin and a bright yellow interior with extra-juicy flesh. Lemon groves thrive on almost two thousand acres of the Sorrento Peninsula, but the number of trees per acre is limited to prevent overcrowding and maintain the quality of the fruit.

The sweet orange we are familiar with today is believed to have appeared in Italy in the fourteenth century. The bitter orange, however, was first enjoyed by the ancient Romans and reappeared in the tenth century. Today many orange varieties, along with their cousin the sweet clementine, are widely grown in the southern region of Calabria. Nearly every variety of citrus fruit thrives in Sicily, but the blood orange is particularly excellent. *Arancia Rossa di Sicilia* has IGP status and includes three varieties of blood oranges grown on the island: Tarocco, Moro, and Sanguinello. Each type has a unique, penetrating orange-red color and a perfumed sweetness that makes it superior to any other blood orange grown in the Mediterranean.

The unique growing conditions of these regions make their citrus crops exceptional, and because such a wealth of citrus is readily available, their flavors have been deeply woven into desserts. You are not likely to find lemons from Italy at your local market, or even in an upscale specialty shop, although you may be lucky enough occasionally to find blood oranges imported from Sicily at a premium price. But do not fret. California, Florida, Texas, and Arizona all provide us with a first-rate citrus harvest. What you must do as a baker is get used to having fresh citrus on hand at all times, since the more your have, the more you will use.

Be picky about what you buy. Do not be tempted by the prettiest, shiniest skin, because that shine is not a product of nature; it comes from the wax that is applied to most fruits sold in American supermarkets. Growers, wholesalers, and retailers are convinced that American consumers are most enticed by the appearance of produce, and regrettably, they have been proved absolutely correct. Fruit is also coated with wax to extend its storage and shelf life, because our food supply must withstand a long period of time between harvest, purchase, and consumption. My advice is to look for fruit that has not been polished like your coffee table. Scratch the surface of a lemon or orange and breathe in the aroma of the oils that should have rubbed off on your fingers. If all you get is a fingernail full of wax, head for the nearest source of organic produce.

Scrutiny should not end with the skin of citrus fruits. Pick them up and feel the weight of the fruit; it should never seem hollow, which is a sure sign of dryness. When you cut into citrus fruits, they should be brightly colored and wet with juices. The flesh should be firm, never dry and never, ever mushy. Do your homework too. Ask your produce purveyor where the fruit comes from, how often a shipment arrives, and, most important, what his or her favorite varieties are. Your questions may raise a few eyebrows, but there are far worse tendencies than a seemingly abnormal relationship with an orange.

POLENTA

The word "polenta" can be confusing. Is it an ingredient, or is it a soft, yummy, carbohydrate-laden side dish with lots of butter and cheese? The answer is that it is both, but in baking, polenta is all about the corn.

Polenta is a stunning example of the continuous thread of time woven through Italian cooking. The first polenta was a thin gruel, made from any number of grains and seeds, including barley, millet, and buckwheat, and cooked only with water. In this case, the word "polenta" meant porridge. It was, along with soup, the food of the poor, from the Middle Ages all the way to the first half of the twentieth century. The basic cooked polenta of modern times is essentially unchanged, prepared today as it has been for centuries—stirred with water, in a pot.

Corn from the Americas was introduced to Italy through the port of Venice in the first half of the sixteenth century and became an agricultural phenomenon. It was enthusiastically cultivated throughout the Veneto, Piedmont, and Lombardy. Italians applied the same cooking techniques to corn as they did to other grains: they dried it, ground it, and cooked it with water, or sometimes milk or meat stock, into a porridge. Corn polenta had become a primary source of nutrition for the working poor of northern Italy by the middle of the eighteenth century, but not without certain consequences. Pellagra is a disease caused by a vitamin deficiency common to people who obtain their nutrition primarily from corn, which lacks niacin as well as protein, a source of the essential amino acid tryptophan. Pellagra epidemics occurred across the northern Italian countryside in the mid-1700s, a time when consumption of corn was at its peak among the poor. Native Americans, who had domesticated corn centuries before, knew how to treat the corn with calcium hydroxide, or slaked lime, an alkali that reduces the risk of contracting pellagra. Consequently, pellagra did not have the same devastating effect in the Americas as it did in Italy.

In spite of the epidemics, polenta never lost its foothold in the north. Today, in the Veneto and especially in Venice, it is just as common to see polenta featured on restaurant menus and on the home dinner table as it is to see pasta. Yet in the south it exists only as a novelty of northern cuisine. Indeed, neither my Calabrian grandmother nor my mother ever once served polenta at our family table, and they would never even consider it an option. So, although many people speak of "Italian cuisine," the truth is that Italy is a country of distinct regions, each holding fast to its own specific culinary traditions, as polenta's story illustrates.

A debate exists within the food community about instant polenta versus so-called real polenta. Purists insist that polenta can be made only from coarsely ground corn, or cornmeal, as we know it here in the States. It takes a heavy pan and strong arms to cook it properly, since it must be stirred continuously for up to an hour as it simmers. Once cooked, traditional polenta retains a bit of its gritty, chewy consistency. Instant polenta, in contrast, is finely ground and precooked. There is a sacrifice in flavor, which is less intensely "corny," as well as in texture, which is somewhat smoother.

The value of polenta as a baking ingredient is measured by its deep corn flavor more than any other characteristic, and in this case, "real" polenta wins. Some brands of polenta have been milled with the germ of the kernels intact. It is the germ that contains the corn oil and carries the lion's share of corn flavor. Retaining the germ of the kernel before milling results in the fullest corn flavor, but with a cost in terms of shelf life. This kind of polenta is highly perishable, and it is most often refrigerated or vacuum-packed. For this reason, the large, industrial mills remove the germ, resulting in a polenta that is less flavorful.

Confused? Don't be. The answer to the great polenta debate is quite simple in terms of baking. Real polenta will impart a deep corn flavor in tart dough, cakes, cookies, or *biscotti*, and impart chewy texture as well. Instant polenta, or fine cornmeal, can be substituted, though the corn flavor won't be as penetrating and the texture will be finer and softer. The bottom line is, you can use either variety, but you will get different results, which you can tailor to your particular tastes.

Zingerman's, a specialty food store in Ann Arbor, Michigan, carries a delicious imported Italian polenta made by the Marino family in Piedmont. Zingerman's also recommends the Italian brands Moretti, Nicoli, and Molino Sobrino, all available in the United States. I use Valsugana instant polenta, a brand from Italy that my local grocery store in Brooklyn happens to carry. Another good source is your local health-food store. Look for either coarse or fine cornmeal; I think organic brands taste best. Read the label carefully—you may need to refrigerate the package after opening it. And for baking, keep in mind that we are talking about polenta as an ingredient; don't grab the cooked polenta from the deli case, which is contained in a sausage-shaped, plastic casing and is indeed the porridge!

NUTS

I love nuts. Italians love nuts. I use the fact that I am an Italian pastry chef as an excuse to eat at least a handful every day. Almonds, pistachios, walnuts, pine nuts, and hazelnuts occupy a huge amount of space in my pantry at Babbo, and pound for pound, I use far more nuts than chocolate on a daily basis. The reason is simple: nuts are an integral part of most Italian sweets. I am grouping an array of nuts into one item, but a multitude of classic Italian desserts feature two or more nuts in combination, and most nuts can be substituted easily for one another in these recipes.

Italy has the distinction of being both a leading world producer of nuts and a leading importer. In other words, the country consumes more nuts than it can produce. Italians eat an enormous portion of the nuts they harvest, leaving only a small amount for export. I will venture to guess that almonds are the most widely used nuts in Italy, and the producers within each region argue that theirs are unquestionably the best. In Agrigento, on the southern coast of Sicily, the almond is celebrated with an Almond Blossom Festival in February, when the abundant almond groves of that area burst into bloom. The province of Bari in Puglia produces more almonds than any other region of Italy, but whether they are the best would probably be challenged by the almond farmers of Ferrara, in Emilia-Romagna. Pontelagoscuro is the Ferrarese town known for its *mandorlini*, the almond macaroons made from the local crop. In Bologna, you are likely to find an almond-topped *ciambella bolognese*, a cake flavored with ground almonds and shaped into a perfect ring, proudly displayed in the window of every *pasticceria*, or pastry shop.

It is difficult to find a region in Italy that does not features almonds in its sweets. In Tuscany candied almonds are enjoyed in Pistoia; the Sienese are famed for their *ricciarelli*, cookies made with sweet almond paste, and *panforte di Siena*, a sweet, spiced honey cake studded with whole almonds. In Prato, the Tuscan city just north of Florence, bakers use almonds in their eponymous *cantucci di Prato,* and in Lombardy almonds are featured in the crumbly *torta sbrisolona* as well as the traditional Easter cake, *columba di Pasqua.* Almonds are used in the layered cake known as *cassata,* from Sicily, and in *fregolotta,* the almond cake of Venice. Nearly every region of Italy makes a version of *torrone,* the beloved nougat candy studded with almonds. And who can forget *marzapane,* found everywhere in Italy but an unmatched specialty of Sicily? Made solely from ground almonds, sugar, and egg whites, shaped into all manner of tiny fruits and vegetables and decorated like works of art, marzipan is a direct almond hit to the taste buds and arguably the ultimate use of an almond.

Walnuts are another popular nut in Italy, and they're my personal favorite. Their flavor is a bit more complex, which is perhaps why I like them so much. The outer skin of the walnut is slightly bitter, which contrasts nicely with the sweet, fatty richness of the nutmeat. I cannot resist them, especially when they are toasted, which intensifies the bittersweet flavor. Walnuts, or *noci,* are grown in several regions of Italy, with the most revered coming from the area around Sorrento, on the coast of Campania. Sorrento's walnuts are slightly darker than those harvested in Umbria, a region that also produces a sizable walnut crop. *Noci* are featured in numerous savory dishes as well as an array of sweets, such as *castagnaccio,* a traditional chestnut and honey cake, and *pan pepato,* a spicy, sweet bread from Umbria made with candied fruits and ground pepper. Green walnuts are the primary ingredient used to make *nocino,* a digestif made annually in June, before the walnuts have fully ripened on the tree.

Perhaps the most highly prized nut in Italy is the hazelnut, harvested in the area surrounding Alba in Piedmont. Piedmontese hazelnuts (*Nocciole del Piemonte*) are the fruit of a noble tree, the *Tonda Gentile delle Langhe,* and their reputation as the best is confirmed by their IGP status, the first such designation bestowed on a product of that region by the European Union. Rounder and plumper than most, Piedmontese hazelnuts have a heady and intense fragrance when roasted. There is not a *pasticceria* in Piedmont that does not boast that its *torta di nocciola,* or hazelnut cake, is the finest in all Italy. Hazelnuts are found in countless confections and desserts, but their best-known use is in Nutella, the wildly popular hazelnut and chocolate spread.

Hazelnuts also grace Piedmontese *torrone* and countless versions of mousses, cakes, tortes, and *biscotti*.

Another fine, IGP-designated hazelnut is the *Nocciole di Giffoni*, which flourishes in the volcanic soil of Campania. This variety is flatter and more spherical, with a darker skin and whiter nutmeat. The demand for *Nocciole del Piemonte* and *Nocciole di Giffoni* has increased over the years, owing to the growth of the confectionery industry in Italy and to stepped-up efforts to export them to American and European chefs and confectioners. Sweet, crunchy, and luxuriously rich, hazelnuts are truly an indulgence.

In Sicily you encounter many desserts and confections studded with pistachios, which are bright green and tinged with hues of pink and red. I can't help but smile whenever I see them. Their exact origin is the subject of some debate; they may have been brought to Sicily by the Phoenicians or by Greek colonizers, and they have historically been grown in the area surrounding Mount Etna. It was the Arab Saracens, the confection-loving invaders who ruled Sicily from the ninth through the early eleventh century, who encouraged the wider cultivation of pistachio trees. Almonds dominate the island agriculturally, but Sicilians never lost their traditional love of pistachios in their sweets. These nuts are an ever-present ingredient in Sicilian cakes, *gelati*, and cookies, despite the fact that Sicily's pistachio harvest has decreased dramatically in the past century. Sicilian pistachios are available in the United States, but they are hard to find. Smaller and softer than domestic pistachios and those imported from the Middle East, Sicilian pistachios have a more pronounced flavor, thanks to the rich volcanic soil.

Also popular are Italian pine nuts, or *pignoli*. Pine nuts aren't really nuts at all, but seeds found within the cones of the Italian stone pine tree. If you have ever spent a ridiculous amount of money on a tiny jar of pine nuts, you can appreciate how labor-intensive the process of harvesting them is. The cones are heated to a specific temperature to dry them and then shaken to remove the seeds, which are then further dried to facilitate removal of their paper-thin skins. The nuts that survive intact are reserved for export (hence those tiny, expensive jars), while the rest are used locally in any number of sweet or savory dishes. The ancient Romans enjoyed their pine nuts. The philosopher Pliny preserved them in honey, and archaeologists have found pine nuts among foods uncovered at the ruins of Pompeii. Today Italian bakers in every region use pine nuts in cakes, tarts, cookies, breads, and candies. You can distinguish Italian pine nuts from their Chinese counterparts by their long, thin shape. Italian pine nuts also possess a more delicate flavor and are rich in heart-healthy monounsaturated oils.

Buying nuts can be an uncertain process. I personally distrust those dusty bags found on the shelves of supermarkets and prefer to shop for nuts at health-food stores that sell them in bulk or at upscale specialty markets. It is important to remember that nuts contain oils, some more than others, which makes them especially perishable. This is particularly true of pistachios and pine nuts. I always store nuts I am not using immediately in an airtight container kept in a cool, dry place. The refrigerator can be too humid, eventually turning nuts soggy and stale-tasting. Some nuts can be frozen, but I am not a big fan of that practice either, as the flavor tends to deteriorate and ice crystals can form on them. My golden rule for nuts is to buy them as you would fresh produce and consume or cook with them right away.

The A. L. Bazzini Company is a beloved fixture in New York, and its store in the TriBeCa neighborhood of lower Manhattan is a nut lover's fantasy. It carries every nut you can imagine, natural or roasted, packaged or in bulk, and of the highest quality. Best of all, the company ships its nuts, as well as an impressive array of dried fruits and other specialty items, to any address in the continental United States.

AMARETTI

Don't be confused—*amaretti* are indeed cookies, not a raw ingredient. But crumbled or crushed, they are often used as a component or final embellishment in many classic Italian desserts. We make and serve *amaretti* daily at Babbo; they are always on the shelf above the pastry station, ready to jump into service when the need arises. I think of *amaretti* as a wonderful and versatile ingredient, worth knowing and worth keeping as a staple in any kitchen.

Amaretti translates as "a little bitter." Meringue cookies, *amaretti* are plump and round, with tiny flecks of crystallized sugar decorating their golden brown, crackled tops. The flavor of the cookies comes from armelline, the oil or essence of kernels found in apricot pits. The most widely known *amaretti* in America, *Amaretti di Saronno*, are produced by the Lazzaroni company. They are immediately recognizable in their distinctive square, bright-red tin canisters in Italian specialty stores. The cookies themselves are packaged in twin sets; two *amaretti* are wrapped together with a pastel tissue, and the legend of how they were invented reveals why. The cardinal of Milan visited the town of Saronno in Lombardy in 1718. A young baker and his lover concocted the recipe for *amaretti* from the only ingredients they could find in Saronno, baking them as a gift for the prelate and his entourage. The cardinal was so pleased that he blessed the young lovers in marriage, and the tradition of baking *amaretti* has been carried forth ever since, with the recipe kept a closely guarded secret by the Lazzaroni family.

Amaretti are made in nearly every region in Italy and are so beloved and ubiquitous, they developed into a popular ingredient in desserts. Crumbled or ground into fine crumbs, *amaretti* are sprinkled over fruit and *gelati*, baked into custards, and folded into mousses, infusing each with their crunchy texture and enduringly familiar taste. That distinctive flavor comes from the armelline, which echoes the sweet flavor of almonds. Since armelline is not commercially available, I bake my *amaretti* with plenty of ground almonds and Amaretto di Saronno, the famous Italian liqueur, which is also made with apricot kernel oil. The liqueur helps my recipe recall the original, but nothing really comes close to the flavor of authentic *Amaretti di Saronno*. Numerous industrial bakers in Italy produce their own versions of *amaretti*, some using both bitter almonds and sweet almonds, but I recommend that you stay with the originals made by Lazzaroni, since they are quite easy to find.

GRAPPA

There is nothing to fear from a bottle of grappa, yet for many Americans, grappa represents the scary monster of spirits. I think the apprehension comes from bad grappa experiences; we are not all lucky enough to have that "first time" be the perfect time. Perhaps tasting Uncle Salvatore's homemade grappa from the old country was not the optimal way to discover it. Admittedly, a grappa hangover is no fun. I remember awakening one morning after a brave encounter with a bottle of grappa the night before and engaging in my very own question-and-answer period: Was it really that strong? *Uh, yeah, about 80 or 90 proof.* I thought it would taste like jet fuel. *It obviously got smoother with the second and third glass.* Did I forget my name? *Maybe, but at least I found my house keys.*

Until recently, much of the grappa available in the United States was mass-produced, cheap, and as flavorful as paint thinner. These days you can walk into any fine Italian restaurant or wine bar in a major American city and find a selection of grappa, beautifully bottled by passionate Italian artisans and made from an impressive range of varietals. An *aquavite,* or "water of life," grappa is made by distilling grape skins and grape pomace, and this characteristic distinguishes it from other distillates made from wine or fruit. There are several dates of importance in the long and rather hotly debated history of grappa. In the tenth century, doctors established the rules for using distillations for medicinal purposes; in the fifteenth century came the first specific mention of *aquavite* by name; and in the seventeenth century, Jesuit monks began to record information about grappa, including methods, recipes, and uses. Many of today's traditional producers point to a long family history of making grappa, dating back to the eighteenth and nineteenth centuries.

Grape pomace is essentially the leftovers of the winemaking process—the skins, pulp, and seeds. The pomace is heated in a still to produce an alcoholic mixture, which is distilled to remove the solids along with water, impurities, methyl alcohol, and any other volatile substances. The grappa is then carefully aged in a multistep process, which ends with a final reduction of alcohol and cold-filtering. Skilled, traditional grappa distillers produce a drink that is filled with nuance and flavor.

Since every region of Italy produces wine, grappa is made in every region on some level or another, and this is where things become tricky. A surprising bit of advice is to be wary of grappa bearing the label of a leading winemaker. The pomace may have come from those vineyards, but the grappa could have been made by anyone. When in doubt, use a compass; grappa is truly a northern passion, and the finest, most impeccably made grappa comes from the small producers of the Veneto and Friuli–Venezia Giulia. Grappa made from red grapes, such as Sangiovese and Refosco, is rounder, softer, and has more clearly defined flavor, while grappa made from white grapes, like Chardonnay and Moscato, is delicate and more floral.

Over the years I have become fond of using grappa in my desserts in place of brandy and other liqueurs, and I find that a truly fine grappa will accent and improve whatever flavor is highlighted on the plate. I especially enjoy adding grappa to fresh fruit desserts; tossing fruit with a dash of grappa before it goes into a tart shell works wonders. And grappa is heavenly when added to a crepe batter or lightly sweetened whipped cream.

Among the best grappa producers are the Nonino family, Jacopo Poli, and Nardini, to name just a few. The best place to purchase distinctive grappa is from wine shops that either specialize in Italian wines or have a large selection of Italian spirits.

SWEET WINES, OR *VINI DOLCI*

My first experience with the sweet wines, or *vini dolci*, of Italy took place when I began working at Babbo. Although I already knew plenty about Italian cooking, I knew little of these Italian wines. I had sampled French Sauternes and had a glass or two of ruby port but had never really been exposed to dessert wines. The architects of Babbo's distinguished and constantly evolving wine program have generously educated me in the delights of *vini dolci* over the years, and the more of these wines I have tasted, the more tempting it has been for me to experiment with them in the kitchen.

Vin santo, or *vino santo,* is a sweet Italian wine to fall in love with. It is produced in several regions of Italy, but the *vin santo* produced in Tuscany, particularly *Vino Santo del Chianti Classico DOC,* is considered the standard-bearer. The method for making *vin santo,* known as *appassimento,* is unique. It begins with a specific blend of white grapes, which varies from region to region but is usually a fifty-fifty blend of *malvasia* and *trebbiano* varietals. The harvested grapes are strung together and hung from the rafters or laid out on special straw matting in a special room, where they dry for three to six months. The dried grapes, which have essentially become raisins, are pressed to extract their highly concentrated juices, which are aged in small wooden casks for three or more years. The sweetness of the wine varies, depending on the sweetness and ripeness of the harvested grapes as well as how long they were dried. It is a wine with lovely viscosity—the color resembles liquid caramel. *Vin santo* is a natural partner for sweets because its acidity balances the sweetness. The classic way to enjoy it is to dip crunchy *biscotti* into a glass after dinner. I have found it to be a fabulous medium for poaching fruit, especially dried fruit, and I like to combine it with marsala when making *zabaione.*

Marsala takes its name from the region where it is produced, in the western corner of Sicily. Too often it suffers the indignity of being slugged into brown gravy and smothered over veal and mushrooms. It is the ideal candidate for an identity makeover in America. Like sherry, *marsala* is a fortified wine, meaning that additional wine or spirits are added during the fermentation process to increase its final alcohol content; in the case of marsala, wine from the previous year's vintage may be added. It can be sweet, semisweet, or dry, and the color ranges from golden to ruby-tinged. The level of sweetness, color, and flavor is determined by the particular blend of grapes used by the vintner. As with any wine, the quality will run from moderately bad to amazing, and the best vintages rival any great sherry or port. Truly fine *marsala* can elevate a dessert as an ingredient or an accompaniment. The nutty, raisiny characteristics give classic *zabaione* its distinctive flair and shine through the other flavors and textures at play in rich, custard-based desserts such as tiramisu.

Italy produces numerous other sweet wines, including sparkling and *frizzante*, or semisparkling, varieties. *Moscato d'Asti* is a delicious sparkling sweet white wine from Piedmont, made with the *moscato*, or Muscat grape. It is lightly sweet yet balanced, with a low alcohol content. There is also *Moscato Rosa*, a slightly less fizzy, rosé variation from Trentino–Alto Adige. *Passito di Pantellaria*, from the island off the coast of Sicily of the same name, is a sweet wine that tastes like a golden raisin in a bottle. *Recioto* from the Veneto and sweet *Brachetto d'Acqui* from Piedmont, sparkling or not, *Malvasia* from Sardinia, fortified or not, and exceptional sweet wines from Orvieto and Montefalco in Umbria are just a few examples from a list that goes on and on.

Pairing these wines with actual desserts is a challenge that can sometimes be met but more often cannot without sacrificing the intent and integrity of either the wine or the food. The best way to enjoy dessert wines is to drink them with something dry and crumbly, which explains why they are so often used for dunking. I find they go exceedingly well with slightly sweet holiday breads and crumbly or spongy cakes. One of my favorite ways to experiment with sweet wines as an ingredient is to sprinkle or brush them directly onto warm cakes just out of the oven. Incorporating them into glazes and icings that go onto breads, cakes, and cookies works well too. *Panna montata*, or whipped cream, is a good foil for certain dessert wines, lacing it with floral notes.

Vino Italiano is an excellent and comprehensive guide to Italian wines by Joseph Bastianich and David Lynch, containing a wealth of information about *vini dolci* as well as numerous resources for selecting and purchasing them.

EQUIPMENT

When I sat down to write this chapter, I initially felt some conflict about it. An image of my Nonni, wearing her embroidered bib apron and standing in her small New York kitchen equipped with appliances dating back to the 1940s, kept floating in front of me. My grandmother did not scratch her head and wonder which size cake pan to use or dig in a drawer for the perfect pastry brush. She used what equipment she had, and she didn't have much. Somehow she constantly turned out *piles* of food, sweets included, for abundant family gatherings, year in and year out.

At the same time, I recalled that my grandmother was no fool. I remember her first encounter with a new appliance my mother received as a gift sometime in the late 1970s—an early-model food processor. Quite frankly, my little Italian grandma was thrilled. I recall some beef cubes going into it and meatballs being shaped soon after. Maybe my Nonni, and all grandmas, would be pretty darn happy with an array of shiny, technologically sound bakeware and ergonomically correct gadgets at their fingertips.

I finally decided that a mixture of the past and the present works best for me. I still have the large, deep cast-iron skillet from my grandmother's kitchen, which is at least fifty years old, and some of her heavy baking pans and her huge wooden dowel for rolling dough. I also have some of the latest and best cookware available sitting alongside them in my cupboard. In my mind, the cook is ultimately the best judge of what is or is not a good pan. Here are a few guidelines for filling in the gaps.

MIXING AND MEASURING

Let's start with the basics. For gathering your ingredients and mixing them, whether by hand or with a mixer, you will need a set of mixing bowls in graduated sizes, ranging from small, to hold a cup or two of ingredients, to extra-large, holding up to 20 cups or 5 quarts, for accommodating large batches of dough or batter. I favor bowls made from ceramic, glass, or heavy stainless steel, since they resist staining and do not absorb odors, but a good set of heavy-duty plastic bowls will work fine too; just be sure to wash them thoroughly, and soak them in a bit of bleach if any food odors or stains appear. A set of measuring spoons is also absolutely necessary, and again, plastic works fine, but I prefer those made of heavy stainless steel, because they are less likely to bend or dent.

It amazes me that some cooks do not realize the difference between dry and liquid measuring cups. There is indeed a difference. A basic set of dry measuring cups will include ¼-cup, ⅓-cup, ½-cup, and 1-cup sizes. I also like to have set of so-called odd-sized cups, which includes ⅔-cup, ¾-cup, 1½-cup, and 2-cup sizes, although none of these measurements are odd. The 2-cup measure is especially handy for recipes calling for large amounts of flour or sugar. Once again, plastic is fine, stainless steel is best.

Liquid measuring cups display the standard American measurements, with cups and ounces, on one side, and the metric measures, in milliliters and liters on the other. It is important to have both, especially since those recipes from your aunt in Palermo will probably be in metric measurements. I like glass cups, but in this case I favor plastic cups, since they are easier to store.

Ten years ago, kitchen scales for home use were a tough find, and digital scales were elusive and expensive to boot, even for professional kitchens. I always wound up improvising with a postal scale from the office supply store, which was usually clumsy and too large for a small kitchen space. Today digital kitchen scales are available everywhere fine cookware is sold. Look for models that measure ounces as well as grams and can take a maximum weight of 5 pounds. Many professional pastry chefs encourage home cooks to weigh all their ingredients. While I agree that weighing is the most accurate way of measuring, I also think that most home cooks are more comfortable with traditional English volume measurements. In some instances I do prefer weight measurements, and I have included them here for ingredients that defy volume measurement, such as butter, chocolate, nuts, and dried fruits. The more baking you do, the more comfortable you will become with weight measurements, making a digital scale an invaluable addition to your kitchen.

This brings us to the actual mixing. An electric standing mixer is the single best investment you can make in your kitchen. Most mixers include a beater, or paddle attachment; a dough hook; and a whisk, or whip, attachment for aerating eggs, beating egg whites, and whipping cream or mascarpone into fluffy peaks. KitchenAid mixers come in 4-, 5-, and 6-quart capacities, in a rainbow of beautiful colors and with an array of useful attachments available. Even my Nonni had a standing mixer, a Sunbeam model from the 1950s that she regarded in the same way I think of a NASA weather satellite—a marvel of modern ingenuity with rewards well worth reaping, even if I don't understand exactly how it works.

It is important for any baker to own a good electric mixer. Hand mixers are functional to a certain degree, and newer models have both flat beaters for batters and dough and wire whips for egg whites and cream. But the handheld models simply do not have enough horsepower to handle large recipes. They rely on you and the power of your arms to mix the ingredients evenly and for the specified amount of time, which is fine for beating a couple of eggs or a cup of whipping cream but a true physical challenge when it comes to dense cookie doughs or large batches of cake batter. A standing mixer simply cannot be compared to a hand mixer in terms of power, functionality, and convenience. If you do invest in a KitchenAid—and I strongly suggest this—then consider purchasing the nifty and quite wonderful pasta rolling attachment too.

MAKING THE CUT

For pastry, I find that a chef's knife, with either an 8-inch blade or a 10-inch blade, is necessary for chopping and dicing, especially nuts, chocolate, herbs, and dried fruits. A paring knife that fits comfortably in your hand is necessary for smaller jobs that require more precision. To keep your knives sharp, regularly hone them on a sharpening stone, which restores the knife's edge, and use a sharpening steel to maintain the edge in between tasks. For slicing *biscotti* and breads, a long, serrated bread knife should also be part of your collection. An offset serrated knife with a thin blade is most effective for delicate *biscotti* and can also be used instead of a chef's knife for chopping nuts and chocolate. It goes without saying that a good cutting board, wooden or heavy-duty plastic, is the only surface suitable for using a knife.

BAKING PANS

When it comes to bakeware, quality makes all the difference. And the single most important factor in determining the quality of a baking pan is its weight, with the materials used to make the pan a close second. It is the weight of the pan, along with its construction, that affects how evenly heat is conducted as an item bakes. In a lightweight, flimsy pan, the heat is not conducted evenly or efficiently during the baking time, so your baked goods are sometimes raw on the inside and scorched on the bottom.

The first rule of thumb is to avoid at all costs thin pans that are made only of aluminum. Instead, look for the words "heavy-gauge," which means that the pans are made with a double or triple ply of metal. Aluminum may indeed be used on an inner layer, but carbon steel or stainless steel has also entered the equation. A tough, durable nonstick coating is another bonus, and over the past several years the quality and variety of nonstick bakeware has increased dramatically so that it is definitely worth the investment. Glass bakeware is another choice, but it does not conduct heat as efficiently as metal. I have experienced browning issues with glass pie plates; the crust never seems to cook enough on the bottom. A far better choice is cast iron coated with enamel. There are several brands to choose from, colorful and attractive as well as functional. In some cases this kind of bakeware conducts heat a bit *too* well, and I find I have to adjust my baking times down a little to compensate for their superconductive powers.

Ultimately, the most reliable way to judge the weight of a particular pan is to hold it in your hands. Compare it to the one sitting next to it and then pick the heavier one. As for the pans you already have, if they work, then by all means use them. I am in no position to decide whether your favorite brownie pan is good or not. If the brownies are good, then chances are you know what you are doing.

Now that you know how to pick your bakeware, it is time to select the sizes. In terms of the recipes in this book, you should make sure you have the following items:

- **TWO HEAVY BAKING SHEETS** are an absolute must. I tend to favor those with a small lip, known in professional terms as half-sheet pans, or jelly-roll pans, which have sides all the way around. I prefer them to baking sheets without a lip, because, truth be told, I am clumsy. I have had an entire batch of cookies slide off a standard cookie sheet and onto the floor or, more painfully, onto my feet because of one of my more graceful moves. I have never found that the lip requires an adjustment in the baking time, but when in doubt, simply bake your cookies until they are done.

- **CAKE PANS** come in a variety of sizes. I use 9- and 10-inch cake pans the most, and my favorites are those that are 3 inches deep, which is more than the standard layer-cake pan. For American-style layer cakes that are filled and frosted, the obvious choice is a standard 9-by-2-inch pan. The cakes in this book are more like tortes; they remain in one layer and are sliced into wedges, so a layer-cake pan will work fine. The other must in this category is the springform pan, preferably either 9, 9½, or 10 inches in diameter and 3 inches deep. In most instances, springform pans can be used interchangeably with layer-cake pans. For bar cookies or square cakes, I like to use a 9- or 10-inch square pan or, for larger recipes, a 13-by-9-inch rectangular pan without sloping sides, such as a lasagne pan. Since loaf cakes are my very favorites, I can't imagine life without two loaf pans. I like to have both 9- and 10-inch ones on hand. The quality and availability of good bakeware have increased dramatically over the past decade, and my favorite brands are Cuisinart, especially the Classic Non-Stick series, NordicWare, and the superb but pricey line of bakeware by All-Clad.

- **TART PANS** are distinctly different from round pie pans. They have fluted straight sides and a removable bottom, which makes it quite easy to pop your finished *crostata* out of the pan and onto a serving plate. I like to use a 9½- or 10-inch tart pan, but for larger tarts, a 12-inch pan works very well. I like nonstick tart pans or those made with heavy black steel; the tarts slide right off, and they clean up easily.

FROM THE SAVORY SIDE OF THE KITCHEN

Saucepans are used as much in making pastry as in making savory dishes. It is a good idea to have 1-, 2-, and 3-quart saucepans in your arsenal for making *gelato* bases, custards, and sweet sauces. The same rule applies here as with bakeware: the heavier the pan is, the more evenly and efficiently the heat will be conducted. For frying, a deep 5-quart stockpot is best, and use it with a deep-fry/candy thermometer, which can clip to the side of the pot. Now and again you will find the need to use a sauté pan, usually a smaller, 8-inch one, but a 10- or 12-inch pan will also come in handy. A large, heavy roasting pan is a must for baking desserts in a water bath; try to get one with a completely even bottom and straight sides. For a stovetop water bath, or double boiler, I like to use a 2- or 3-quart saucepan to hold simmering water, with a stainless steel or glass bowl that fits snugly on top.

GADGETS AND GIZMOS

It is easy to become mesmerized by the gadget section of your favorite kitchenware emporium. The next thing you know, you have convinced yourself that you cannot live without that strawberry huller. Feel free to splurge and fill your drawers with all manner of gadgets; they certainly can make life in the kitchen a bit more fun. Personally, I like to think in terms of quality rather than quantity, so be sure to include the following items in your collection:

- **WIRE WHISKS**, both the balloon kind, for whipping egg whites or cream by hand, and the straight kind, for combining dry ingredients and gently cooking custards. Try to have two sizes of each variety, large and medium, to accommodate your bowls and saucepans.

- **RUBBER SPATULAS**, also found in a variety of sizes. Heatproof silicone spatulas are better; they remain flexible but won't crack and deteriorate after prolonged exposure to the high heat of stovetop cooking.

- **A PASTRY BAG**, size 12, 14, and/or 16, necessary for piping ganache and icings as well as doughnut and *bigne* doughs. As for pastry tips, I prefer to use the larger kind that fits directly into the bottom of the bag, rather than the smaller tips that require a coupler attachment. Plain round tips in several sizes and one or two star tips will get the most use for the recipes in this book.

- **SHARP VEGETABLE PEELERS.** I prefer the Y-type to the straight, vertical kind.

- **A GOOD GRATER**, nowadays known as a microplane. Microplanes are wonderful because they don't shred and tear citrus zest as box graters do. Their unique design and super-sharp blades allow the food to fall from the grater instead of getting stuck in between notches. They come in a variety of lengths and with different degrees of grating, and are a must for your gadget collection.

- **METAL TONGS** are perfect for gently picking up roasted fruit or turning fritters in a sauté pan.

- **A WOODEN-HANDLED CHINESE SKIMMER OR A SLOTTED SPOON**—ideal for removing deep-fried items from hot oil or fruits from poaching liquid.

- **A CHINOIS**, which is a conical sieve, and **A SMALL, 2-OUNCE LADLE**, for straining *sorbetto*, *gelato,* and custard bases.

- **A SIFTER OR A FINE-MESHED SIEVE**, for sifting dry ingredients and dusting confectioners' sugar. I particularly like sifters with three layers of screen mesh, also known as triple-sifters.

- **AN OFFSET SPATULA**, or several, in graduated sizes, for spreading batters evenly into cake pans and for icing and glazing cakes and cookies.

- **A PASTRY BRUSH**, for glazing cookies and cakes and brushing excess flour off the surface of dough. Silicone brushes are a godsend, because the individual brush hairs won't fall out and into your food, and the brushes clean up very easily.

- **A CANDY/DEEP-FRY THERMOMETER**, for determining the temperature of boiling sugar and/ or honey and of oil for frying. I prefer the flat, rectangular type that clips easily to the side of the pan.

- **A COOLING RACK FOR COOKIES AND CAKES.** I prefer large rectangular grid-type racks. One is good but two are better, as any baker of dozens of cookies at a time can attest.

- **PARCHMENT PAPER,** now widely available in supermarkets—the ideal medium for helping to ease baked goods out of or off their pans.

COUNTERTOP MUSTS

In addition to a standing mixer, two appliances are worthy of precious space on your kitchen countertops: a canister blender and a food processor, both indispensable. Many people make the mistake of choosing either one or the other. I regard both as basics. With a standard chopping blade, a food processor finely chops nuts and chocolate, and nothing makes better tart dough. Blenders have smaller, more powerful blades, perfect for giving fruit purees, sauces, and soups a superfine, silky consistency. A heavy-duty canister blender is the only appliance powerful enough for this task. Hand blenders, also known as immersion blenders, are great for quick jobs, but do not expect them to pack the same punch as a canister blender. I prefer Cuisinart food processors and have found that KitchenAid and Waring make the best blenders. The rule of thumb for blenders and food processors is that you get what you pay for. You can pick up an inexpensive blender or food processor at a discount store for $20 to $40, but it will not stand the test of time. Always approach the purchase of food processors and blenders as a long-term investment.

Set aside a coffee grinder to use exclusively for grinding spices. It is an inexpensive friend that will come in quite handy for grinding your own spices and dried citrus zest.

An electric countertop fryer is useful if you have the space to spare and love frying fritters and doughnuts. Look for models by DeLonghi and T-Fal for superior quality.

Last but not least, you will need an ice cream machine to churn *gelato*. The nonelectric kind, which utilizes a frozen canister and hand cranking, rarely lives up to its promise. If you are seriously interested in experimenting with making *gelato*, try a countertop electric machine. They come in a range of prices and sizes, so research them carefully before making a purchase.

Now that you are fully equipped, *andiamo;* let's go into *la cucina.*

COOKIES
biscotti

COOKIES EMBODY THE CONCEPT OF BAKING AS AN ACT OF SHARING. Who can possibly make an entire batch and keep them all? It is impossible. When they are warm from the oven, their irresistible aroma wafting through the house instantly draws a crowd to the kitchen. Packed in a tin or sealed in a jar, an unexpected gift of cookies epitomizes the spirit of generosity.

The word *biscotti* has a different meaning in Italy than it does here in the United States; cookies of all shapes, flavors, and sizes are commonly referred to as *biscotti* in *pasticcerie,* or pastry shops. The origin of the word can be traced back to the Roman Empire. In Latin, *bis* means "twice," and *coctum,* which means "baked," eventually morphed into *cotto,* or "cooked." The original *biscotti* were more about function than flavor. Unleavened wafers were first baked to cook them and baked again to dry them out completely, making them suitable nourishment during the long journeys that were the life of a Roman soldier. The Roman philosopher Pliny boasted that *biscotti* would be edible for centuries, a theory that I hope was not tested on an unsuspecting medieval duke.

Italians enjoy crumbly, dry-textured cookies that are perfect for savoring with a glass of wine, and I don't argue with the concept. My favorite ending to a meal is undoubtedly a few almond *biscotti* dipped into a glass of *vin santo,* the golden, slightly sweet dessert wine of Tuscany. The austerity of an unadorned butter cookie is uncommon in Italy, because Italians love to embellish their *biscotti* with fruit, nuts, chocolate, and icings, featuring their local ingredients. In this chapter you will find a range of flavors, textures, and ingredients from every corner of Italy: polenta from the Veneto, honey from Tuscany, almonds and pistachios from Sicily, chestnuts and lemons from Campania. The recipes are a mix of the old and the new, of favorites from my personal cookie jar and some popular choices from the Babbo cookie plate. Be prepared to make a double batch of your favorites; the joy of sharing is contagious.

Cookies are often the fledgling baker's first foray into desserts, because they are relatively easy to master. There are a few things to remember when baking cookies. First, you will probably bake the cookies in batches, staggering the forming or rolling, baking, and cooling. If a recipe calls for working with only one portion of the cookie dough at a time, keep the remaining portions refrigerated until you are ready to work with them. It is your decision how many sheets of cookies to bake at once. If you bake only one sheet at a time, you will get the best results from positioning the rack in the center of the oven. When making large batches of cookies, I prefer to bake two or even three sheets at a time, and in that case I move the sheets from the top rack to the bottom rack, and vice versa, halfway to three quarters of the way through the baking time, to ensure that the cookies bake evenly. I also turn the pans 180 degrees for even browning. Always allow your cookies to cool and firm up for several minutes before using a spatula to slide them gently off the baking sheet and onto a wire rack to cool completely. Store cookies in an airtight container and keep them in a cool, dark, dry place. If they are decorated or iced, layer them between sheets of parchment paper to protect them. To keep soft cookies moist, place a few apple peels in the container.

CHOCOLATE KISSES
baci di cioccolato

This is one of the first recipes I created for Babbo, so these cookies carry fond memories for me. I also love them because they are intensely chocolatey without being too sweet. Baci means "kisses" in Italian, and here two chocolate cookies are sandwiched with a kiss of chocolate ganache. It is highly likely that the lucky people who devour them will kiss you for making them. If you prefer, you can pipe a small rosette or star of ganache onto each cookie instead of making sandwiches, but the kisses are a bit more difficult to store that way. I must admit that I also like them without the chocolate ganache—a simple kiss of chocolate, which isn't a bad thing at all. MAKES APPROXIMATELY 2 1/2 DOZEN SANDWICHES OR 5 DOZEN SINGLE COOKIES

FOR THE COOKIES

½ cup whole blanched almonds

1 tablespoon granulated sugar, plus more
    for rolling

1½ cups plus 1 tablespoon unbleached
    all-purpose flour

⅓ cup unsweetened Dutch-processed cocoa
    powder

¼ teaspoon baking powder

½ teaspoon kosher salt

1 cup (2 sticks/8 ounces) unsalted butter,
    softened

1 cup confectioners' sugar

2 teaspoons pure vanilla extract

1 tablespoon dark rum

FOR THE GANACHE FILLING

8 ounces bittersweet or semisweet chocolate,
    chopped

1 tablespoon unsalted butter, softened

¾ cup heavy cream

2 teaspoons dark rum, grappa, cognac,
    or your favorite liqueur (optional)

To make the cookies: Preheat the oven to 325°F. Spread the almonds in a single layer on a baking sheet and toast them until they are light golden brown and fragrant, 14 to 16 minutes. Remove the almonds from the oven and turn off the oven until you are ready to form the cookies. Allow the almonds to cool completely, then grind them in a food processor with the 1 tablespoon sugar until they are finely chopped.

In a medium bowl, whisk together the flour, cocoa powder, baking powder, and salt and set aside.

Using an electric mixer fitted with the paddle attachment, beat together the butter and confectioners' sugar on medium speed until creamy and light, about 2 minutes, then beat in the vanilla extract and rum and scrape down the sides of the bowl. On low speed, beat in the dry ingredients, followed by the ground almonds. Remove the dough from the bowl, flatten it into a disk, wrap it in plastic, and chill for about 1 hour, until it is firm enough to handle.

Preheat the oven to 325°F. Lightly grease two baking sheets with nonstick cooking spray or butter or line them with parchment paper. On a lightly floured surface, divide the dough into 3 pieces. Work with 1 piece at a time, keeping the others wrapped and refrigerated. Roll 1 portion of dough into a small log about ¾ inch in diameter. Cut each log into ½-inch lengths and roll each piece into a ball, then roll the balls in granulated sugar to coat them completely. Place the cookies on the prepared baking sheets, spaced ½ inch apart. Repeat with the remaining portions of dough.

Bake the cookies, rotating the sheets 180 degrees to ensure even browning, until they are puffed and cracking slightly on top, 12 to 15 minutes. Allow the cookies to cool on the sheets for 1 or 2 minutes, then use a spatula to remove them gently to a wire rack to cool completely.

While the cookies are cooling, make the ganache filling: Place the chopped chocolate and butter in a medium bowl. Heat the heavy cream in a saucepan until it comes to a boil and pour it over the chocolate and butter. Allow the mixture to sit for a few moments, then whisk until smooth and glossy. Whisk in the rum, if you like. Allow the ganache to cool, whisking it occasionally, until it is firm enough to pipe.

To assemble the kisses: Pair up the cookies according to size. Turn one cookie upside down and, using a pastry bag fitted with a plain or star tip, pipe a small amount of ganache onto the flat side, then place the bottom of the second cookie on the ganache to form a sandwich; the two round tops of the cookies should be facing outward. Repeat until all the cookies have been used. Allow the ganache to firm up, at room temperature or in the refrigerator if necessary, then transfer the kisses to a serving plate.

The cookies can be stored, layered between sheets of parchment paper, in an airtight container kept in a cool place for up to 3 days.

ALMOND FINGERS
ditti di mandorle

Almond flour gives these tasty lemon-scented cookies a very tender texture, while the crunch of the sliced almond coating provides a perfect contrast. Dusted with confectioners' sugar and piled on a cake stand or antique plate, they make an elegant presentation. I especially love them with a cup of hot, lemony tea.

MAKES APPROXIMATELY 4 DOZEN COOKIES

2 cups unbleached all-purpose flour

¾ cup almond flour

¼ teaspoon baking powder

½ teaspoon kosher salt

1 cup (2 sticks/8 ounces) unsalted butter, softened

1 cup granulated sugar

1 large egg, separated

Freshly grated zest of 1 lemon

1 teaspoon pure vanilla extract

2 cups sliced blanched almonds

Confectioners' sugar, for dusting

In a medium bowl, whisk together the all-purpose flour, almond flour, baking powder, and salt and set aside.

Using an electric mixer fitted with the paddle attachment, beat together the butter and granulated sugar on medium speed until light and fluffy, about 2 minutes. Beat in the egg yolk, followed by the lemon zest and vanilla extract, scraping down the sides of the bowl after each addition. Beat in the dry ingredients on low speed to make a stiff dough. Remove the dough from the bowl, flatten it into a disk, wrap it in plastic, and chill until it is firm enough to roll, about 1 hour.

Preheat the oven to 325°F. Lightly grease two baking sheets with nonstick cooking spray or butter or line them with parchment paper.

Place the almonds in a shallow bowl. In another shallow bowl, lightly beat the egg white with a fork until frothy.

Divide the dough into 3 equal pieces. Work with 1 piece at a time, keeping the other portions wrapped and refrigerated. Roll the piece of dough into a narrow log ½ inch in diameter. Cut the log into cylinders about 1½ inches long. Roll each cylinder in the beaten egg white, then in the sliced almonds to coat it completely. Place the cookies on the prepared sheets, spacing them evenly, about ½ inch apart. Repeat with the remaining portions of dough.

WHAT EXACTLY IS ALMOND FLOUR?

Professional pastry chefs often use almond flour in their recipes, and increasingly you will find it included in recipes for the home chef. Almond flour imparts a subtle, sweet almond flavor and tender texture to cakes, cookies, and pastry dough. It is nothing more than blanched almonds milled into a powder, but that definition is deceptively simple. It is nearly impossible to duplicate the texture of almond flour by simply grinding some blanched almonds at home. A food processor or standard blender can grind the nuts to a certain point, but the blades of these appliances are neither sharp enough nor powerful enough to create a flourlike consistency. Instead, the nuts are pummeled until their oils are released, producing a greasy paste—fine for a sandwich, but not for a cake or cookie recipe. Commercially milled almond flour is uniformly ground to a super-fine consistency. Thanks to the current craze for cooking, almond flour is much easier to find than it used to be. Health-food stores and upscale food markets usually carry it, as do some of the merchants listed in Sources (pages 285–87).

Bake the cookies until they are firm and the almonds are lightly golden brown, 14 to 16 minutes, rotating the sheet 180 degrees halfway through the baking time to ensure even browning. Allow the cookies to cool on the sheets for 1 or 2 minutes, then use a spatula to remove them gently to a wire rack to cool completely. Dust the cookies generously with confectioners' sugar.

The cookies can be stored in an airtight container, layered between sheets of parchment paper, in a cool, dry place for up to 4 days.

MOSTACCIOLI

So many versions of this beloved cookie exist that researching the recipe made my head spin. A pasta shape that goes by the same name only added to the confusion. The mostaccioli I remember from my childhood were soft, formed from a flat log, bias-cut into diamonds, covered in chocolate and a drizzle of icing. From there, I discovered numerous variations. Some were round, some were longer and thinner; some were made with dried fruits, such as citron, figs, and orange peel, while others were less chocolatey and more spicy; some were much sweeter than others, or denser. In Italian cooking, the confusing use of the same name for different things throughout the country's twenty regions is common, but this example took the cake—or actually the cookie.

The story behind the cookies changed from region to region as well. Many Italian Americans know them as "mostachoulli," which seems to have something to do with a comparison to a mustache, which I don't quite get. I eventually heard a story that makes the most sense: the cookies were originally baked during the grape harvest and sweetened with grape must, or mosto. *In Tuscany they are less a cookie than a blob of* mosto-*sweetened bread dough. In Abruzzo and Molise the cookies are made with a combination of chocolate and grape must.*

Since anything goes when it comes to mostaccioli, *I decided to make up my own version. I go along with the use of chocolate, I like to use a bit of spice, and in place of the grape must, I substitute some* vincotto *and honey. The texture is soft and almost cakelike. You can make these cookies in the fall, to celebrate the grape harvest, or at Christmastime, as an unusual addition to your holiday cookie plate.*

MAKES ABOUT 3 DOZEN COOKIES

FOR THE COOKIES
1 heaping cup whole blanched almonds
4 ounces unsweetened chocolate, chopped
½ cup (1 stick/4 ounces) unsalted butter
2 cups unbleached all-purpose flour
1½ cups cake flour
1½ cups granulated sugar
1 tablespoon baking powder
1 teaspoon kosher salt
1 teaspoon ground cinnamon
½ teaspoon ground nutmeg
¼ teaspoon ground cloves

½ cup unsweetened Dutch-processed cocoa powder
½ cup honey
½ cup whole milk
4 large eggs
½ cup *vincotto* (page 93)
¾ cup finely chopped candied citron, candied orange peel, or dried currants

FOR THE ICING
1 cup confectioners' sugar
2 tablespoons whole milk
½ teaspoon pure almond extract

To make the cookies: Preheat the oven to 350 °F. Spread the almonds in a single layer on a baking sheet and toast them until they are light golden brown and fragrant, 14 to 16 minutes. Remove the almonds from the oven and turn off the oven until you are ready to form the cookies. Allow the almonds to cool completely, then chop them into medium-sized pieces with a sharp knife.

Melt the chocolate and butter together in a medium bowl set over a pan of simmering water, whisking to combine them. Set the mixture aside in a warm spot.

In a mixer fitted with the paddle attachment, beat the all-purpose flour, cake flour, sugar, baking powder, salt, spices, and cocoa powder on low speed for 10 seconds to mix thoroughly.

In a medium bowl, whisk together the honey, milk, eggs, and *vincotto*. Add the wet ingredients to the mixer and beat on medium speed until the two mixtures are thoroughly combined, about 1 minute. Add the melted chocolate and butter mixture and beat well on low speed. Add the almonds and the candied fruit and beat just to incorporate them into the dough. Remove the bowl from the mixer, cover it with plastic wrap, and chill the dough for 30 minutes.

Preheat the oven to 325°F. Lightly grease two baking sheets with nonstick cooking spray or butter or line them with parchment.

Remove the dough from the refrigerator. To shape each cookie, roll a heaping teaspoonful of the dough into a ball with floured fingers and place it on the baking sheet, flattening it slightly with your fingers. Repeat with the remaining dough, spacing the cookies ½ inch apart. Bake the cookies for 13 to 15 minutes, or until they are puffed and cracking, rotating the sheets 180 degrees halfway through the baking time to ensure even baking. Allow the cookies to cool for 1 or 2 minutes on the baking sheets, then use a spatula to transfer them gently onto a rack to cool completely.

While the cookies are cooling, make the icing: In a medium bowl, combine the confectioners' sugar with the milk and whisk until the mixture is smooth and free of lumps. Whisk in the almond extract. Keep the icing covered with plastic wrap until you are ready to use it.

To decorate the cookies, drizzle a small amount of icing in a zigzag pattern over the top of each cookie, or glaze the top of each cookie with a pastry brush.

The cookies can be stored in an airtight container between sheets of parchment paper for up to 1 week.

LEMONY SEMOLINA COOKIES
biscotti di limone e semolino

I adore the flavor of fresh lemons, so much so that I seek it out wherever I can, on a restaurant menu or in a pastry shop. It has taken me a number of years to develop my own ultimate lemon cookie recipe, and finally, here it is. The semolina gives these cookies a golden hue and chewy texture. Limoncello *is a delightful lemon liqueur that evokes the sunny coast of Amalfi with every sip. It is made from the rind of fresh lemons, which probably come from Amalfi, Sorrento, or even Sicily, and it is increasingly easy to purchase here in the United States. After you make the cookies, the bottle won't last long in your refrigerator once you take to enjoying a glass of chilled* limoncello *on hot summer evenings. As for the cookies, a perfectly pulled shot of strong espresso is the ideal accompaniment.* **MAKES 5 DOZEN COOKIES**

2 cups unbleached all-purpose flour	1 cup granulated sugar, plus more for rolling
⅔ cup semolina	1 large egg
1 teaspoon baking powder	1 large egg yolk
½ teaspoon baking soda	Freshly grated zest and squeezed juice of 1
½ teaspoon kosher salt	lemon
½ cup (1 stick/4 ounces) unsalted butter,	2 tablespoons *limoncello*
softened	½ teaspoon pure vanilla extract
2 tablespoons extra-virgin olive oil	

In a medium bowl, whisk together the all-purpose flour, semolina, baking powder, baking soda, and salt and set aside.

Using an electric mixer fitted with the paddle attachment, cream together the butter, olive oil, and 1 cup sugar on medium speed until very light and fluffy. Beat in the egg and the egg yolk, followed by the lemon zest and juice, *limoncello,* and vanilla extract, scraping down the sides of the bowl after each addition.

On low speed, beat the dry ingredients into the wet ingredients to make a soft dough. Remove the dough from the bowl, flatten it into a disk, wrap it in plastic, and chill until it is firm enough to roll, about 1 hour.

Preheat the oven to 325°F. Lightly grease two baking sheets with nonstick cooking spray or butter or line them with parchment.

Place the additional granulated sugar in a small bowl. With lightly floured fingers, break off teaspoonfuls of dough and roll them into 1-inch balls. Roll each ball in the granulated sugar to coat evenly. Place the cookies on the baking sheets, evenly spacing them 1 inch apart.

Bake the cookies until they have collapsed and are crinkled and pale golden brown, 14 to 15 minutes, rotating the sheets 180 degrees halfway through the baking time to ensure even browning. Allow the cookies to cool for 1 or 2 minutes on the baking sheets, then use a spatula to transfer them gently onto wire racks to cool completely.

The cookies can be stored in an airtight container, layered with parchment paper, in a cool, dry place for up to 4 days.

HAZELNUT COOKIES
nocciolati

This recipe is my attempt to duplicate some wonderful cookies I sampled from a Roman bakery near the Campo de' Fiori. On the last morning of a visit to the Eternal City a few years ago, I bought a bagful and took them to the train station with me. By the time I got to Florence, they were all gone. My version comes close, but when I make them, I can't help but wish I was back in Rome, munching on them as I wander through the tangle of streets that surround the campo.

MAKES 4 DOZEN COOKIES

1½ cups unbleached all-purpose flour

½ teaspoon baking powder

½ teaspoon kosher salt

2 cups whole hazelnuts, skinned (see page 53)

1¼ cups granulated sugar

2 large eggs

1 teaspoon pure vanilla extract

4 tablespoons (½ stick/2 ounces) unsalted butter, melted and cooled

1 cup confectioners' sugar, for rolling

Preheat the oven to 325°F. Lightly grease two baking sheets with nonstick cooking spray or butter or line them with parchment.

In a large bowl, whisk together the flour, baking powder, and salt and set aside. Place the hazelnuts in the bowl of a food processor with 2 tablespoons of the granulated sugar and process until they are finely chopped.

Using an electric mixer fitted with the paddle attachment, beat the eggs and the remaining 1⅛ cups sugar on medium speed until the mixture is very light in color, about 2 minutes. Add the vanilla extract and then the melted, cooled butter. On low speed, beat in the dry ingredients followed by the ground hazelnuts to make a firm dough, about 30 seconds.

Place the confectioners' sugar in a medium bowl. Using lightly floured fingers, form the dough into 1-inch balls. Roll each ball in the confectioners' sugar to coat evenly. Place the cookies on the baking sheets, evenly spaced ½ inch apart, and lightly press them with your fingers to flatten them slightly.

Bake the cookies until they are puffed, cracked, and lightly golden brown, 16 to 18 minutes, rotating the sheets 180 degrees halfway through the baking time to ensure even browning. Allow the cookies to cool on the baking sheets for 1 or 2 minutes and then use a spatula to transfer them gently onto a wire rack to cool completely.

Store the cookies in an airtight container kept in a cool, dry place for up to 4 days.

HAZELNUTS: TO SKIN, OR NOT TO SKIN?

Some of my most traumatic memories as a fledgling baker are of my first attempts at skinning hazelnuts. I can clearly remember one session when I spent a considerable amount of time rubbing the skins off a seemingly insurmountable number of hot hazelnuts, only to throw them into some brownie batter a few minutes later, where they would be obscured by the chocolate and no one would ever realize whether they had skins or not.

Skinning hazelnuts is often a matter of aesthetics. Leaving the skin on means that your finished dessert will be dotted with dark flecks of skin, which does not necessarily detract from the beauty of your cookie or cake or tart dough. Remember when your mom told you that your freckles made you look "special"?

I have always found that skinning hazelnuts is a task to be approached with an open mind and a cool temper, since hazelnut skin can be especially stubborn. The standard method is to roast the hazelnuts in a single layer in a hot (350° to 375°F) oven for 12 to 15 minutes, or until the skins appear to crack. Then transfer the nuts in batches to a dish towel, fold it over them, and rub them back and forth inside the towel to remove the skins. Be prepared: not all the skins will flake away, and it is not your fault.

Fortunately for bakers, more and more markets are offering hazelnuts that have been blanched, roasted, and then put into large machines that literally vibrate the skin off the nuts. If you cannot find roasted, skinned hazelnuts, you can certainly decide to leave the skins on for any of the recipes in this book, and if you decide to remove the skins yourself, don't worry if some of nuts have a little, or even all, of their skins still attached. It is the heavenly fragrance and rich flavor of hazelnuts that truly matter in any recipe.

BITTERSWEET CHOCOLATE AND HAZELNUT COOKIES
biscotti di cioccolato a nocciole

The recipe for this cookie originally appeared in The Babbo Cookbook, *by Mario Batali. Mario asked me to include it in the dessert chapter I contributed to that book because of its iconic status on the cookie plate featured at Babbo. I have been baking these cookies every day since we first opened our doors in 1998, and they are still my favorites. They are not too sweet, slightly crumbly, and have a deep chocolate flavor and a nutty crunch from the hazelnuts. I am obliged to bake extras every day to compensate for the ones that inexplicably disappear from my cookie box.*

MAKES ABOUT 5 DOZEN COOKIES

2 cups unbleached all-purpose flour

⅓ cup unsweetened Dutch-processed cocoa
   powder

½ teaspoon baking powder

½ teaspoon kosher salt

½ cup whole hazelnuts, skinned or unskinned
   (see page 53)

1 cup (2 sticks/8 ounces) unsalted butter,
   softened

½ cup granulated sugar

1 large egg

1 teaspoon pure vanilla extract

5 ounces semisweet or bittersweet chocolate,
   finely chopped

1½ cups confectioners' sugar, for dusting

In a medium bowl, whisk together the flour, cocoa powder, baking powder, and salt. Place the hazelnuts in the bowl of a food processor and pulse them 2 or 3 times to chop them medium-fine. Add the hazelnuts to the bowl with the dry ingredients and stir to combine them.

In the bowl of an electric mixer fitted with the paddle attachment, cream together the butter and granulated sugar on medium speed until pale and fluffy, about 2 minutes. Beat in the egg and vanilla extract and scrape down the sides of the bowl. On low speed, beat in the dry ingredients, followed by the chocolate, and beat just until combined. Cover the bowl with plastic wrap and chill the dough until firm, about 30 minutes.

Preheat the oven to 325°F. Lightly grease two baking sheets with nonstick cooking spray or butter or line them with parchment.

Place the confectioners' sugar in a shallow bowl. To form the cookies, roll 1 scant tablespoon of dough into a 1-inch ball, then flatten it slightly with your fingertips

DUTCH-PROCESSED COCOA POWDER

Whenever I read this on the label of a box of unsweetened cocoa, I imagine attractive blond people in colorful costumes and clogs processing it in mysterious ways. The facts are much less romantic. "Dutched" cocoa has been alkalized, meaning that an alkali has been added to remove acidity. Most of the cocoa from Europe is processed this way, so it is lighter in color and has a more delicate, milder flavor than natural cocoa powder (including the American brands Hershey's and Scharffen Berger), which is darker and has a deeper, bitter chocolate flavor. The difference between Dutch-processed and natural cocoa powder is more than a matter of taste. It also affects the leavening, or rising, of the recipe. You may use baking soda, an alkali, as the leavening agent in a recipe only if another ingredient contains an acid. Baking soda will react with the acid present in natural cocoa powder to produce the carbon dioxide that gives your cookies or cakes a lift. If a recipe calls for Dutch-processed cocoa powder, you must use baking powder, either alone or in addition to baking soda, for leavening. Baking powder already contains the acid, usually in the form of cream of tartar, necessary for that important chemical reaction.

to form a small disk. Roll the cookie in the confectioners' sugar to coat it evenly and place it on the baking sheet. Repeat until all of the dough is used, spacing the cookies 1 inch apart on the baking sheets.

Bake the cookies until they are puffed and cracking, 8 to 10 minutes. Rotate the baking sheets 180 degrees halfway through the baking time to ensure that the cookies bake evenly. Allow the cookies to cool on the baking sheets for 1 to 2 minutes, then use a spatula to transfer them gently to a wire rack to cool completely. If desired, dust them with additional confectioners' sugar.

The cookies can be stored in an airtight container, layered between sheets of parchment paper, and kept in a cool, dry place for up to 1 week.

HONEY CLOUDS
nuvole di miele

The inspiration for these soft, pillowy cookies, glazed with honey and garnished with sliced almonds, comes from my grandmother. She made delicious honey cookies that became the subject of hot debate in my family after she passed away, since all of us seem to have different memories of them. They were long, they were short, they were firm, they were soft—the argument has yet to be completely settled. I decided to create a new page of family history by inventing my own honey cookie. Mine are completely different from Nonni's but were created in honor of the lovely person she was. Any kind of honey will work well, Italian or not, especially one with delicate, flowery notes. MAKES APPROXIMATELY 3 DOZEN COOKIES

FOR THE COOKIES

¾ cup sliced blanched almonds

¼ cup granulated sugar

1½ cups unbleached all-purpose flour

½ teaspoon baking powder

½ teaspoon kosher salt

½ cup (1 stick/4 ounces) unsalted butter, softened

⅔ cup mild-flavored honey, such as acacia or orange blossom

1 large egg

1 large egg yolk

Freshly grated zest of 1 small orange

FOR THE GLAZE AND GARNISH

1½ cups confectioners' sugar

¼ cup mild-flavored honey, such as acacia or orange blossom

1 tablespoon freshly squeezed orange juice

¼ cup sliced blanched almonds, toasted and cooled

Preheat the oven to 325°F. Lightly grease two baking sheets with nonstick cooking spray or butter or line them with parchment.

To make the cookies: Place the almonds and the granulated sugar in the bowl of a food processor and process for about 20 seconds, until the almonds are finely ground. In a medium bowl, whisk together the flour, baking powder, and salt.

Using an electric mixer fitted with the paddle attachment, cream the butter and honey together on medium speed until smooth and creamy, about 2 minutes. Beat in the egg and the egg yolk until incorporated, scraping down the sides of the bowl after each addition. On low speed, beat in the dry ingredients, followed by the ground almonds and orange zest, to make a soft dough. Remove the bowl from the mixer, cover the dough with plastic wrap, and chill for about 1 hour, or until firm enough to handle.

TOAST YOUR NUTS

Why do professional bakers always advise you to toast nuts? Because nuts taste better that way, plain and simple. Toasting deepens and draws out the nuts' aromatic flavors, taking your recipe to its full potential.

As a general rule, toast and cool your nuts before assembling the rest of your ingredients. Spread them in an even layer on a baking sheet, which you can line with parchment if you like, and bake them in a preheated oven at 325° to 350°F for 10 to 15 minutes, or until they are golden brown and fragrant. The nuts will cool faster if you remove them from the baking sheet, but try to keep them in a single layer. I like to transfer them to a clean piece of parchment paper on my kitchen counter.

In the case of hazelnuts, roasting the nuts in order to remove the skins toasts them too, so a second toasting is not necessary. Every nut toasts at a different rate, so it is important to keep an eye on them. All nuts contain oils, and those with a higher concentration of oils, such as pine nuts, will toast faster than those with fewer oils; the same is true for nuts that are slender or thin, such as slivered or sliced almonds.

To form the cookies: Use lightly floured fingers to roll teaspoonfuls of dough into balls about ½ inch in diameter. Place the cookies about a 1 inch apart on the prepared baking sheets and flatten them slightly with your fingertips.

Bake the cookies until they are golden brown and puffed, 12 to 14 minutes, rotating the sheets 180 degrees halfway through the baking time to ensure even browning. Allow the cookies to cool slightly on the baking sheets before using a spatula to remove them gently to a wire rack to cool completely.

While the cookies are cooling, prepare the glaze: Place the confectioners' sugar, honey, and orange juice in a bowl and whisk together until smooth.

Spoon a small amount of the glaze onto each cooled cookie and top it with a few toasted sliced almonds. Allow the glaze to set and dry before serving or storing.

Store the cookies in an airtight container, layered with sheets of parchment paper, for up to 3 days.

POLENTA COOKIES FROM THE VENETO
zaletti

I love, love, love these cookies. The combination of flavors and textures—the corny, chewy polenta, the sweet, grappa-soaked currants, and the aromatic lemon zest— makes them perfectly yummy and comforting. I imagine that children in the Veneto ask for exactly this kind of cookie when they come home from school. During my last visit to Venice, I spotted the biggest zaletti I had ever seen in the window of a pastry shop; they were at least six inches long, which is pretty hefty for a cookie. I like to make them a bit smaller—the length of my pinkie always seems like a good call.

An easy way to shape diamonds is to roll a bit of dough into a small log, flatten it, and then pinch and taper the ends. You can also roll the dough out on a lightly floured surface and cut it into diamonds with a knife or a cutter. You don't have to form these cookies as diamonds, but I think it is nice to keep the spirit of tradition with them—it just feels right. MAKES 3 1/2 TO 4 DOZEN COOKIES

¾ cup dried currants

¼ cup boiling water

3 tablespoons grappa

1¾ cups unbleached all-purpose flour

1 cup instant or fine polenta

¾ cup granulated sugar, plus more for garnish

1 teaspoon kosher salt

1 teaspoon baking powder

1 large egg

1 large egg yolk

½ cup (1 stick/4 ounces) unsalted butter, melted and cooled

Finely grated zest of 1 lemon

Place the currants in a small heatproof bowl, pour the boiling water and grappa over them, and stir briefly to combine. Set the bowl aside to let the currants plump and cool.

Place the flour, polenta, sugar, salt, and baking powder in the bowl of an electric mixer fitted with the paddle attachment and beat on low speed for 30 seconds to combine them. In a medium bowl, whisk together the egg and egg yolk to break them up, then whisk in the melted butter and lemon zest. Add the egg mixture to the dry ingredients and beat on medium speed to combine thoroughly, about 1 minute. Add the currants and their liquid and beat them into the dough on medium speed for about 30 seconds. Remove the dough from the bowl, flatten it into a disk, wrap it in plastic, and chill until it is firm enough to roll, about 1 hour.

Preheat the oven to 325°F. Lightly grease two baking sheets with nonstick cooking spray or butter or line them with parchment paper.

To form the cookies, use lightly floured fingers to pull off tablespoonfuls of dough and shape each one into a small, plump log about 1½ inches long. Press the log down to flatten it and pinch the ends together to taper them, creating a diamond shape. Place the diamonds on the baking sheets, spaced 1 inch apart. Sprinkle the tops of the cookies lightly with granulated sugar.

Bake the cookies for 15 minutes, or until they are lightly golden brown around the edges and firm to the touch, rotating the sheets 180 degrees halfway through the baking time to ensure even browning. Allow the cookies to cool on the baking sheets for 1 or 2 minutes, then use a spatula to remove them gently to a wire rack to cool completely.

The cookies can be stored in an airtight container for up to 1 week.

SICILIAN PISTACHIO BARS

Bar cookies are really easy, especially in a small apartment kitchen like mine. Simply spread out the dough, bake, and cut for instant gratification. Be sure to use a sharp knife when cutting these, and feel free to use your imagination—they can be rectangles, squares, or even diamonds, depending on your creative impulses. Sicilian pistachios are hard to find, but if you do come across them, give them a try. They have an intense green color and a sweet, mellow flavor. MAKES 24 TO 36 BARS

2 cups unbleached all-purpose flour

½ teaspoon kosher salt

1 cup shelled, whole, unsalted pistachios, Sicilian if available

1 cup (2 sticks/8 ounces) unsalted butter, softened

1 ¼ cups plus 2 teaspoons granulated sugar

2 large eggs

1 teaspoon pure vanilla extract

1 teaspoon amaretto or ½ teaspoon pure almond extract

Freshly grated zest of 1 lemon

Preheat the oven to 325°F. Lightly grease a 13-by-18-inch jelly-roll pan and line it with parchment; then lightly grease the paper, using nonstick cooking spray or butter.

In a medium bowl, whisk together the flour and salt and set aside. Place ½ cup pistachios in the bowl of a food processor and process for 20 to 30 seconds, until the nuts are finely ground. Stir the ground pistachios into the flour mixture.

Using an electric mixer fitted with the paddle attachment, cream the butter with the 1¼ cups sugar until very light and fluffy, about 2 minutes. Beat in the eggs, one at a time, followed by the vanilla extract, amaretto, and lemon zest, scraping down the sides of the bowl after each addition.

On low speed, mix in the dry ingredients to make a soft dough. Use an offset spatula to spread the dough evenly in the pan, smoothing the surface as much as possible. Coarsely chop the remaining ½ cup pistachios in the food processor and sprinkle them evenly over the surface of the dough. Sprinkle the remaining 2 teaspoons sugar evenly over the nuts.

Bake for 35 to 45 minutes, or until the dough is firm and just turning golden brown at the edges, rotating the pan 180 degrees halfway through the baking time to ensure even browning. Allow the pan to cool on a wire rack for 30 to 45 minutes before cutting the cookies into rectangular bars, about 1½ inches long and ½ inch wide. The cookies can be stored in an airtight container, layered between sheets of parchment paper, and kept in a cool, dry place for up to 3 days.

CHESTNUT LORE

Chestnuts are not actually nuts but seeds in their pods. High in energy-fueling complex carbohydrates, low in fat, and blessedly versatile, they have been a staple of the Mediterranean diet for centuries. Look for imported Italian chestnuts in your local market, unless you are fortunate enough to live in an area where chestnuts grow locally. More than half a dozen varieties of fresh chestnuts are found in Italy, but only two are commonly exported to the United States. *Castagne* are small, rounded on one side, and flat on the other, while *Marroni* are larger and voluptuously rotund. Only purchase chestnuts from a market that displays them in the refrigerated produce section, since they are perishable and must be handled with the utmost care. They should be plump, firm, and shiny. Press the chestnuts to be sure that there are no air pockets between the shell and the flesh underneath, and be wary of a mottled or spotty appearance, which may indicate the presence of mold.

To roast chestnuts properly, you must first score them, making an X or a horizontal slash with a sharp paring knife across the rounder side of each nut. Place the scored chestnuts in a single layer in a shallow metal baking dish and sprinkle them with a little water. You can toss in a few strips of orange or tangerine zest to enhance their flavor. Roast them in a hot oven, 400° to 425°F, for 20 to 25 minutes. Be sure to shake the pan every 5 minutes or so to prevent them from charring in one spot. They are perfect when the scored X has flowered, curling back to reveal a bit of the chestnut flesh, which should be golden brown and toasted. When you pry off the shell, most of the furry skin should come off, but for baking, whatever doesn't come off is never a problem. Above all, serve and enjoy roasted chestnuts while they are still hot and easy to peel. They are well worth a few burned fingers.

Chestnut flour is made from chestnuts that are milled to a powder. You can find it at Italian specialty food shops, in health-food stores, and from online retailers (see Sources, pages 285–87). Chestnut flour contains absolutely no gluten, so when baking with it, you must also include wheat flour—all-purpose, bread, cake, or whole wheat—in the recipe to produce the proper texture. Although chestnut flour is sold in relatively small packages, you might have some left over after you have made your favorite recipe. If so, store it in a zippered freezer bag in your refrigerator or freezer to prevent it from spoiling.

CHESTNUT BROWNIES

After an autumn Sunday dinner, my family, like many Italian families, enjoys linger-ing at the table with fresh roasted chestnuts and lively conversation. We often wind up roasting a few more than we eat, and these brownies are a perfect way to use up the leftovers. I am always surprised by how much chestnut flavor is present in the company of so much chocolate, and the slightly chewy texture of the chestnuts evokes memories of the night before. Fresh chestnuts are available seasonally, usu-ally from October through December, so enjoy them while you can. If I am rushed for time, I buy a bag of hot roasted chestnuts from a street vendor, and if I success-fully resist the temptation to eat them on the subway ride home, all I have to do is peel them and I am ready to go. MAKES 16 BROWNIES

15–17 whole roasted chestnuts, shells and
    skins removed (see page 61)

4 ounces unsweetened chocolate

10 tablespoons (1¼ sticks/5 ounces) unsalted
    butter

½ cup unbleached all-purpose flour

½ cup chestnut flour

1 tablespoon unsweetened Dutch-processed
    cocoa powder

2 teaspoons baking soda

¼ teaspoon kosher salt

¾ cup granulated sugar

½ cup packed dark brown sugar

4 large eggs

1 teaspoon pure vanilla extract

1 tablespoon grappa or cognac

Preheat the oven to 350°F. Lightly grease a 9-inch square pan with nonstick cooking spray or butter or line with parchment paper.

Using a sharp chef's knife, coarsely chop the chestnuts; you should have 1 heaping cup.

Melt the chocolate and butter together in a heatproof medium bowl set over a pan of simmering water, whisking to combine them. Set the bowl aside in a warm spot. In a clean medium bowl, whisk together the all-purpose flour, chestnut flour, cocoa pow-der, baking soda, and salt and set aside.

Transfer the chocolate and butter mixture to the bowl of an electric mixer fitted with the paddle attachment. Add the sugars and beat on medium speed to combine the ingredients thoroughly, about 30 seconds. Beat in the eggs, one at a time, followed by the vanilla extract and grappa, scraping down the sides of the bowl after each addi-tion. On low speed, beat in the dry ingredients, followed by the chestnuts.

Pour the batter into the prepared pan and spread it evenly with an offset spatula. Bake the brownies until a toothpick inserted in the center comes out clean and the brownies have begun to pull away from the sides of the pan, 20 to 25 minutes. Rotate the pan 180 degrees halfway through the baking time to ensure even baking.

Allow the brownies to cool completely in the pan on a wire rack before cutting them into squares or rectangles. They are easiest to cut after being chilled several hours or overnight; after cutting the chilled brownies, allow them to come to room temperature before serving.

The brownies can be stored in an airtight container kept in a cool, dry place for up to 3 days.

ALMOND, ANISE, AND ORANGE BISCOTTI
biscotti di mandorle, anis, e arancia

These biscotti *are wonderfully aromatic, thanks to anise seeds and orange zest. If you can't find anise seeds, fennel seeds make a fine substitute. I like to the chop the almonds into fairly large pieces, which look pretty when the* biscotti *are sliced and provide a satisfying crunch. A serrated knife is the best way to chop roughly by hand, or you can crush the nuts with a heavy saucepan or pound them in a mortar with a pestle. A food processor will chop the nuts too unevenly, pulverizing some of them into a powder while leaving others whole.*

The fun part of making biscotti *is being creative with the slices. You can flatten your logs of dough slightly to create thinner* biscotti *or leave them round for a plumper shape. Slicing the* biscotti *on a sharp diagonal as opposed to a slight bias produces different shapes and sizes too. Long and thin makes for easy dunking into coffee or vin santo, while thicker, rounder* biscotti *are better for packing up and sending afar.* MAKES ABOUT 4 DOZEN *BISCOTTI*

3½ cups unbleached all-purpose flour	2 cups granulated sugar, plus 1½ tablespoons
1 teaspoon baking powder	for glaze
1 teaspoon kosher salt	2 teaspoons pure vanilla extract
4 cups whole blanched almonds	1 tablespoon whole anise seeds
4 large eggs	Freshly grated zest of 1 large orange
2 large egg yolks, plus 1 egg white for glaze	

Place the flour, baking powder, and salt in a medium mixing bowl and whisk to combine thoroughly. Using a sharp knife, coarsely chop the almonds and set them aside.

In the bowl of an electric mixer fitted with the paddle attachment, beat together the eggs, the egg yolks, and the 2 cups sugar on medium speed until light, about 2 minutes. The mixture will look somewhat curdled. Beat in the vanilla extract, anise seeds, and orange zest. Beat in the dry ingredients, then the chopped nuts, to make a soft dough. Remove the dough from the bowl, wrap it in plastic, and chill for 2 hours, or until it is firm enough to handle.

Preheat the oven to 325°F. Lightly grease two baking sheets with nonstick cooking spray or butter or line them with parchment paper.

Divide the dough into 5 equal portions. On a lightly floured surface, shape each portion of the dough into a log about 1½ inches in diameter and 10 inches long. Place 2 of the logs on one of the baking sheets, 3 inches apart, and 3 of the logs on the second baking sheet, also 3 inches apart. In a small bowl, beat the egg white with a fork until frothy. With a pastry brush, glaze each log with the beaten egg white and sprinkle with 1 teaspoon sugar.

Bake the logs until they are lightly golden brown, firm to the touch, and just beginning to crack slightly, 20 to 25 minutes. Rotate the sheets 180 degrees halfway through the baking time to ensure even browning. Allow the logs to cool on the baking sheets on a wire rack until they are cool to the touch, about 40 minutes. Reduce the oven temperature to 200°F.

With a sharp, serrated knife, slice the cooled *biscotti* slightly on the bias into ¼-inch-wide slices. Lay the slices on the baking sheets in a single layer. Return them to the oven and cook for 20 minutes more, or until they are toasted, dry, and crisp. Cool the *biscotti* completely on the baking sheets, then store them in an airtight container kept in a cool, dry place for up to 2 weeks.

MOSAIC BISCOTTI

biscotti di mosai

Everyone loves these biscotti *because they are substantial and flavorful, with a firm, crunchy texture that is ideal for dunking. The nuts and chocolate form pretty patterns that remind me of mosaic tiles. As with the recipe for Almond, Anise, and Orange Biscotti on page 64, avoid using a food processor to chop the nuts, because it will invariably turn some of the nuts into a fine powder. These* biscotti *are great keepers, if you can resist eating them in one sitting.*

MAKES ABOUT 4 DOZEN *BISCOTTI*

3½ cups unbleached all-purpose flour
1 teaspoon baking powder
1 teaspoon kosher salt
4 large eggs
2 large egg yolks, plus 1 egg white for glaze
2 cups granulated sugar, plus 1½ tablespoons for glaze
2 teaspoons pure vanilla extract
12 ounces semisweet or bittersweet chocolate, coarsely chopped
2 cups skinned or unskinned hazelnuts (see page 53), coarsely chopped
2 cups whole, unsalted pistachios, coarsely chopped

In a medium bowl, whisk together the flour, baking powder, and salt and set aside.

Using an electric mixer fitted with the paddle attachment, beat together the eggs, egg yolks, and 2 cups sugar on medium speed until pale and thick, about 2 minutes. Beat in the vanilla extract, followed by the dry ingredients and then the chocolate and nuts, until the dough is thoroughly mixed.

Preheat the oven to 325°F. Lightly grease two large baking sheets with nonstick cooking spray or butter or line with parchment.

Using floured hands, divide the dough into 5 equal portions. On a lightly floured surface, shape each portion of the dough into a log about 1½ inches in diameter and 10 inches long. Place 2 of the logs on one of the baking sheets, 3 inches apart, and 3 of the logs on the second baking sheet, also 3 inches apart. In a small bowl, beat the egg white with a fork until frothy. With a pastry brush, glaze each log with the beaten egg white and sprinkle with 1 teaspoon sugar.

Bake the logs until they are lightly golden brown, firm to the touch, and just beginning to crack slightly, 20 to 25 minutes. Rotate the sheets 180 degrees halfway through the baking time to ensure even browning. Allow the logs to cool on the baking sheets on

BISCOTTI DAYS

The steps to making good *biscotti* are numerous but not at all difficult. At Babbo, the entire pastry staff pulls together in a marathon session of rolling, baking, slicing, and toasting in order to make hundreds of *biscotti* at once. At home, lacking the appropriate team of assistants, I make *biscotti* on gloomy, rainy days. It cheers me up, simultaneously occupying my hands and freeing my mind, and I never feel guilty about taking my time. When I am finished, I stand back and survey the stacks of perfectly formed and toasted *biscotti*, as pretty as those in the corner coffee shop, and much tastier. After patting myself on the back, I may even find myself packing up some for a neighbor to share the bounty.

a wire rack until they are cool to the touch, about 40 minutes. Reduce the oven temperature to 200°F.

With a sharp, serrated knife, slice the *biscotti* slightly on the bias into ¼-inch-wide slices. Lay the slices on the baking sheets in a single layer. Return them to the oven and cook for 20 minutes more, or until they are toasted, dry, and crisp. Cool the *biscotti* completely on the sheets, then store them in an airtight container kept in a cool, dry place for up to 2 weeks.

POLENTA AND SESAME BISCOTTI
biscotti di polenta e sesamo

Sesame seeds and cornmeal are a fantastic combination. The butter in this recipe provides a tender-crisp rather than crunchy texture. To make these biscotti with a snowy-white interior, try using white cornmeal or polenta and white sesame seeds. Believe it or not, these are especially pretty at Christmas, when they match the color of the first dusting of snow and make a welcome and unusual addition to your holiday cookie collection. MAKES ABOUT 6 DOZEN *BISCOTTI*

3¼ cups unbleached all-purpose flour

1 cup instant or fine polenta

1 teaspoon baking powder

1 teaspoon kosher salt

1 cup (2 sticks/ 8 ounces) unsalted butter, softened

1⅓ cups granulated sugar, plus 1 tablespoon for glaze

4 large eggs

3 large egg yolks, plus 1 egg white for glaze

2 teaspoons pure vanilla extract

¾ cup white sesame seeds

In a large bowl, whisk together the flour, polenta, baking powder, and salt and set aside.

In the bowl of an electric mixer fitted with the paddle attachment, cream the butter and 1⅓ cups sugar on medium speed until light and fluffy, about 2 minutes. Add the eggs, one at a time, and then the egg yolks, one at a time, beating well after each addition. Scrape down the sides of the bowl, then beat in the vanilla extract. Add the dry ingredients and beat on low speed to form a soft dough. Beat in ½ cup of the sesame seeds until they are thoroughly incorporated. Cover the dough with plastic wrap and chill for 2 hours, or until firm enough to handle.

Preheat the oven to 325°F. Lightly grease two baking sheets with nonstick cooking spray or butter or line them with parchment.

Remove the dough from the refrigerator; it will be quite sticky, so use a well-floured board and floured hands to handle it. Divide the dough into 4 equal portions and roll each portion into a log about 1½ inches in diameter and 12 inches long. Place 2 logs, spaced 3 inches apart, on each baking sheet. In a small bowl, beat the egg white with a fork until it is frothy. With a pastry brush, glaze the surface of the logs with egg white, then sprinkle the logs with the remaining ¼ cup sesame seeds and the remaining 1 tablespoon sugar.

Bake the logs until they are golden brown and feel somewhat firm to the touch, 30 to 35 minutes, rotating the sheets 180 degrees halfway through the baking time to ensure even browning. Allow the logs to cool on the baking sheets on a wire rack until cool to the touch, about 40 minutes. Reduce the oven temperature to 200°F.

With a sharp, serrated knife, slice the *biscotti* slightly on the bias into ¼-inch-wide slices. Lay the slices on the baking sheets in a single layer; you may need an additional baking sheet to acccomodate all the slices. Return the *biscotti* to the oven and cook for 20 minutes more, or until they are toasted, dry, and crisp. Cool the *biscotti* completely on the sheets, then store them in an airtight container kept in a cool, dry place for up to 2 weeks.

LA BEFANA'S STARS
befanini

I think it is fun to have another cookie to bake after the rush of Christmas. These cookies symbolize the story of La Befana (pronounced La Bay-fah-nah), who travels around Italy on the Feast of the Epiphany, which falls on January 6 and celebrates the visit of the three Magi to the Christ Child. I like to bake these on the eve of Epiphany and eat them the next day, when I take the Christmas tree down. Rich, rolled sugar cookies spiked with a bit of anisette, they are superb with a cup of hot chocolate.

The traditional shape of these cookies is a star, to signify the Star of Bethlehem and La Befana's quest for the baby Jesus. I think most kids will agree with my belief that multicolored sprinkles are absolutely necessary; the glaze brushed on top of the cookies helps the sprinkles adhere and gives the cookies a pretty sheen.

MAKES ABOUT 4 DOZEN COOKIES

FOR THE COOKIES
3½ cups unbleached all-purpose flour
½ teaspoon baking powder
½ teaspoon kosher salt
1½ cups (3 sticks/12 ounces) unsalted butter, softened
1¼ cups granulated sugar
1 large egg

2 large egg yolks
1 teaspoon pure vanilla extract
2 teaspoons anisette
Freshly grated zest of 1 orange

FOR THE GLAZE
1 large egg yolk
2 tablespoons heavy cream
Multicolored sprinkles

To make the cookies: In a medium bowl, whisk the flour, baking powder, and salt together and set aside.

In the bowl of an electric mixer fitted with the paddle attachment, cream the butter and sugar together on medium speed until creamy and light, about 2 minutes. Beat in the egg and egg yolks, one at a time, scraping down the sides after each addition, followed by the vanilla extract, anisette, and orange zest. Beat in the dry ingredients on low speed to form a stiff dough. Remove the dough from the bowl, flatten it into a disk, wrap it in plastic, and chill until it is firm enough to roll, about 1 hour.

Preheat the oven to 350°F. Lightly grease two baking sheets with nonstick cooking spray or butter or line them with parchment paper.

Divide the dough into 3 equal pieces; work with 1 piece at a time, keeping the remaining pieces refrigerated. On a floured surface, roll the dough to a thickness of ⅛ inch. Using a floured 2-inch star-shaped cookie cutter, cut the dough into stars. Place the cookies ½ inch apart on the baking sheets. Gather the scraps together and repeat rolling and cutting until you have used all the scraps; it may be necessary to refrigerate the scraps until they are firm enough to roll again.

To make the glaze: In a small bowl, whisk the egg yolk with the cream. Using a small pastry brush, lightly brush the surface of the cookies with a bit of glaze and decorate them with the sprinkles.

Bake the cookies until they are lightly golden brown, 12 to 14 minutes, rotating the baking sheets 180 degrees halfway through the baking time to ensure even browning. Allow the cookies to cool slightly on the baking sheets, then gently remove them with a spatula to a wire rack to cool completely.

The cookies can be stored in an airtight container, layered between sheets of parchment paper, for up to 4 days.

THE STORY OF LA BEFANA

When I was a mite, my mom kept a strange-looking cloth doll perched on a shelf in the kitchen, seemingly to keep her company as she cooked. It resembled an old woman dressed a bit like a gypsy; a scarf was tied around her head, and she was riding a broom. I didn't really notice her until the year Mom bought me a book about Christmas celebrations around the world. I devoured that book, and being a little Italian kid, I loved the chapter on Christmas in Italy the most. I remember sprawling on the floor of our living room while I read about La Befana, the Christmas "witch" of Italy, who rode on her broom and delivered goodies to Italian children. I was astounded. I knew about Santa Claus, but how could I have missed out on another kindly gift-giver, and an Italian one to boot? I ran into the kitchen to ask my mother about this generous witch, and she nodded toward her doll: "There she is—La Befana."

The legend of La Befana has a few variations on a basic theme. Befana is a hunched old woman, usually depicted either carrying or riding on her broom. The story goes that Befana was tending to her housework when a commotion erupted in her village. Mysterious travelers from foreign lands were passing through; it was the three kings, the Magi, on their journey to visit the newborn Christ Child. Befana watched the procession cautiously from her door, sweeping all the while. The Magi paused and asked her if she wanted to join them on their journey. Befana replied that she was too busy tending to her housework to go on a frivolous search, and the procession passed. Not long after, Befana came to realize that the Magi were searching for the Christ Child, and she began to have regrets about her refusal. She quickly packed up her meager gifts for the baby Jesus, rolling them up in a cloth which she tied to the end of her broom, and then she set off to catch up with the Magi. Befana never found the Magi or the Christ Child, and every year she continues her journey on January 5, the eve of Epiphany. She stops at every house on her search, leaving gifts of oranges, books, cookies, and trinkets for the good children and coal, onions, and garlic for the bad children.

The story is bittersweet, tinged with regret and the agony of an unfulfilled quest. Other versions of the legend are even more poignant. When King Herod decreed the Slaughter of the Innocents, ordering the murder of all male babies in his kingdom, one young mother was so stricken with grief that she convinced herself that her baby son had been lost rather than killed. She rolled up all of his belongings into a cloth and set out to find him, searching from house to house. Befana continued her search for what to her seemed like only a few days. Eventually she came across a newborn baby boy in a manger. She knew that at last she had found her son, and she lovingly laid his belongings down in front of the manger. The baby's father looked upon her and wondered where this gray-haired old woman had come from. The father was Joseph of Nazareth, and the baby was the infant Jesus. To reward the old woman for her kindness, God blessed her in a special way. For all eternity she would be known as La Befana, or "giver of gifts," and on the night of January 5 she would adopt all the children of the world as her own and visit them with gifts of clothes and toys.

As with all legends, La Befana's has been embellished with the passage of time and the application of local customs. In some versions she is larger than life, dressed in a sooty black shawl from the chimneys through which she enters houses. Some versions say that Befana grew tired while carrying her broom with its sack of goodies, and when she could no longer walk, she was swept into the air by a mysterious wind that lifted her onto her broom, which she rode from that point on. Others have her arriving on a donkey, an entirely appropriate entrance into the remote villages of the mountainous southern regions of Italy.

Since Epiphany was a pagan ritual long before it was a Christian feast, "Befana" or "Befania" could be derived from the Greek *epifania*. Epiphany was a festival of purification and benediction, rituals that would ward off ills and evils that might befall the household in the coming year. The Etruscans may have seen a Befana-like figure as a harbinger of ill fortune and bad luck, and used the rite of Epiphany as a way to rid themselves of her presence. A nineteenth-century Tuscan incantation to be recited along with the burning of incense and spices offers a bit of proof:

In the name of heaven
And of the stars and moon,
May this trouble change
To better fortune soon!
Befania! Befania! Befania!
Should this deed be thine,
Befania! Befania!
Take it away, bring luck, I pray,
Into this house of mine!

Whether you choose to think of La Befana as a somewhat creepy witch or a kindly holiday icon, her story teaches an important lesson to all children, speaking of the importance of family, the strength of faith, and the never-ending devotion of a mother's love.

COCONUT SHORTBREAD
biscotti di cocco

Italians enjoy fresh coconut, and in my many trips to Rome, I have seen it offered at countless open-air markets and produce stands. A cute little box-shaped contraption holds wedges of fresh coconut with the shell attached, spraying them with a fine mist of water to keep the coconut meat moist and fresh in the noonday sun. I love coconut in anything, and these cookies are a terrific way for me to get my fix. I like to use a combination of unsweetened shredded dried coconut and sweetened flaked coconut to get the full impact of flavor. Cake flour and "oo" flour (see page 84) impart a sandy, delicate texture. These cookies go nicely with a steaming cup of hot chocolate on a chilly day. They also pair well with lemonade on a sunny day. It's nice to have a cookie recipe that spans the seasons, isn't it?
MAKES 3 TO 4 DOZEN COOKIES

2¼ cups "oo" flour

½ cup cake flour

1 teaspoon kosher salt

¾ cup (1½ sticks/6 ounces) unsalted butter, softened

1¼ cups confectioners' sugar

½ cup packed light brown sugar

2 large eggs

1 large egg yolk

1 teaspoon pure vanilla extract

1⅓ cups unsweetened shredded dried coconut

1 cup sweetened flaked coconut

½ cup raw or turbinado sugar, for garnish

In a medium bowl, whisk together the "00" flour, cake flour, and salt and set aside.

In the bowl of an electric mixer fitted with the paddle attachment, beat the butter with the confectioners' sugar and light brown sugar on medium speed until creamy and light, about 2 minutes. Add the eggs and the egg yolk, one at a time, beating well after each addition and scraping down the sides of the bowl. Beat in the vanilla extract.

Add the dry ingredients and beat them in on low speed, followed by both kinds of coconut. Beat briefly on medium speed to fully incorporate all the dry ingredients into the dough. Remove the dough from the bowl, flatten it into a disk, wrap it in plastic, and chill until it is firm enough to roll, about 1 hour.

Preheat the oven to 325°F. Lightly grease two baking sheets with nonstick cooking spray or butter or line them with parchment.

On a lightly floured board, roll the dough to a thickness of ⅛ inch. Use a round or scalloped 1½- or 2-inch cookie cutter to cut the cookies, then place them on the baking sheets, evenly spaced ½ inch apart. Gather the scraps together and repeat rolling and cutting until you have used all the scraps; it may be necessary to refrigerate the scraps until they are firm enough to roll again. Sprinkle the tops of the cookies with the raw sugar.

Bake the cookies until they are lightly golden brown, 14 to 16 minutes, rotating the sheets 180 degrees halfway through the baking time to ensure even browning. Allow the cookies to cool for a minute or two on the baking sheets, then use a spatula to remove them gently to wire racks to cool completely.

The cookies can be stored in an airtight container kept in a cool, dry place for up to 5 days.

CAKES
torte

TALIANS HAVE A LEGENDARY LOVE FOR SWEETS THAT REVEALS ITSELF IN the number of *pasticcerie* that seem to appear around every corner in both big cities and small towns. What always compels me to gaze into the window of an Italian pastry shop is the unassuming nature of the cakes that are lined up in neat rows or perched on a lone pedestal or two. Elaborate and heavily embellished confections are certainly present, especially during feast days and holidays, but they are generally far outnumbered by rustic, simple presentations. Gobs of sugary frosting are noticeably absent, replaced by the sheen of a glaze or a light dusting of confectioners' sugar; nuts and fresh or candied fruits may be strategically placed as garnish to provide a seductive hint of the flavor that lies within. The quiet nature of this sort of cake speaks much more loudly to me than the tall, fluffy, layered cakes.

Too often it is easy to make the mistake of narrowly defining cakes in terms merely of chocolate or vanilla. In Italy, the flavor and texture of a cake makes its own strong statement. Usually a specific ingredient—ground nuts, orange or lemon zest, fresh cheese, butter, lard, or olive oil—defines the texture and character of a cake. Will it be buttery and rich, creamy and smooth, or crumbly and light? A simple, unfrosted cake can stand by itself next to a glass of dessert wine. If it is embellished with custard, cream, or *zabaione,* the purpose is to complement the cake itself, not to mask its shortcomings.

The recipes in this chapter offer a wide array of textures and flavors, drawing on the history, traditions, and ingredients of the Italian regions that inspired their creation. Cakes are my favorite dessert to have when company calls and on special occasions; they always seem to create a sense of excitement and anticipation. No matter how grand the meal, be sure to remind yourself and your guests to save some room for cake.

MOSTACCIOLI WITH A GLASS OF
SAGRANTINO PASSITO, PAGE 48

POLENTA
AND SESAME
BISCOTTI,
PAGE 68

CITRUS-GLAZED POLENTA CAKE, PAGE 86

CHOCOLATE KISSES, PAGE 44

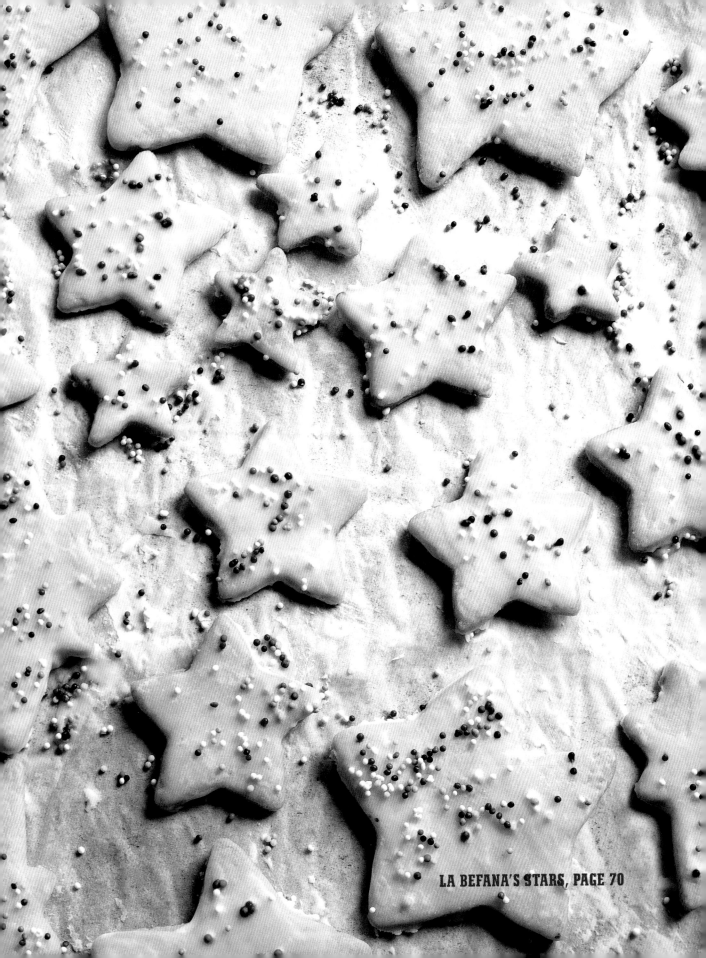

LA BEFANA'S STARS, PAGE 70

CLOCKWISE FROM TOP: MOSAIC
BISCOTTI, PAGE 66; POLENTA AND
SESAME BISCOTTI, PAGE 68; ALMOND
FINGERS, PAGE 46; POLENTA COOKIES
FROM THE VENETO, PAGE 58; LEMONY
SEMOLINA COOKIES, PAGE 50

GRAPPA-SOAKED MINI
SPONGE CAKES, PAGE 80

CHOCOLATE AND WALNUT TORTE FROM CAPRI, PAGE 92

PAN DI SPAGNA

The historical connection between Italy and Spain comes alive when you bake an Italian sponge cake, otherwise known as *pan di Spagna*. From the Middle Ages on, Spanish monarchs carved out areas of conquest throughout Italy, especially from Naples southward to Sicily. The Spanish left their imprint on the country's language, art, architecture, and food; one such contribution was the so-called Spanish sponge. In the early eighteenth century, the city of Parma in Emilia-Romagna was united with the Spanish court of King Philip V through the marriage of the king to a Parmese duchess. *Pan di Spagna* became all the rage in convent and court kitchens, catering to the chic, internationally minded clergy and nobility of northern Italy. It makes perfect sense to me why this cake became so popular. The delicate texture and airiness make *pan di Spagna* the ideal medium to soak up flavored syrups and layer with creamy fillings. If it becomes stale, it can be toasted until crisp, like *biscotti*.

I have taken a few liberties with the classic *pan di Spagna* recipe, adding some butter to make the cake more tender and flavorful; cake flour provides a light texture. It is important to use the proper technique when making any sponge cake: both the egg yolks and the egg whites should be beaten with the whisk attachment of your mixer to their fullest, most voluminous potential, and the dry ingredients should be folded in lightly and efficiently, since too many strokes will make the cake tough and rubbery.

GRAPPA-SOAKED MINI SPONGE CAKES
pan di spagna con grappa

I can't think of a better use for miniature Bundt molds than these moist, light sponge cakes, a variation on the classic Italian sponge cake, pan di Spagna. *Don't be afraid of the grappa syrup; the alcohol will cook off as the syrup boils. You can add even more flavor to the syrup if you wish simply by adding half a vanilla bean or the zest of an orange or a lemon to the pot. Whipped cream, or even tangy crème fraîche, is a divine accompaniment, perhaps with some fresh fruit and a* caffè correto—*a shot of espresso "corrected" with a dash of grappa.* MAKES 12 MINI SPONGE CAKES

FOR THE GRAPPA SYRUP
¾ cup granulated sugar
3 tablespoons grappa
¼ cup water

FOR THE SPONGE CAKES
2 cups sifted cake flour
1½ teaspoons baking powder
1 teaspoon kosher salt
8 large eggs, separated

1¼ cups granulated sugar
2 tablespoons honey
1 tablespoon grappa
1 teaspoon pure vanilla extract
½ cup (1 stick/4 ounces) unsalted butter, melted and cooled
Pinch of kosher salt
¼ teaspoon cream of tartar

Preheat the oven to 350°F. Grease two mini Bundt pans, each with six 4-by-2 inch molds, 1 cup capacity (12 cakes total), with nonstick cooking spray, dust the pans with flour, and tap to knock out the excess.

To make the grappa syrup: Stir together the sugar, ½ cup grappa, and the water in a medium saucepan. Place the saucepan over medium heat and bring the contents to a boil, then lower the heat slightly and allow the syrup to simmer for 5 minutes. Remove the pan from the heat and allow the syrup to cool.

To make the sponge cakes: Sift together the cake flour, baking powder, and salt into a medium bowl and set aside.

In the bowl of an electric mixer fitted with the whisk attachment, beat the egg yolks together with the sugar and honey on medium speed until very light, pale yellow in color, and doubled in volume, about 3 minutes. Beat in the grappa and vanilla extract, followed by the melted butter. Transfer the egg mixture to a large, clean mixing bowl. Fold in the dry ingredients quickly and lightly, using a rubber spatula, stopping just before they are fully incorporated.

Clean the whisk attachment and mixing bowl. Place the egg whites and salt in the cleaned bowl. Using the whisk attachment on medium-high speed, beat the egg whites until they are foamy and light. Add the cream of tartar and continue beating until stiff peaks form. Fold the egg whites into the batter quickly and lightly; this will also incorporate any streaks of dry ingredients that remain.

Spoon the batter into the prepared pans, filling them ¾ full and smoothing the tops with the back of the spoon. Bake the cakes for 20 to 25 minutes, or until a cake tester inserted in the center comes out clean and the cakes have begun to pull away from the sides of the pans. Allow the cakes to cool for 5 minutes in the pans, then carefully turn them out onto a wire rack.

Gently brush the grappa syrup over the entire surface of the warm cakes, until all the syrup has been used. Allow the cakes to cool completely before serving.

Serve the cakes with whipped cream or *gelato* and fresh fruit or simply dusted with confectioners' sugar. Any leftover cakes may be wrapped in plastic or stored in an airtight container and served the following day.

ITALIAN CRUMBLY CAKE
sbrisolona

Sbrisolona *is a classic, crumbly cake created in the pastry shops of Mantova in Lombardy. It is compact, in contrast to the airy, fluffy layer cakes that are more common in the United States. The cake explodes with the flavor of its crown of toasted almonds and a hint of cinnamon. The kitchen staff at Babbo used to fight over the leftovers to enjoy with morning coffee. I can't say I blame them— this is one of those cakes that tastes even better the day after you make it.*

MAKES ONE 10-INCH CAKE, APPROXIMATELY 10 SERVINGS

FOR THE CAKE

1¼ cups "00" flour (see page 84)

¼ cup almond flour

½ teaspoon kosher salt

½ teaspoon baking powder

½ teaspoon ground cinnamon

1 large egg

4 large egg yolks

1 cup granulated sugar

1 teaspoon pure vanilla extract

½ cup (1 stick/4 ounces) unsalted butter, melted and cooled

FOR THE TOPPING

1½ cups sliced blanched almonds

1 large egg white

3 tablespoons granulated sugar

Preheat the oven to 325°F and position a rack in the center. Lightly grease a 10-inch springform pan with nonstick cooking spray or butter, dust it with flour, and tap to knock out the excess.

To make the cake: In a medium bowl, whisk together the "00" flour, almond flour, salt, baking powder, and cinnamon and set aside.

In an electric mixer fitted with the paddle attachment, beat the egg, egg yolks, and sugar on medium speed until they are thick and pale yellow, about 3 minutes. On low speed, add the dry ingredients and beat well, scraping down the sides of the bowl. Beat in the vanilla extract, followed by the melted butter. Switch to medium speed and beat for 30 seconds.

Spread the batter evenly in the prepared pan and smooth the top with a spatula.

To make the topping: Put the sliced almonds in a medium bowl. Lightly beat the egg white in small bowl with a fork until it is foamy and light, then pour half of it over the almonds, stirring to coat them evenly (discard the rest of the egg white). Sprinkle the almonds with the sugar and toss to coat them. Spread the almond topping evenly over the surface of the batter.

Bake the cake for 25 to 30 minutes, or until it is springy to the touch and golden brown on top and a cake tester inserted in the center comes out clean. Allow the cake to cool for 10 minutes in the pan, then remove the sides and allow the cake to cool completely on a wire rack.

To serve, carefully remove the bottom of the springform pan with an offset spatula and transfer the cake to a serving plate. Any leftover cake can be wrapped in plastic and served the next day.

FLOUR ARRANGEMENT

Purchasing a simple sack of flour can be an unexpectedly complicated experience, but armed with a bit of knowledge, you will find it far less mysterious. I generally wind up using all-purpose, cake, or Italian "oo" flour in my recipes to achieve a particular texture or density. Once you understand the properties of each type, you can begin to experiment and create your own recipes.

The term "flour" can be applied to any grain that is finely ground, and in most baking recipes, "flour" means wheat flour. The wheat contains gluten, the protein that forms an elastic structure within which cakes and breads are able to rise and take shape. The wheat kernel also contains the germ, the sprouting part, as well as the bran, its skin. Most flour is ground using high-pressure, heat-generating steel rollers that remove the germ and its nutritious vitamins, oils, and enzymes. To remedy this, the U.S. Food and Drug Administration mandates that niacin, riboflavin, thiamin, and iron be added to flour after it is ground; this is where the word "enriched" comes from.

Your local supermarket will carry all-purpose flour, available either bleached or unbleached, and yes, you can use either one without adversely affecting the outcome of your recipe. Obviously, bleaching agents have been used in bleached flour, resulting in a pure, bright white effect; unbleached flour has a creamy ivory color, which lends a subtle difference in some cakes and breads. All-purpose flour is made with a combination of high-gluten hard wheat and low-gluten soft wheat.

High-gluten bread flour is unbleached and made mostly from hard wheat, with a bit of malted barley thrown in to improve the oomph of yeast. Cake flour, in contrast, is made with soft wheat and is always bleached—you will notice the snow-white color immediately. Cake flour has a lower starch content, which gives cakes and pastries a softer, more tender texture.

Be careful to read labels—some cake flours are also self-rising, which means that a leavening agent like baking powder has already been added. Pastry flour may be bleached or unbleached and has a slightly higher starch content than cake flour. Using it is a matter of preference; some chefs like it for cookies, crackers, and layered, or laminate, doughs.

"oo" flour is a staple in Italian bakeries and pizzerias. In Italy, flour is classified numerically as 1, 0, or 00, referring to how much of the bran and germ have been removed and how finely the flour has been processed. "oo" flour, with the bran and germ removed, is the finest and whitest, with a texture similar to that of talcum powder. The protein (gluten) content of "oo" flour is similar to that of all-purpose flour; it has been milled finer but is not interchangeable with cake flour, which is both softer and lower in protein than all-purpose flour. I love the distinct texture "oo" flour gives to cookies, cakes, and *biscotti*—firm, but with a fine crumb—and I find myself using it more and more. Look for it at Italian specialty shops and in better supermarkets. It is also widely available from online vendors (see Sources, pages 285–87).

Semolina flour is actually a by-product of the processing of white flour—the gritty, coarse particles of hard durum wheat that are left over after the finer flour has passed through. Very high in protein, semolina is used in the making of bread, dry pasta, and gnocchi. I have to admit that I am a bit obsessed with using semolina flour in my recipes. It may be that I feel obligated, since huge drums of it lurk in the corner of the Babbo kitchen where the pasta is being made. I also am a sucker for the color, a soft, muted yellow that turns ivory when cooked in milk, like faded polenta. Usually I wind up tossing it into a recipe because I am curious to see how it will affect the flavor and texture. Experimentation often yields the happiest results.

CITRUS-GLAZED POLENTA CAKE
torta di polenta con agrumi

I love this sunny yellow cake, which gets its bright flavor from an array of citrus fruits used in both the cake and the tangy glaze. This is a great cake for those deadly winter months after the holidays, when piles of citrus fruit are all you see at the supermarket and you've just about had it with making banana bread. I like to pair this cake with coffee or espresso-flavored gelato; omit the cinnamon from the recipe on page 183 and you have the perfect partner.

MAKES ONE 9-INCH CAKE, APPROXIMATELY 10 SERVINGS

1½ cups plus 1 tablespoon unbleached
    all-purpose flour, plus more for dusting
    the pan
1 lemon
1 lime
1 orange
¾ cup instant or fine polenta

2 teaspoons baking powder
1 teaspoon kosher salt
4 large eggs
1 cup granulated sugar
¾ cup extra-virgin olive oil
2 cups confectioners' sugar, plus more for
    dusting (optional)

Preheat the oven to 325°F and position a rack in the center. Lightly grease a 9-inch springform pan with butter or nonstick cooking spray, dust the pan with flour, and tap to knock out the excess. Grate the zest from the lemon, lime, and orange, setting the zests aside for the cake batter and reserving the fruit for the glaze.

In a medium bowl, whisk together the flour, polenta, baking powder, and salt and set aside. In the bowl of an electric mixer fitted with the whisk attachment, beat the eggs and granulated sugar together on medium-high speed until they are pale yellow and have tripled in volume, 3 to 4 minutes. Beat in the reserved citrus zests.

Alternate adding the dry ingredients and the olive oil to the egg mixture; begin with one third of the dry ingredients, then add half the oil, followed by another third of the dry ingredients, beating only until each addition is incorporated. Stop the mixer and briefly scrape down the sides of the bowl. Beat in the remaining olive oil, followed by the last third of the dry ingredients.

Pour the batter into the prepared pan and smooth the top with a spatula. Bake the cake for 25 to 30 minutes, rotating it 180 degrees halfway through the baking time to ensure even browning. The cake is done when it springs back lightly when touched and pulls away from the sides of the pan, and when a cake tester inserted in the center comes out clean. Cool the cake in the pan on a rack for 12 to 15 minutes, then carefully remove the sides of the pan and allow the cake to cool completely.

While the cake is cooling, make the glaze: Sift 2 cups confectioners' sugar into a large bowl. Squeeze 1 tablespoon of juice from each of the reserved citrus fruits. Add the citrus juices to the bowl and whisk until smooth. If the glaze seems too thick, add a few drops of water until it falls easily from a spoon. Drizzle the glaze over the cooled cake and allow it to set until it is completely dry.

Carefully remove the bottom of the springform pan with an offset spatula and transfer the cake to a serving plate. If desired, dust the cake with additional confectioners' sugar before serving. Any leftover cake may be wrapped in plastic and served the following day.

CHESTNUT SPICE CAKE WITH MASCARPONE CREAM
torta di castagne con crema di mascarpone

Filled with aromatic spices, this is an ideal treat for a chilly autumn day. The chestnut flour gives it a soft, tender texture, and the chestnut honey contributes a subtle, lingering flavor. I like to serve this cake to company during the holidays; the dollop of mascarpone cream on the side adds a luxurious touch, perfect for a festive get-together.

MAKES ONE 9-INCH CAKE, APPROXIMATELY 10 SERVINGS

FOR THE CAKE

1¾ cups unbleached all-purpose flour, plus more for dusting the pan

¾ cup chestnut flour (see page 61)

1½ teaspoons baking powder

½ teaspoon baking soda

1 teaspoon salt

2 teaspoons ground cinnamon

1 teaspoon ground ginger

½ teaspoon ground nutmeg

½ teaspoon ground cardamom

¼ teaspoon ground cloves

¾ cup (1½ sticks/6 ounces) unsalted butter, softened

1 cup granulated sugar

½ cup chestnut honey (see page 129)

3 large eggs

1 teaspoon pure vanilla extract

1 tablespoon cognac or brandy

1 cup whole milk

Confectioners' sugar, for dusting (optional)

FOR THE MASCARPONE CREAM

2 cups mascarpone

¾ cup heavy cream

2 tablespoons granulated sugar

Preheat the oven to 350°F and position a rack in the center. Grease a 9-inch springform pan with nonstick cooking spray or butter, dust it with flour, and tap to knock out the excess.

To make the cake: In a medium bowl, sift together the all-purpose flour, chestnut flour, baking powder, baking soda, salt, and spices and set aside. Using an electric mixer fitted with the paddle attachment, cream together the butter, granulated sugar, and honey until creamy and light, about 2 minutes. Beat in the eggs, one at a time, scraping down the sides of the bowl after each addition. Beat in the vanilla extract and cognac and scrape down the sides.

Add one third of the dry ingredients to the egg mixture and beat on low speed to incorporate them. Add half the milk and beat on low speed, then increase to medium speed for 10 seconds and scrape down the sides of the bowl. Add another third of the dry ingredients and repeat, followed by the rest of the milk and the remaining third of the dry ingredients. Scrape down the sides of the bowl after each addition, and finish the batter by beating for 10 to 20 seconds on medium speed to ensure that all the ingredients are thoroughly combined.

Pour the batter into the prepared pan, smoothing the top with a spatula. Bake the cake for 35 to 40 minutes, or until it springs back when lightly touched and has pulled away from the sides of the pan. Allow the cake to cool in the pan for about 10 minutes on a rack, then carefully remove the sides of the pan and let the cake cool completely.

Before serving, remove the bottom of the springform pan and transfer the cake to a serving plate. If desired, dust the cake with confectioners' sugar.

To make the mascarpone cream: Place the mascarpone, heavy cream, and sugar in the bowl of an electric mixer fitted with the whisk attachment. Beat the ingredients on medium speed to combine them, then switch to high speed, beating until the cream forms stiff peaks, 20 to 30 seconds.

To serve the cake, cut in wedges, place each wedge on a plate, and serve with a dollop of mascarpone cream alongside. Refrigerate any leftover cream in an airtight container. Any leftover cake may be wrapped in plastic or stored in an airtight container for up to 2 days.

ALMOND AND RAISIN CAKE
torta di mandorle e sultane

Oenophiles may shudder at the thought, but I think it is perfectly fine to surrender one glass from a bottle of vin santo *to make this delicious cake. (For a brief primer on* vin santo, *see page 31.) The cake gets a double shot of moistness from both the wine-plumped golden raisins and the almond paste. This is a cake that needs no adornment; you can linger over it with the rest of the bottle of wine.*

MAKES ONE 9-INCH ROUND CAKE, 8 TO 10 SERVINGS

2 cups unbleached all-purpose flour, plus more
    for dusting the pan

¾ cup *vin santo*

½ cup golden raisins

¼ cup almond flour

2 teaspoons baking powder

½ teaspoon kosher salt

½ cup (1 stick/4 ounces) unsalted butter,
    softened

¾ cup granulated sugar

3 ounces almond paste

2 large eggs

½ teaspoon pure vanilla extract

¼ teaspoon pure almond extract

¼ cup whole milk

Confectioners' sugar, for dusting

Preheat the oven to 325°F and position a rack in the center. Lightly grease a 9-by-2-inch round cake pan with nonstick cooking spray or butter, dust it with flour, and tap to knock out the excess.

Combine the *vin santo* and raisins in a small saucepan and place over medium heat until the wine just begins to simmer. Remove the pan from the heat and allow the raisins to plump and the mixture to cool.

In a medium bowl, whisk together the all-purpose flour, almond flour, baking powder, and salt and set aside. In the bowl of an electric mixer fitted with the paddle attachment, beat together the butter and sugar on medium speed until creamy and light, about 2 minutes. Add the almond paste and beat on medium speed until the mixture is fluffy and lump-free, about 1 minute.

Beat in the eggs, one at a time, followed by the vanilla and almond extracts, scraping down the sides of the bowl after each addition. On low speed, add half the dry ingredients, beating well. Scrape down the sides of the bowl and add the milk, beating well. Beat in the remaining dry ingredients on low speed, then switch to medium speed and beat for 30 seconds. Switch back to low speed and beat in the raisins and *vin santo*.

Pour the batter into the prepared pan, smoothing the surface with a spatula. Bake the cake for 35 to 40 minutes, or until a cake tester inserted in the center comes out clean. Allow the cake to cool in the pan for 10 minutes, then invert it onto a wire rack to cool completely.

Transfer the cake to a plate and dust with confectioners' sugar before serving. Any leftover cake may be wrapped in plastic and served the next day.

CHOCOLATE AND WALNUT TORTE FROM CAPRI
torta caprese

I've sampled many versions of this cake, a specialty of the island of Capri, off the Amalfi Coast of Campania. Some contain almonds along with or instead of walnuts, but since walnuts are my favorite, the choice is easy for me. Brown sugar is an unusual addition here, since it is not an ingredient found or used in Italy, but I am willing to depart from tradition because it deepens the flavor of the chocolate. This flourless torte is moist and fudgy and tastes even better the next day. I love to adorn a wedge of torta caprese *with a dollop of unsweetened whipped cream and a drizzle of* vincotto. *This cake is flourless, which makes it perfect for Passover.* MAKES ONE 9-INCH CAKE, 12 TO 15 SERVINGS*

1¼ cups walnut pieces	¾ cup packed light brown sugar
1 tablespoon unsweetened Dutch-processed cocoa powder	1 tablespoon dark rum or grappa
8 ounces bittersweet or semisweet chocolate	½ teaspoon kosher salt, plus a pinch
¾ cup (1½ sticks/6 ounces) unsalted butter	3 large egg whites
6 large egg yolks	1 tablespoon plus 1 teaspoon granulated sugar

Preheat the oven to 350°F and position a rack in the center. Lightly grease a 9-inch springform pan with nonstick cooking spray or butter, dust it with flour, and tap to knock out the excess.

Place the walnut pieces on a baking sheet and toast them until they are golden brown and aromatic, 12 to 14 minutes. Allow the walnuts to cool completely, then place them in a food processor with the cocoa powder and pulse until the nuts are finely ground.

Melt the chocolate and butter together in a large, heatproof bowl over a pan of simmering water, stirring often to prevent scorching. Remove the bowl from the heat and allow the mixture to cool to lukewarm. In an electric mixer fitted with the paddle attachment, beat the egg yolks with the light brown sugar on medium speed until very thick and pale in color, about 3 minutes. Beat in the rum and the ½ teaspoon salt. Using a spatula, fold the egg mixture into the cooled chocolate and butter mixture, then fold in the walnuts and cocoa.

Clean the mixing bowl. Place the egg whites and the pinch of salt in the cleaned bowl and, using the whisk attachment, beat on medium speed until the whites are thick but not peaking, about 2 minutes. Continue beating while you gradually add the granu-

VINCOTTO

The process of making wine yields many gifts aside from the wine itself, and *vincotto* is undoubtedly one of my favorites. Literally translated, the name means "cooked wine," which doesn't sound very appealing. But do not be fooled by words; open your first bottle of *vincotto* and you will become an instant convert.

Vincotto is made from the cooked must, or *mosto*, of black Negroamaro and Malvasia grapes. The grapes are dried and then gently boiled down until they have only one fifth of their original volume. The liquid is then aged for four or more years in oak barrels, along with some of the "mother," or original, batch. No acid or sugar is added to it, yet *vincotto* is sweet and tangy all at once, with pronounced pruney, caramel notes. It is perfect with soft young cheeses, such as fresh robiola or goat cheese, or drizzled over fresh, succulent fruit; try it with peaches, plums, cherries, nectarines, figs, or pears. Better yet, drizzle some over a dish of vanilla *gelato* or mix it into plain or sweetened yogurt. Ultimately, my favorite way to enjoy *vincotto* is with chocolate desserts, since it brings out the fruity qualities of the chocolate while balancing the sweetness.

Vincotto is produced on a small scale by a handful of artisans. Without question, Gianni Calogiuri makes the finest and most flavorful *vincotto*. The family estate also makes *vincotto* infused with fruits, such as raspberry, fig, lemon, and orange. More information is available at its website, www.vincotto.com.

lated sugar, then switch to high speed, beating the whites until they are softly peaking, about 1 minute.

Fold the whites into the cake batter, then immediately pour the batter into the prepared pan, smoothing the surface with a spatula. Bake the cake for 40 to 45 minutes, or until it is slightly puffed and just beginning to crack. Rotate the cake pan gently halfway through the baking time to ensure even browning. Allow the cake to cool in the pan for 20 minutes, then remove the sides of the pan and cool the cake completely; the center may sink a bit.

Carefully remove the bottom of the springform pan and transfer the cake to a serving plate. Any leftover cake may be wrapped in plastic and served the following day.

ZUCCHINI-OLIVE OIL CAKE WITH LEMON CRUNCH GLAZE

So what do you do when your garden produces a profusion of summer squash? Zucchini pizza, zucchini pasta, zucchini frittata. . . . Eventually your family is going to call you out. At that point I suggest trying this moist, tasty cake chock full of spices and walnuts and then glazed with a crunchy, lemony icing. Don't even mention the zucchini if your family is on squash overload. I use the finer side of my box grater to shred the zucchini, with the skin on; it will disappear into the cake while imparting all of its moisture and a subtle flavor.

MAKES ONE 10-INCH CAKE, APPROXIMATELY 12 SERVINGS

FOR THE CAKE

1 cup walnut pieces

2 cups unbleached all-purpose flour

1 teaspoon baking powder

½ teaspoon baking soda

1 teaspoon kosher salt

2 teaspoons ground cinnamon

1 teaspoon ground ginger

½ teaspoon ground nutmeg

3 large eggs

1¾ cups granulated sugar

1 cup extra-virgin olive oil

2 teaspoons pure vanilla extract

2½ cups grated zucchini (about 2 small zucchini)

Confectioners' sugar, for dusting (optional)

FOR THE LEMON CRUNCH GLAZE

¼ cup freshly squeezed lemon juice

⅓ cup granulated sugar

1 cup confectioners' sugar

To make the cake: Preheat the oven to 350°F and position a rack in the center. Grease a 10-cup Bundt pan using nonstick cooking spray or butter, then dust it with flour to coat it completely, tapping out the excess flour.

Place the walnuts in a single layer on a baking sheet and toast them until they are golden brown and aromatic, 12 to 14 minutes. Cool the walnuts completely, then finely chop them in the food processor and set aside.

Sift the flour, baking powder, baking soda, salt, and spices into a medium bowl and set aside. In an electric mixer fitted with the paddle attachment, beat the eggs, sugar, and olive oil together on medium speed until light and fluffy, about 3 minutes, then beat in the vanilla extract. Scrape down the sides of the bowl with a spatula after each addition. Beat in the dry ingredients all at once on low speed until they are thoroughly combined, then switch the mixer to medium speed and mix for 30 seconds. Beat in the zucchini and the walnuts on low speed until they are completely incorporated, scraping down the sides of the bowl.

Pour the batter into the prepared pan, smoothing the top with a spatula. Bake the cake for 45 to 50 minutes, rotating the pan halfway through the baking time to ensure even browning. The cake is done when a tester inserted in the center comes out clean and the cake has begun to pull away from the sides of the pan.

While the cake is baking, prepare the glaze: In a medium bowl, whisk together the lemon juice and granulated sugar, then whisk in the confectioners' sugar until the glaze is completely smooth.

Allow the cake to cool in the pan for 10 minutes, then carefully invert it onto a wire rack. Using a pastry brush, immediately brush the glaze over the entire surface of the warm cake, using all of the glaze; it will adhere to the cake and set as the cake cools. Allow the cake to cool completely and the glaze to dry completely.

Transfer the cake to a stand or serving plate and, if desired, lightly dust it with confectioners' sugar. Any leftover cake may be wrapped in plastic and served the following day.

OBSESSIVE RICOTTA CHEESECAKE
torta di ricotta

I am obsessed with ricotta cheesecake. I sample it from every pastry shop I stumble upon, and I have begged for recipes from every long-lost cousin in my extended family. I must have made dozens of attempts before arriving at my own recipe. The surprise for me was the benefits that came from adding American cream cheese. An Italian purist might insist on using mascarpone or only ricotta, but cream cheese gives this cake a creamy texture and tames the graininess of the ricotta. The almonds in the crust add another layer of flavor and nutty texture. As for the candied fruits, I find that most people are firmly on one side of the fence or the other. If you choose to omit them, you can substitute the grated zest of one orange. Just reading this recipe makes me want a slice.

MAKES ONE 9-INCH CAKE, APPROXIMATELY 12 SERVINGS

FOR THE CRUST

¾ cup sliced blanched almonds, toasted and cooled

¼ cup unbleached all-purpose flour

3 tablespoons granulated sugar

Pinch of kosher salt

1 large egg yolk

2 tablespoons (¼ stick/1 ounce) unsalted butter, melted and cooled

½ teaspoon pure vanilla extract

FOR THE FILLING

1 8-ounce package cream cheese

¾ cup granulated sugar

¼ teaspoon kosher salt

4 cups (30 ounces) fresh whole-milk ricotta

3 large eggs

1 teaspoon pure vanilla extract

1 tablespoon amaretto

1 tablespoon cornstarch

2 tablespoons finely chopped candied orange rind (optional)

2 tablespoons finely chopped candied lemon rind or candied citron (optional)

Preheat the oven to 325°F and position a rack in the middle. Lightly grease a 9-inch springform pan with butter or nonstick cooking spray, dust it with flour, and tap to knock out the excess.

To make the crust: Place the almonds, flour, sugar, and salt in a food processor and process until the nuts are finely chopped. In a small bowl, lightly whisk together the egg yolk, melted butter, and vanilla extract. Add the liquids to the nut mixture and pulse several times to moisten and combine the ingredients thoroughly. The mixture should come together easily between your fingers when pinched.

To form the crust, press the mixture onto the bottom and about an inch up the sides of the springform pan. Place the pan in the refrigerator for 15 to 20 minutes to firm up the crust, then bake for 10 to 15 minutes, or until the crust is light golden brown. Remove the pan from the oven and allow the crust to cool completely on a wire rack.

To make the filling: In an electric mixer fitted with the paddle attachment, beat the cream cheese with the sugar and salt on medium speed until soft and creamy, about 1 minute. Add the ricotta and beat until the mixture is smooth and light, another 2 minutes. Beat in the eggs, one at a time, scraping down the sides of the bowl with a spatula. Beat in the vanilla extract, amaretto, and cornstarch. Fold in the candied fruits, if desired, with the spatula.

Pour the filling into the cooled crust, smoothing the top with the spatula. Bake the cheesecake for 45 to 50 minutes, or until the center is set; it should be jiggly but not liquid. Remove the cheesecake from the oven and allow it to cool completely in the pan on a wire rack.

Chill the cooled cheesecake for at least 4 hours before serving; it is best served fully chilled on the following day. To serve, remove the sides of the springform pan and cut the cheesecake into wedges with a long, thin-bladed knife. Any leftover cake should be wrapped in plastic and stored in the refrigerator for up to 3 days.

RICOTTA POUND CAKE

Sometimes I like to eat fresh ricotta by the bowlful, so I can fully savor its creamy goodness. One Saturday morning I was sneaking around Babbo with a little bowl of ricotta for an impromptu breakfast snack, and as I indulged myself, the thought of pound cake jumped into my head. I may have been delusional or inspired—either way, I was driven enough to go straight into the kitchen and create this cake. Two hours later we were all standing around eating it, marveling at the rich flavor and moist texture. Ricotta in pound cake—who knew?

MAKES ONE 9-INCH CAKE, APPROXIMATELY 10 SERVINGS

1½ cups cake flour

2½ teaspoons baking powder

1 teaspoon kosher salt

¾ cup (1½/sticks/6 ounces) unsalted butter, softened

1½ cups fresh whole-milk ricotta

1½ cups granulated sugar

3 large eggs

½ vanilla bean

1 teaspoon pure vanilla extract

Confectioners' sugar, for dusting

Preheat the oven to 350°F and position a rack in the center. Grease a 9-inch loaf pan with nonstick cooking spray or butter, dust it with flour, and tap to knock out the excess.

In a medium bowl, sift together the cake flour, baking powder, and salt and set aside. In an electric mixer fitted with the paddle attachment, cream together the butter, ricotta, and sugar on medium speed until smooth and light, about 2 minutes. Beat in the eggs, one at a time, scraping down the sides of the bowl after each addition. Split the vanilla bean lengthwise and scrape out the seeds with the blunt side of a small knife, then beat them into the batter along with the vanilla extract. On low speed, beat in the dry ingredients to combine them, scrape down the sides of the bowl, and beat the batter for 30 seconds on medium speed.

Pour the batter into the prepared pan and use a spatula to smooth the top. Give the pan a few gentle whacks on the counter to remove any air pockets. Bake the cake for 15 minutes, then turn the pan 180 degrees to ensure even browning. Lower the temperature to 325°F and continue baking until the cake springs back lightly when touched, the sides have begun to pull away from the pan, and a cake tester inserted in the center of the cake comes out clean, about 25 minutes more. Allow the cake to cool in the pan on a wire rack for 15 minutes, then carefully invert it onto the rack to cool completely.

Dust the cake lightly with confectioners' sugar before serving it; the flavor is best on the next day. Any leftover cake may be wrapped in plastic and kept at room temperature for up to 3 days.

YOGURT CHEESECAKE WITH PINE NUT BRITTLE

Every time I put a cheesecake on the dessert menu at Babbo, it is a guaranteed sellout. People can't seem to get enough of it, and I try to satisfy this demand by creating different and unique versions of this universal favorite. Deliciously thick and creamy Greek-style yogurt is everywhere these days, and it is a far cry from the thin, watery yogurt I used for so many years. It harmonizes perfectly with the rich, buttery texture of mascarpone. This is a crustless cheesecake, more like a custard than anything else. For a contrast in texture, I like to serve it garnished with some crushed pine nut brittle, or crocante.

MAKES ONE 10-INCH CHEESECAKE, 10 TO 12 SERVINGS

¾ cup granulated sugar, plus more for dusting the pan	3 large eggs
	6 large egg yolks
3 cups (24 ounces) plain Greek-style yogurt	½ teaspoon kosher salt
1½ cups mascarpone	1½ teaspoons pure vanilla extract
3 tablespoons confectioners' sugar	Pine Nut Brittle (recipe follows)

Preheat the oven to 350°F and position a rack in the center. Lightly grease a 10-inch springform pan with nonstick cooking spray or butter. Sprinkle a couple of tablespoons of granulated sugar into the pan and swirl it around to coat the bottom and sides evenly, tapping out the excess sugar. Line the outside of the pan with a sheet of aluminum foil to guard against any leaks. The cheesecake will be baked in a water bath, so have ready a deep roasting pan that is large enough to accommodate the springform pan with an inch of space on all sides.

In an electric mixer fitted with the paddle attachment, beat together the yogurt, mascarpone, remaining ¾ cup granulated sugar, and confectioners' sugar on medium speed until very smooth and creamy, about 1 minute, stopping once to scrape down the sides of the bowl. Beat in the eggs and egg yolks one at a time, followed by the salt and vanilla extract, scraping down the sides of the bowl after each addition.

Pour the batter into the prepared pan, smoothing the top with a spatula. Place the spring form pan in the roasting pan and carefully fill the roasting pan with enough hot water to come halfway up the sides of the springform pan. Cover both pans with a single piece of aluminum foil, tenting the foil so it does not touch the top of the springform pan and being sure to cover the roasting pan completely. Very carefully transfer the roasting pan to the oven.

Bake the cheesecake for 20 minutes, then carefully rotate the pan 180 degrees to ensure that the cake bakes evenly. Bake for another 20 minutes, then remove the foil tent. The cake should be puffed but not cracked, jiggly but not liquid in the center. If necessary, continue baking the cake without the foil until it is set.

Remove the roasting pan from the oven and allow the cake to cool in the water bath until the water is lukewarm. Carefully remove the springform pan from the roasting pan and continue cooling the cake on a rack until it is cool to the touch. Remove the foil from the outside of the pan and chill the cake in the refrigerator 8 hours or overnight.

Before serving, remove the sides of the springform pan; you may have to run a knife around the edges. Transfer the cheesecake to a serving plate or cake stand and sprinkle the top with some chopped pine nut brittle. To serve, cut the cheesecake into wedges with a long, thin-bladed knife. Any leftover cake may be wrapped in plastic and stored in the refrigerator for up to 3 days.

PINE NUT BRITTLE (*CROCANTE*)

MAKES ABOUT 4 CUPS *CROCANTE*

2 cups granulated sugar

¼ cup water

4 tablespoons (½ stick/2 ounces) unsalted butter

4 tablespoons light corn syrup

2 teaspoons kosher salt

2 cups pine nuts

Line a 13-by-9-inch jelly-roll pan with parchment or wax paper, then lightly grease the paper with nonstick cooking spray or butter.

In a large, heavy-bottomed saucepan, stir the sugar and water together. Add the butter and corn syrup and clip a candy thermometer to the side of the pan. Place the pan over medium-high heat and bring the mixture to a boil. Turn up the heat to high and continue to cook until the mixture turns deep golden brown and registers 350°F on the candy thermometer.

Immediately turn off the heat and very carefully remove the candy thermometer. Stir in the salt with a large wooden spoon, a slotted metal spoon, or a heatproof spatula, then stir in the pine nuts. Make sure the caramel coats all the nuts.

Turn the mixture out onto the jelly-roll pan and, using a spatula, spread it toward the sides of the pan so the nuts are in a single layer. Let the brittle cool completely before breaking it into pieces and storing in an airtight plastic container. Keep in a cool, dry place for up to 2 weeks.

To prepare the brittle for a garnish or topping, break it into small pieces and then chop it using a large chef's knife.

THE SPICE MARKET

Spices made their first appearance in Italian cooking during the glory days of Rome, when they were brought back from the far reaches of the Roman Empire to grace the tables of emperors. Though they became scarce during the Middle Ages, interest in and desire for exotic spices never fully died, and when the Crusades brought Europe directly into contact with the East, the spice trade exploded. The Italian port cities of Venice and Genoa became the gateways for exotic goods from the East to reach not only Italy but all of Western Europe, and the merchants of Venice became power players in the trade of spices.

By the fourteenth century the use of spices was widespread and well documented. A Florentine merchant's manual from the early 1300s contains a long list of spices available for trade, including numerous varieties of pepper and ginger, cinnamon, cloves, nutmeg and mace, cardamom, cumin, turmeric, caraway, saffron, and aniseed, as well as many others. Italian cookbooks from this period also recommend using spices in cooking. Spices were valued for their perceived medicinal value; the "heat" was thought to greatly aid the digestive process, allowing foods to be efficiently "cooked" by the stomach. Spices were dusted onto or infused in nearly everything—meats and soups, wine, and sweets and confections that were enjoyed after a large meal.

Spices, like sugar, were a symbol of status and fashion and a luxury of the elite. Despite this, it is important to note that the primary reason for their popularity in the cooking of this period was that spices, again like sugar, simply made foods taste better. There is a false belief that spices were used to cover up the flavor of bad or rancid foods. On the contrary, they were available only to persons of wealth and status who already enjoyed the best of foods, properly cooked. Peasants may indeed have had a need to improve the flavor of their simpler foods with spices, but they did not have access to them. Spices became ingredients for the same reasons they are used today—they improved the taste of food, and people found that pleasing. Cooks and chefs from the fourteenth and fifteenth centuries applied considerable thought and technique to the use of spices in their cooking. Early recipe collections offer proof, providing specific instructions about when the spices should be added to achieve the finest flavor (later was better) as well as the most healthful benefits.

Ironically, the generous use of spices in cooking fell out of fashion just as they became more available to the general population, in the eighteenth century. Much like today, the trends came and went as wealthy people found new culinary delights to place in vogue. In Venice, however, where spices made their grand entrance, they maintained their presence, if not outright dominance. Today you will find the exotic flavors of ginger, cinnamon, clove, nutmeg, mace, and saffron still perfuming the cuisine of Venice, and when you are wandering along the narrow streets, it is not unusual to find merchants stacking piles of spices to entice those with a bit of money to spend, just as they did centuries ago.

ALMOND CAKE FROM ABRUZZO
parrozzo

Parrozzo *is a traditional cake from the region of Abruzzi, where it is glazed with melted chocolate and decorated with whole almonds. I like to chop my chocolate fine and fold it into the cake batter instead, resulting in a speckled* parrozzo. *The bits of chocolate make a pretty contrast to the cake's pale yellow interior, colored by semolina. Finishing the cake with a chocolate glaze makes for a sleek presentation, or you can drizzle the glaze in a zigzag pattern for a more rustic approach. Either way, the cake is oh-so-soft and tender. Try it with a scoop of Toasted Almond Gelato (page 177).* MAKES ONE 9-INCH CAKE, 8 TO 10 SERVINGS

FOR THE CAKE

1 cup sliced blanched almonds, plus ½ cup for garnish (optional)

1½ cups cake flour

½ cup semolina

2 teaspoons baking powder

½ teaspoon kosher salt

½ cup (1 stick/4 ounces) unsalted butter, softened

¾ cup granulated sugar

2 large eggs

1 teaspoon pure vanilla extract

½ teaspoon pure almond extract

Finely grated zest of 1 lemon

¼ teaspoon ground nutmeg

½ cup finely chopped semisweet or bittersweet chocolate (3½ ounces)

FOR THE CHOCOLATE GLAZE

6 ounces bittersweet or semisweet chocolate, chopped

2 ounces unsweetened chocolate, chopped

2 tablespoons (¼ stick/1 ounce) unsalted butter, softened

2 tablespoons amaretto

Preheat the oven to 325°F and position a rack in the center. Grease a 9-by-2-inch round cake pan with nonstick cooking spray or butter, dust it with flour, and tap to knock out the excess.

To make the cake: Place all the almonds in a single layer on a baking sheet and toast them until they are golden brown and aromatic, 12 to 14 minutes. Allow the almonds to cool completely, then place 1 cup in the bowl of a food processor. Add the cake flour, semolina, baking powder, and salt and process until the almonds are finely ground.

In an electric mixer fitted with the paddle attachment, beat together the butter and sugar on medium speed until very light and creamy, about 2 minutes. Beat in the eggs, one at a time, scraping down the sides after each addition. Beat in the vanilla and almond extracts and the lemon zest. Add the dry ingredients and the nutmeg and beat on low speed until the dry ingredients are moistened, then switch to medium speed and beat until the batter is thick and emulsified, about 1 minute. Beat in the chopped chocolate.

Pour the batter into the prepared pan, smoothing the top with a spatula. Bake the cake for 25 to 30 minutes, or until it springs back lightly when touched, the sides have pulled away from the pan, and a cake tester inserted near the center comes out clean. Cool the cake in the pan on a wire rack for 10 minutes, then invert it onto the rack to cool completely.

While the cake cools, make the glaze: Place both chocolates in a heatproof bowl, place it over a pan of simmering water, and whisk until the chocolate has melted. Remove the bowl from the water and whisk in the butter and amaretto. Allow the glaze to cool to room temperature.

Pour the cooled glaze onto the middle of the cake and spread it to the sides with a spatula, allowing some of the glaze to dribble over the edge and down the sides of the cake. Carefully transfer the cake to a serving plate or cake stand and, if desired, decorate with the remaining ½ cup toasted almonds. Any leftover cake may be wrapped in plastic and stored at room temperature for 2 days.

VENETIAN APPLE CAKE

This is a great, quick cake to make for unexpected company or an after-school snack for the kids. I decided it was Venetian because it contains spices, which came through Venice during the height of its power as a trading port, and polenta, which is popular throughout the Veneto region. This is not the usual gooey, apple-laden coffee cake; instead, one large apple is grated and folded into the batter. The apple flavor infuses the cake, blending perfectly with the spices and honey. The prep is a snap—simply peel the apple and grate it on all sides until you reach the core.
MAKES ONE 9-INCH CAKE, 8 TO 10 SERVINGS

1½ cups unbleached all-purpose flour
½ cup instant or fine polenta
2 teaspoons baking powder
1 teaspoon kosher salt
½ teaspoon ground cinnamon
½ teaspoon ground ginger
¼ teaspoon ground nutmeg
1 large Granny Smith or Golden
   Delicious apple

8 tablespoons (1 stick/4 ounces) unsalted
   butter, softened
2 tablespoons extra-virgin olive oil
¾ cup granulated sugar
½ cup honey
2 large eggs
1½ teaspoons pure vanilla extract
¼ cup whole milk
Confectioners' sugar, for dusting (optional)

Preheat the oven to 350°F and position a rack in the center. Grease a 9-by-2-inch round cake pan with butter or nonstick cooking spray, dust it with flour, and tap to knock out the excess.

In a medium bowl, whisk the flour, polenta, baking powder, salt, and spices together and set aside. Peel the apple and grate it, using the medium side of a box grater. Place the grated apple in a bowl, cover it with plastic wrap, and set aside.

In an electric mixer fitted with the paddle attachment, cream the butter, olive oil, and sugar together on medium speed until light and fluffy, about 1 minute. Scrape down the sides of the bowl and beat in the honey until the mixture is smooth and creamy, about 1 minute. Beat in the eggs, one at a time, scraping down the sides of the bowl, followed by the vanilla extract.

On low speed, beat in half the dry ingredients, followed by all the milk. Scrape down the sides of the bowl and beat in the remaining dry ingredients. Switch the mixer to medium speed and beat for 30 seconds to emulsify the batter. Using a rubber spatula, gently fold in the grated apple.

Pour the batter into the prepared pan, smoothing the top with the spatula. Bake for 35 to 40 minutes, or until a cake tester inserted near the center of the cake comes out clean and the cake springs back when lightly touched. Allow the cake to cool in the pan on a wire rack for 10 minutes, then invert it onto the rack to cool completely.

Transfer the cake to a serving plate or cake stand and, if desired, garnish the top with a dusting of confectioners' sugar. Any leftover cake may be wrapped in plastic and stored for up to 2 days.

SPOON DESSERTS
budini

T HE RECIPES IN THIS CHAPTER SHARE THE COMMON CHARACTERISTIC of being enjoyed with a spoon. Here in America, a spoon suggests a certain level of comfort, which makes this my personal collection of Italian comfort desserts. *Budino* means "pudding," and while some of these dishes slide easily into that category, I have expanded the definition to encompass any dessert that fits my idea of luxurious, soft, and sometimes creamy comfort.

This chapter gives you an opportunity to have fun with serving pieces. In many instances you will need a good set of custard cups to cook some of the *budini*. Heavy ceramic or porcelain ramekins are the best choice for a caramelized custard such as Mocha-Cinnamon Bônet; these days you can find them in an array of colors, not just the traditional white or ivory, making them dramatic tableware as well as entirely functional. Decorative ceramic teacups and demitasse or espresso cups also make imaginative choices for cooking and/or serving. Here is your chance to bring out your favorite crystal bowls and stemmed serving glasses, or to show off treasures you may have collected on a trip to Florence or to the Umbrian towns of Gubbio, Deruta, and Orvieto, each known for its handmade ceramics.

Comfort can be an entirely subjective and highly elusive ideal, but to me it means lazy weekends, nights in front of the tube or a fire, with close friends or a good book, shoes off, feet encased in slippers or curled around soft sand. Even if not enjoyed under such romantic conditions, comfort foods are ultimately transformative. When you feel like you are hurtling down a mountain at breakneck speed, your favorite version of a *budino* can provide a perfectly soft landing spot.

ZUCCHINI–OLIVE OIL
CAKE WITH LEMON
CRUNCH GLAZE, PAGE 94

YOGURT CHEESECAKE WITH
PINE NUT BRITTLE, PAGE 100

A SLICE OF YOGURT CHEESECAKE
WITH PINE NUT BRITTLE, PAGE 100

CHOCOLATE AND DATE PUDDING
CAKES, PAGE 124

MOCHA-CINNAMON BÔNET,
PAGE 112

HEAVENLY PANNA COTTA WITH
VINCOTTO, PAGE 128

FRESH FIG TART,
PAGE 162

HONEY AND PINE NUT TART,
PAGE 145

A GENTLE BATH

In cooking, the term "bain-marie" refers to either baking in a water bath or cooking over a pot of simmering water. In either case it is a gentle, even way to cook delicate foods such as custards. The origin of this term, which translates as "Mary's bath," was explained by the Académie des Gastronomes as a reference to the "gentle name of Mary." The technique was developed during the fourteenth century, a time of particular devotion to the Virgin Mary. As food writer Waverley Root explains it, the *bagno maria*, as it is known in Italian, was an invention of the alchemist and saint Maria di Cleofa, who was, according to legend, a descendent of the Virgin Mary and who used it in her studies of medicine and cooking.

Regardless of which tale you choose to believe, baking in a water bath is essential for custard desserts. A bain-marie is nothing fancy; it merely consists of a pan large enough and deep enough to hold small custard cups or a larger vessel such as a springform pan. Deep roasting or lasagne pans are good choices because they have flat rather than sloping sides. Be sure to pick a pan that is flat on the bottom, since some roasting pans are grooved, which may make your custard cups tilt and sit unevenly. Restaurants use "hotel pans," large rectangular pans with straight sides. Hotel pans can be purchased at restaurant supply stores in standard sizes and depths; I like a 6-inch-deep one, the ideal depth for baking custards.

The depth of your bain-marie is an important consideration; if your custard cups are taller than the pan's sides, you'll find it very difficult to cover them. Many custard recipes require you to protect the custards from developing a skin with a tent of aluminum foil during baking. Ideally, your bain-marie will be deep enough to hold the custard cups and still allow an inch or two of headroom, over which you can easily tent the foil.

Always remember to fill your bain-marie with very hot tap water before baking. Cold water will take some time to heat up and will unnecessarily slow down the cooking process. When you remove your custards from the oven, leave them in the bain-marie to cool, which will help any custards that are slightly underdone to continue cooking in the residual heat from the bath.

MOCHA-CINNAMON BÔNET
bônet alla piemontese

Bônet (pronounced beau-nay) is possibly the ultimate custard dessert and a special-ty of the region of Piedmont. Tucked in the northwestern corner of Italy, Piedmont shares a long border with France and produces some of Italy's finest wines and cheeses. Although Bologna is reputed to be the heart of Italian cuisine, the Piedmontese are justly confident that their cooking is unsurpassed. Bônet combines the richness of a crème brûlée, the gush of caramel from a flan, and that unique bit of Italian ingenuity, crushed amaretti. As it bakes, the amaretti crumbs float to the top of the custard, forming a soft crust on the bottom when the bônet is unmolded. Traditionally, bônet is a chocolate dessert, but I have opted for a mocha twist, using some espresso beans and cocoa powder with a touch of cinnamon. This dessert was selling out on my Babbo menu every night for a whopping seven months. It is that good. MAKES 6 SERVINGS

2½ cups heavy cream

½ cup whole milk

2½ cups granulated sugar

2 cinnamon sticks

¼ cup whole espresso beans, coarsely
   chopped in a food processor

1 teaspoon Dutch-processed cocoa powder

5 large egg yolks

1 large egg

Pinch of kosher salt

½ cup water

1 cup crushed *amaretti*

Whipped cream, for garnish

Preheat the oven to 325°F and position a rack in the center. Have ready a large, flat-bottomed roasting pan that can comfortably hold six 4- to 5-ounce ramekins with an inch of space in between them.

Place the heavy cream, milk, ¼ cup sugar, cinnamon sticks, chopped espresso beans, and cocoa powder in a medium saucepan and whisk briefly to combine. Place the saucepan over medium heat and bring the mixture to a boil, stirring occasionally. Remove the pan from the heat and allow the mixture to steep for 30 minutes.

In a medium bowl, whisk together the egg yolks, egg, salt, and ¼ cup sugar. Remove the cinnamon sticks from the saucepan, then slowly pour the warm milk mixture into the egg mixture, whisking constantly. Return the mixture to the pan and whisk thor-oughly. Strain the custard through a chinois or fine-meshed sieve to strain out the espresso beans. Set aside the custard to cool while you caramelize the ramekins.

Have ready a bowl of ice water. Prepare the caramel for the ramekins by placing the remaining 2 cups sugar and ½ cup water in a heavy medium saucepan, stirring to moisten the sugar completely; the mixture should resemble wet sand. Place the pan over high heat and bring the mixture to a boil. Continue to cook until it turns light golden. Remove the pan from the heat. The caramel will continue to deepen in color after it has been removed from the heat. When it has turned a deep amber, after about 6 minutes, carefully pour about ¼ cup* into each of the ramekins, one at a time. Quickly swirl the caramel halfway up the sides of the ramekin in a circular motion. If you have poured too much caramel into a ramekin, pour it back into the pan. (If you happen to burn your fingers or hand on the caramel, immediately plunge them into the bowl of ice water.) Allow the caramel to cool in the ramekins for about 10 minutes.

Arrange the ramekins in the roasting pan. Sprinkle 2 heaping tablespoons of *amaretti* crumbs on the bottom of each ramekin. Pour the custard into the ramekins until it reaches about ⅛ inch from the top. Create a bain-marie, or water bath, by adding enough hot water to the roasting pan to come halfway up the sides of the ramekins. Cover the roasting pan with aluminun foil, tenting it slightly so it does not touch the top of the ramekins.

Carefully place the roasting pan on the oven rack and bake the custards for 35 minutes, then rotate the pan 180° to ensure even baking. Bake them for another 15 minutes and then check them for doneness. The custards are ready when the centers are no longer liquid but jiggly like gelatin. Depending on your oven, they will bake for a total of 1 hour, give or take 10 minutes.

Remove the pan from the oven, remove the foil, and allow the custards to cool in the water bath until you can safely pick up the ramekins, then allow them to cool to room temperature. Chill the custards thoroughly for at least 4 hours before serving.

To unmold, run the tip of a sharp knife around the edge of each ramekin. Turn it over and shake it until you feel the custard begin to loosen, then turn it onto a serving plate, allowing the caramel to pool around each *bônet*. Serve with softly whipped cream.

---

* Do not attempt to measure this, since the caramel is too hot to handle and will harden quickly. An "eyeball" measurement will be sufficient. There should be enough caramel to cover the bottom and coat the sides of each ramekin halfway.

VANILLA BEAN AND BAY LEAF CUSTARDS

The leaves of the evergreen bay tree are also known as laurel and were used by the ancient Romans to crown their victorious leaders and heroes. Laurus nobilis, also known as true laurel, is native to the Mediterranean region and favored by Italian cooks for seasoning both savory and sweet dishes. I love the flavor of fresh bay leaves, especially in combination with the finest vanilla beans. The rich, creamy texture of these custards is the perfect medium for both. It is important to use fresh bay leaves for this recipe—dried bay leaf has a milder flavor profile and is simply not up to the task. MAKES 4 SERVINGS

2½ cups heavy cream

½ cup whole milk

¼ cup plus 2 tablespoons granulated sugar

1 vanilla bean

3 fresh bay leaves

5 large egg yolks

Pinch of kosher salt

Toasted pine nuts, for garnish (optional)

Place the heavy cream, milk, and ¼ cup granulated sugar in a medium saucepan. Split the vanilla bean lengthwise and scrape out the seeds with the blunt side of a paring knife. Add the seeds and the bean to the pan, along with the fresh bay leaves. Whisk the ingredients together briefly, place the saucepan over medium heat, and heat the mixture until it scalds or bubbles slightly. Turn off the heat and let the mixture sit for 30 minutes to infuse it with the flavor of the bay leaves.

Preheat the oven to 325°F and position a rack in the center. Arrange four 4-ounce ramekins or custard cups in a flat-bottomed roasting pan large enough to accommodate them with ¾ inch of space in between them.

Place the egg yolks in a large bowl and whisk them with the salt and the remaining 2 tablespoons of sugar. Remove the bay leaves and vanilla bean from the cream mixture and discard. Whisk the cream mixture into the egg yolks in a steady stream. Strain the custard through a chinois or fine-meshed sieve to remove any lumps of egg yolk.

Evenly divide the custard among the ramekins. Carefully add enough hot water to the roasting pan to come one third up the sides of the ramekins. Cover the roasting pan with aluminum foil, tenting it slightly so the foil does not touch the top of the ramekins.

Carefully place the pan in the oven and bake the custards for 35 minutes, then rotate the pan to ensure even baking. Bake them for another 15 minutes and then check for

doneness. The custards are finished when the centers are no longer liquid but jiggly like gelatin. Depending on your oven, they should bake for a total of 50 minutes to 1 hour.

Remove the pan from the oven, remove the foil, and allow the custards to cool in the water bath until you can safely pick them up, then allow them to cool to room temperature. Chill the custards thoroughly in the refrigerator for at least 4 hours before serving.

If desired, serve each custard with a sprinkling of toasted pine nuts.

RICOTTA AND ROBIOLA CUSTARDS
budini di ricotta e robiola

This simple cheese custard is a perfect example of the straightforward nature of Italian desserts. The texture is creamy, light, and ethereal; the flavor of the two cheeses is perfectly complemented by a mere drizzle of warm honey and a dusting of cinnamon—or, in summer, a compote of fresh berries tossed with a bit of sugar. Robiola cheese is primarily produced in the regions of Piedmont and Lombardy. Fresh robiola is made with cow's milk and is similar to fresh goat cheese but softer, with an extra-fine curd and super-creamy texture. Don't confuse it with aged robiola, which is a soft-ripened cheese that can be quite assertive. Fresh robiola is available at some upscale markets and cheese shops, or see Sources, pages 285–87. It comes packaged in cubes weighing 100 grams each. Osella is the brand most commonly imported to the United States. If you cannot find it, fresh goat cheese makes a fine substitute. MAKES 6 SERVINGS

1 cup fresh whole-milk ricotta	2 tablespoons whole milk
2 cubes (200 grams) fresh robiola	¼ cup heavy cream
2 large eggs	Honey, warmed, for garnish
¼ cup granulated sugar	Ground cinnamon, for garnish
1 teaspoon pure vanilla extract	

Preheat the oven to 325°F and position a rack in the center. Arrange six 4-ounce ramekins or custard cups in a flat-bottomed roasting pan large enough to accommodate them with ¾ inch of space between them.

Place the ricotta, robiola, and sugar in the bowl of a food processor and pulse several times, until the cheeses are creamy and smooth. Add the eggs, vanilla extract, milk, and heavy cream and pulse to combine. Scrape down the sides of the bowl and pulse one more time to ensure that all the ingredients are fully incorporated and the mixture is smooth.

Divide the mixture among the ramekins, tapping each ramekin once or twice on the counter to even the top. Add enough hot water to the roasting pan to come halfway up the sides of the ramekins. Cover the roasting pan with aluminum foil, tenting it slightly so the foil does not touch the top of the ramekins.

Carefully place the pan in the oven and bake the custards for 35 minutes, then rotate the pan to ensure even baking. Bake them for another 15 minutes and then check for doneness. The custards are finished when the centers are no longer liquid but jiggly like gelatin. Depending on your oven, the custards should bake for a total of 1 hour, give or take 10 minutes.

Remove the pan from the oven, remove the foil, and allow the custards to cool in the water bath until you can safely remove them to continue cooling to room temperature. Chill the custards thoroughly in the refrigerator, for at least 4 hours, before serving.

Serve the custards with a drizzle of warm honey and a dusting of ground cinnamon.

CREAMY PUMPKIN CUSTARD
crema di zucca

When autumn finally hits New York and the morning carries a crisp little breeze that makes you reach for a woolly sweater, I know it is time to turn my sights toward my fall lineup of desserts. This creamy pumpkin and cheese custard leads the pack; it is light and flavorful, bursting with the colors of autumn. I am particularly fond of the golden raisins plumped with orange juice and rum that are spooned over the top of the custard. They are also terrific over Ginger Honey Gelato (page 182). MAKES 6 SERVINGS

¼ cup granulated sugar, plus more for dusting the ramekins

2 pieces crystallized ginger (about 1 ounce)

4 ounces cream cheese, softened

½ cup packed light brown sugar

¼ cup mascarpone

3 large egg yolks

1 teaspoon pure vanilla extract

¼ teaspoon kosher salt

1 cup fresh pumpkin puree (see page 120) or canned pumpkin

Unsweetened or lightly sweetened whipped cream or crème fraîche, for garnish

Golden Raisin Compote (recipe follows), for garnish

Preheat the oven to 325°F and position a rack in the center. Grease six 4-ounce ramekins or custard cups with nonstick cooking spray, then coat the bottoms and sides with some granulated sugar, shaking out the excess. Have ready a flat-bottomed roasting pan large enough to accommodate the ramekins with ¾ inch of space in between them.

Place the granulated sugar and crystallized ginger in the bowl of a food processor and process until the ginger is finely ground. Place the mixture in the bowl of an electric mixer fitted with the paddle attachment and add the cream cheese and light brown sugar. Cream the ingredients together on medium speed until smooth and lump-free, about 2 minutes. Beat in the mascarpone, followed by the egg yolks, one at a time, scraping down the sides of the bowl after each addition. Beat in the vanilla extract and salt, then beat in the pumpkin puree just until combined.

Divide the mixture among the ramekins, filling them ¾ full and tapping each one once or twice on the counter to even the top. Place the ramekins in the roasting pan and add enough hot water to come halfway up the sides of the ramekins. Cover the roasting pan with aluminum foil, tenting it slightly so the foil does not touch the top of the ramekins.

Carefully place the pan in the oven and bake the custards for 25 minutes, then rotate the pan to ensure even baking. Bake them for another 15 minutes and then check for doneness; the custards should appear slightly puffy and their surfaces should be matte. Remove the pan from the oven and allow the custards to cool for 10 minutes, then remove them from the bain-marie and chill until firm, at least 4 hours.

To serve, run the tip of a knife around the edge of each custard and flip it onto a serving plate. Top each serving with a dollop of whipped cream or crème fraîche and a spoonful of golden raisin compote.

GOLDEN RAISIN COMPOTE

MAKES ABOUT 1 1/2 CUPS
1 heaping cup golden raisins
¾ cup orange juice
¼ cup golden or dark rum
⅓ cup granulated sugar
2 tablespoons unsalted butter, softened

Place the raisins, orange juice, rum, and sugar in a small saucepan over medium heat. Simmer until the raisins are soft and plump, then pour the liquid through a chinois or fine-meshed sieve to strain out the raisins and place them in a small bowl. Return the liquid to the pan and continue simmering until it is syrupy and reduced to about ½ cup. Remove the pan from the heat and whisk in the butter. Combine the sauce with the raisins and cool to room temperature.

THE BEST WAY TO ROAST A PUMPKIN

To produce a thick, flavorful pumpkin or butternut squash puree, start with a hot oven rather than a pot of water. Boiling a squash or pumpkin adds far too much water to the equation, resulting in a watery, mushy puree, while roasting brings out the natural sweetness and vibrant color of the vegetable.

The steps are quite simple. Cut your pumpkin or squash into quarters; in the case of an extremely large pumpkin, you may want to cut the quarters in half. Remove the seeds and pulp with a large, heavy spoon; it isn't necessary to peel the skin, but you can if you wish, using a sharp knife. Place the pieces of pumpkin or squash in a large roasting pan and brush them generously with some good olive oil. Turn them cut side down, pour about 1 cup or ½ inch water into the pan, and cover it tightly with aluminum foil. Place the roasting pan in a preheated 400°F oven and roast the pumpkin or squash for about 45 minutes, or until the pieces are soft and fork-tender. You can remove the foil during the last 10 minutes or so to let some of the water evaporate and allow the flesh to caramelize ever so slightly. Allow the pumpkin or squash to cool completely in the pan, then scrape the pulp away from the skin and into a food mill or the bowl of a food processor and puree in batches until smooth.

The most flavorful pumpkins are small sugar pumpkins; their name perfectly describes their taste. I am also fond of cheese pumpkins, which have a skin that is similar in color and texture to that of butternut squash and flesh that is brilliant orange. After Thanksgiving it is sometimes difficult to find pumpkins at the market; in that case, I heartily recommend using butternut squash, which also yields a wonderful-tasting puree for Creamy Pumpkin Custard (page 118) or any other recipe calling for a pumpkin puree.

YOGURT WITH CARAMEL, AGED BALSAMIC, AND PINE NUT BRITTLE

The brittle, or crocante, *as it is known in Italy, is simple to make and difficult to keep around; one bite never seems to be enough for me. Making your own caramel sauce is addictive as well, and having leftovers around to pour over* gelato *for an impromptu sundae is a pleasant habit to form. Beyond that, all you need is* aceto balsamico, *the fine, aged balsamic vinegar from Modena (see page 122). Surprisingly, when it is all presented in fine glass or china dessert bowls, this makes a very pretty and unusual dessert for company.* **MAKES 4 TO 6 SERVINGS**

FOR THE CREAMY CARAMEL SAUCE

2¼ cups granulated sugar

¼ cup light corn syrup

¾ cup water

1½ cups heavy cream

½ cup (1 stick/4 ounces) unsalted butter, cut in small pieces

2 cups Greek-style yogurt

Pine Nut Brittle (page 102)

4–6 teaspoons *aceto balsamico tradizionale di Modena* or *aceto balsamico condimento*

To make the creamy caramel sauce: Place the sugar, corn syrup, and water in a medium saucepan and stir together just enough to moisten the sugar. Place the pan over medium-high heat and cook at a slow boil until the sugar begins to caramelize. When the sugar has turned a uniformly light golden color, turn off the heat.

The caramel will continue to darken as it sits. When it has turned a deep mahogany, gently pour in the cream, a tablespoonful at a time. The caramel will bubble up, so stand back from the pan. Continue adding the cream gradually, then add the butter, a few pieces at a time. When the caramel is no longer bubbling, gently stir the mixture with a whisk to combine the ingredients. If the caramel is no longer hot enough to melt all the butter, turn on the heat to low for a few moments and continue whisking until the butter is melted and the sauce is creamy and smooth. The caramel sauce may be cooled and then chilled until you are ready to use it.

To assemble the dish: Stir the yogurt to make it creamy and spoonable. Heat the caramel sauce until it is warm and pourable. With a sharp knife, finely chop the pine nut brittle. For each serving, pour a small pool of warm caramel sauce into a dessert bowl. Place a pretty dollop of yogurt on top, drizzle a bit more caramel over the top, and sprinkle on a generous amount of the brittle. Anoint each serving with a teaspoon of the aged balsamic vinegar.

THE REAL DEAL

Aceto Balsamico Tradizionale di Modena. Just the number of words involved should give you a clue as to how important and wondrous this product is. The traditional balsamic vinegar of Modena is made from grape must, or *mosto*, and its production is complex and controlled, with centuries of tradition behind it. The vinegar's status as an exported product is relatively recent; for hundreds of years it remained a specialty of Emilia-Romagna, enjoyed exclusively in and around the provincial areas of Modena and Reggio Emilia, where it is made. The consortium that governs its production, marketing, and export was formed in 1979, and clearly the producers were forward-thinking, given the tremendous surge in tourism to Italy in the past two decades, the accompanying interest in regional Italian cuisine, and the inevitable demand for regional products. In 2000, the European Union bestowed the coveted DOP status on *aceto balsamico* of Modena, bringing to the rest of the world a treasure previously hidden in the attics of Modenese families for generations.

The consortium of producers that exports *aceto balsamico* of Modena (its full name is quite a mouthful: Consorzio Produttori Aceto Balsamico di Modena) controls every aspect of production, from the harvesting of the grapes to the packaging and labeling of the bottles.

The grapes can be only of the Trebbiano and Lambrusco varietals (though a few others are allowed in small quantities) and must be entirely harvested from the vineyards of the region. The grapes are pressed, and in accordance with the regulations of the *consorzio*, they must be cooked relatively quickly thereafter in an open vat until the *mosto* is reduced in volume by about half. Then the vinegar is aged progressively in wooden barrels for a minimum of twelve years; some balsamic has been aged for well over one hundred years.

As the aging process proceeds, the balsamic is carefully transferred to barrels of decreasing volume and made from differing woods, namely oak, chestnut, and juniper. The smallest cask provides the first few liters of volume; the rest comes from newly cooked *mosto* added to the largest barrel. The balsamic continues to reduce and concentrate as it ages, and the result is a viscous, rich, and syrupy liquid, with a glossy sheen and an aromatic bouquet. The final product has a bit to do with the blending and decanting of the vinegar from barrel to barrel, as well as some blind luck. Two different producers may follow exactly the same method of barreling yet wind up with two entirely different vinegars in terms of volume, flavor, and density.

Before the *aceto balsamico* is bottled, a

panel of five masters of the *consorzio* tastes it to ensure that it meets the standards of production and quality. The vinegars are judged using a point system, and if the balsamic does not earn enough points, it is sent back to the barrels. Once it has been approved for sale, it is bottled in a standard size of 100 milliliters, to just under 4 liquid ounces. The bottles are numbered, labeled, and sealed and then released for sale and exportation. *Aceto balsamico* must be aged for at least twelve years to be labeled *vecchio*, or old; vinegar that is at least twenty-five years old earns the designation *stravecchio* or *extravecchio*.

Your first taste of *Aceto Balsamico Tradizionale* can stop you in your tracks; it is the ultimate balance of acidity with an almost smoky sweetness, which makes it an ideal partner for fruits and cheeses. Whatever you choose to serve with it, *aceto balsamico* takes center stage. The classic suggestions are to present it with components of equally superior quality. Dribble it onto a rib-eye steak or a grilled veal chop. Try a few drops on fresh pasta with the finest olive oil and a hint of sautéed garlic. For dessert, it is heavenly with perfect, ripe strawberries or cherries dusted with a bit of confectioners' sugar, shards of Parmigiano-Reggiano, or a dollop of mascarpone, and with fresh, creamy vanilla *gelato* or *semifreddo*. *Aceto balsamico* elevates even the finest products to a new level.

There are a number of alternatives to authentic *Aceto Balsamico Tradizionale* that echo the rich flavor and sweet, balanced acidity. Look for bottles labeled *balsamico condimento*, or balsamic condiment, which are made by producers that do not adhere completely to the strict guidelines of the consortium yet remain true to the traditional methods and standards of quality. If you can read the label or information included with the bottle, try to determine whether the *condimento* is made from 100 percent Trebbiano grape must, with no other vinegars added, and aged from five to ten years; some may even be blended with a percentage of *Aceto Balsamico Tradizionale* for the best flavor.

Aceto Balsamico Tradizionale di Modena, the traditional balsamic vinegar of Modena, is something that any fan of Italian cuisine and culture should taste at least once; it is food history in a bottle, considered special because it truly is. It isn't particularly hard to find if you know where to look, but be prepared for the price. A bottle of *vecchio* vinegar can cost upwards of $75, and *stravecchio* vinegars can climb past $200. If you do treat yourself to a bottle of the real deal, do not burden yourself with even a moment of guilt—it is worth every precious drop.

CHOCOLATE AND DATE PUDDING CAKES

I call these pudding cakes because they are very soft and tender in the middle, begging to be dug into with a spoon. True to my love of chocolate and fruit, I include moist Medjool dates in this recipe; they contribute a deep caramel flavor that holds hands with the chocolate like a smitten teenager. Medjool dates are everywhere these days, from health-food stores to upscale markets and major supermarket chains, and are usually available from late fall through spring. You may find them in the refrigerated produce section or alongside other fruits. Be sure to pick Medjool dates that are plump and soft, with a papery matte skin. Dried dates are quite different, shriveled and hard, and may be coated with natural sugars that have crystallized; I find them to be too sweet and lacking in flavor, so I avoid them.

I think the best way to bake these budini *is in custard cups or ramekins, and I serve them right in the cup. I especially like to enjoy one with a tall glass of milk. You can serve them either inside the ramekins or popped out of the ramekins or a muffin pan and inverted onto a plate. They can be made a day in advance; simply pop them in a hot oven or the microwave to warm them gently before serving with a scoop of your favorite* gelato *or a generous blob of freshly whipped cream.*

MAKES 6 TO 8 SERVINGS

1 cup walnut pieces

8 large Medjool dates (6 ounces)

½ cup whole milk

4 ounces bittersweet or semisweet chocolate, chopped

4 tablespoons (½ stick/2 ounces) unsalted butter

¾ cup unbleached all-purpose flour

2 tablespoons unsweetened Dutch-processed cocoa powder

¼ teaspoon baking powder

¼ teaspoon baking soda

½ teaspoon kosher salt

2 large eggs

¼ cup granulated sugar

¼ cup packed dark brown sugar

1 teaspoon pure vanilla extract

¾ cup heavy cream

Preheat the oven to 325°F and position a rack in the center. Lightly grease eight 6-ounce ramekins or custard cups or a 6-cup muffin tin.

Place the walnuts in a single layer on a baking sheet and toast them until they are golden brown and aromatic, 12 to 14 minutes. Set the walnuts aside to cool, then finely chop them in a food processor. Remove and set aside.

Cut the dates in half lengthwise and remove and discard the pits. Roughly chop the dates and place them in the food processor. In a small saucepan, heat the milk over medium-high heat to scald it, then add it to the dates and process to make a puree; it will be a bit lumpy. Place the chocolate and butter in a heatproof bowl placed over a saucepan of gently simmering water and melt, whisking to combine them.

In a medium bowl, whisk together the all-purpose flour, cocoa powder, baking powder, baking soda, and salt and set aside.

In an electric mixer fitted with the paddle attachment, beat the eggs and sugars together on medium speed until they are thick and light-colored, about 4 minutes. Beat in the vanilla extract, followed by the chocolate and butter mixture. Scrape down the sides of the bowl and beat in the dry ingredients on low speed. Beat in the date puree, followed by the heavy cream and then the walnuts.

Divide the batter among the ramekins or cups and place them on a baking sheet, evenly spaced about an inch apart. Bake the pudding cakes for 20 to 25 minutes, rotating the baking sheet halfway through the baking time to ensure they bake evenly. The cakes should be puffed and cracked on top, but the centers will sink as they cool, remaining soft and slightly wet.

Remove the pudding cakes from the oven and cool on a rack for about 15 minutes before serving them warm. You may also refrigerate them for up to 24 hours and reheat them before serving.

LIME BAVARIANS
bavarese di calce

Bavarese *is the Italian version of Bavarian cream; it is basically custard, lightened with both whipped cream and egg whites and strengthened with a bit of gelatin. The texture is airy and delicate, melting in your mouth with an intense, limey zing—perfect after a heavy meal. Individualizing the custards makes them easy to serve and such fun to eat; I love to present them in pretty china espresso or tea cups. They are fabulous with Coconut Shortbread (page 74).* MAKES 6 TO 8 SERVINGS

4 limes

3 sheets gelatin (see page 127)

2 large eggs

1 tablespoon confectioners' sugar

¾ cup whole milk

1½ cups heavy cream

¼ cup plus 2 teaspoons granulated sugar

¼ teaspoon pure vanilla extract

Pinch of kosher salt

Toasted unsweetened coconut, for garnish
  (optional)

Grate the zest from 1 of the limes and squeeze the juice from all 4 into a small bowl; set aside. Place the gelatin sheets in a bowl of cold water to soften them.

Separate the eggs, placing the yolks in a medium bowl and reserving 1 of the whites in another medium bowl. Whisk the yolks with the confectioners' sugar until thoroughly blended.

Place the milk, ½ cup heavy cream, the ¼ cup granulated sugar, and the grated zest into a small saucepan over medium heat and bring to a boil. Remove the pan from the heat and whisk a splash of the mixture into the egg yolks. Gradually whisk in the remaining hot liquid, then return the custard to the pan and whisk for a minute or two.

Remove the gelatin from the cold water, pat away the excess water with a soft cloth, and add the gelatin to the saucepan, whisking it in thoroughly. Strain the custard through a chinois or fine-meshed sieve to remove any lumps of egg or bits of gelatin. Whisk in the vanilla extract, then transfer the custard to a clean bowl to cool. Set the bowl in a larger bowl half filled with ice water. Whisk the custard every few minutes as it cools in the ice bath; when it has cooled to room temperature, about 5 minutes, remove the bowl from the ice bath. (Be careful not to let the custard remain in the ice bath too long, or the gelatin will begin to set.)

In an electric mixer fitted with the whisk attachment, beat the remaining 1 cup heavy cream until stiff peaks form. Remove from the mixer and replace with the bowl con-

SHEET GELATIN VERSUS POWDERED GELATIN

Sheet or leaf gelatin is the standard in Europe and the preferred choice of professional pastry chefs. It is now becoming available to home cooks, which is good news, since it is much easier to use than powdered gelatin. Four sheets are equal in gelling power to one ¼-ounce package of powdered gelatin. Both kinds need to be softened before they are added to a recipe, and heat is used to dissolve the gelatin into the other ingredients; the recipe is eventually chilled to cause the gelling action.

Pastry chefs favor sheet gelatin because it is incredibly easy to use. Simply place the dried sheets of gelatin in a bowl of cold tap water (make sure that it is cold or the gelatin will start to dissolve into the water). After 2 or 3 minutes, the sheets of gelatin will become limp, with the consistency of very soft noodles. Remove them from the water, allowing the excess water to drip off, then place them on a paper or linen towel and gently pat them once

or twice. You can then whisk the sheets into the hot liquid of your recipe.

Powdered gelatin is a bit trickier. If there is water in the recipe, place half of it in a small bowl and sprinkle on the gelatin to soften. Heat the remaining water to scald it, then whisk it in to dissolve the gelatin. Another option is to combine the gelatin in a small saucepan with a portion of the sugar from the recipe. Add some of the liquid from the recipe, whisking to combine, and place over low heat to scald the mixture. It is important to check the mixture with a spoon, allowing it to fall away and examining the spoon to make sure there are no undissolved particles of gelatin.

Sheet gelatin is found in some supermarkets and most specialty markets, even in some health-food stores. There are numerous online and mail-order sources, including the Baker's Catalogue from King Arthur Flour Company (see Sources, pages 285–87).

taining the egg white. Beat the white with the salt until it is white and foamy, then whisk in the remaining 2 teaspoons granulated sugar, one at time. When all of the sugar has been added, increase the speed to high and beat the white until stiff, glossy peaks form.

Whisk the lime juice into the cooled custard. Next fold in the egg white, followed by the whipped cream. You may find it easier to use a whisk to do most of the folding, then finish with a spatula. Pour the mixture into 6 chilled espresso or 8 tea cups. Chill the bavarians in the refrigerator until firm, 3 to 4 hours.

Serve the bavarians in the cups. Garnish with toasted unsweetened coconut, if desired, or serve with *biscotti*.

HEAVENLY PANNA COTTA

This is panna cotta in the modern sense. The translation is literally "cooked cream," and the original format of the dessert was essentially reduced heavy cream cooked with sugar until thick and spoonable. Nowadays we make panna cotta with gelatin, which results in a texture that is both creamy and feather-light. This version involves the addition of fresh sheep's-milk ricotta, which is what makes it so heavenly. Its flavor just sings of Italy. If you cannot get your hands on sheep's-milk ricotta, fresh cow's-milk ricotta will do just fine. This recipe comes together effortlessly, making it the ultimate no-fuss dessert. MAKES SIX SERVINGS

1 cup fresh sheep's-milk ricotta or whole cow's-milk ricotta

1 cup whole milk

1½ cups heavy cream

½ cup plus 2 tablespoons granulated sugar

½ vanilla bean

4 sheets gelatin (see page 127)

Chestnut honey (see page 129) or *vincotto* (see page 93), for garnish

Place the ricotta and ½ cup milk in a medium bowl and whisk vigorously until the ricotta is smooth and lump-free. Place the heavy cream and sugar in a medium saucepan. Scrape the seeds from the vanilla bean with the flat side of a small knife and add them to the pan along with the bean. Place the mixture over medium heat and bring just to the boiling point, whisking occasionally. In the meantime, place the gelatin sheets in a bowl of cold water to soften them.

When the cream mixture has scalded, turn off the heat. Remove the gelatin from the water, pat away the excess water with a soft towel, and add the gelatin to the cream mixture, whisking it in thoroughly to dissolve it. Whisk in the remaining ½ cup milk.

Gradually pour the liquid into the bowl with the ricotta, whisking constantly until the mixture is completely smooth. Remove the vanilla bean and strain the mixture through a chinois or fine-meshed sieve. Divide the *panna cotta* among 6 dessert glasses and refrigerate until set, about 4 hours.

Before serving, drizzle the surface of each *panna cotta* with 1 or 2 teaspoons of warm chestnut honey or a few drops of *vincotto*.

CHESTNUT HONEY

Italian chestnut honey is a gift from the forest. The dark amber color only hints at the rich, layered flavor and strong, penetrating aroma, which mingles notes of leather and hay with the woodsy undertones of chestnut. The honey is not as syrupy-sweet as typical honeys and even has a tinge of spice, which I find addictive. It is particularly suited to baking, especially with nuts, complementing their flavor and contributing a denser, moister texture to breads and muffins. Chestnut honey makes a splendid partner for the grand mountain cheeses of Piedmont, such as the piquant Mountain Gorgonzola and the enormously flavorful Castelmagno.

Numerous chestnut honeys are imported from Italy, and they vary in intensity of color and flavor; the differences depend on the methods by which the bees are moved among the blossoming chestnut trees as well as how or even whether the honey is refined after it is harvested. A decade ago chestnut honey was a rare find on this side of the Atlantic, but today it is one of the more common imported varieties found in gourmet shops and online (see Sources, pages 285–87). I recommend the following way to enjoy it for the first time: Lightly toast a slice of Italian semolina bread, spread it liberally with sweet, unsalted butter, and drizzle the surface with just enough of the chestnut honey to make it glisten. I guarantee you will never want for a better breakfast.

ROSE AND ALMOND PANNA COTTA

The gentle perfume of a few drops of rose water brings out the floral qualities of fresh milk and is simultaneously balanced by the flavor of toasted almonds. I owe the creation of this dessert to my dear assistant Brian Levy, who longed for an understated use for the flavor and scent of roses on our menu. Rose water is a common ingredient in Middle Eastern cooking. If you cannot find a Middle Eastern market in your neighborhood, you can order it from Kalustyan's, New York City's finest purveyor of exotic spices (see Sources, pages 285–87). MAKES 6 SERVINGS

½ cup sliced blanched almonds	3 sheets gelatin (see page 127)
1¼ cups heavy cream	1 cup whole milk
⅓ cup plus 1 tablespoon granulated sugar	1 teaspoon rose water (see headnote)

Preheat the oven to 400°F. Spread the almonds in a single layer in a small, ovenproof baking dish or on a baking sheet and toast until they are golden brown and aromatic, about 10 minutes.

Remove the almonds from the oven and immediately place them in a medium saucepan. Add the heavy cream and sugar and stir to combine. Place the saucepan over medium heat and bring the mixture to a boil. Remove the pan from the heat and allow the contents to sit for 30 minutes to infuse the liquid with the flavor of the almonds. In the meantime, place the gelatin sheets in a bowl of cold water to soften them.

Return the saucepan to medium heat to bring the cream mixture to scalding, then take it off the heat again. Remove the gelatin from the water, pat away the excess water with a soft towel, and add the gelatin to the pan, whisking it in thoroughly to dissolve it.

Strain the cream and almond mixture through a chinois or a fine-mesh sieve to remove the sliced almonds. Whisk in the milk and rose water. Divide the mixture among 6 dessert glasses and refrigerate until set, about 4 hours.

ZABAIONE AL MOSCATO

You may already be familiar with this deliciously foamy dessert, which is often spelled zabaglione *in Italian cookbooks, or* sabayon *in French. Here I am using the spelling common in Piedmont, where the delightful concoction was born. However you spell it, this is most definitely a recipe that has been localized throughout Italy; the type of wine used varies from region to region, with marsala being the classic choice. The technique is easy (see page 132), so don't feel even a twinge of fear— Italian mothers and daughters have been making this for centuries!*

This is my favorite variation, using Moscato d'Asti, *the sweet, bubbly dessert wine from the winemaking Piedmontese area of Asti. I have added a bit of lemon juice to the basic formula, which balances the sweetness of the wine. Zabaione is perfect with fresh berries or peaches in the summer, and particularly wonderful with the Chocolate Salami on page 252 at any time of year.*

MAKES ALMOST 2 CUPS, OR 4 SERVINGS

4 large egg yolks

¼ cup granulated sugar

¼ cup Moscato d'Asti

1 teaspoon freshly squeezed lemon juice

Create a double boiler with a saucepan and a large heatproof stainless steel or copper mixing bowl that will sit comfortably on top of it. The saucepan should be able to hold 3 to 6 inches of water below the bottom of the bowl, so it does not touch the bowl when simmering. Add the water to the saucepan, place over medium heat, and bring the water to a gentle boil.

Place the egg yolks in the bowl and add the sugar, whisking them together well with a large, balloon-shaped whisk. Slowly whisk in the *Moscato d'Asti* and the lemon juice.

Place the bowl on top of the saucepan and immediately begin whisking at a steady, moderate pace. The *zabaione* will become frothy and thick. Continue whisking until the *zabaione* falls from the whisk and mounds on top of itself, keeping and holding its shape for a few seconds. Remove the bowl from the saucepan and whisk for a few more seconds.

Immediately divide the *zabaione* among 4 dessert dishes and serve warm, with *biscotti* or fresh fruit.

FROM A TO ZABAIONE

Zabaione is one of those recipes that truly survive the ages; the basic formula has remained virtually the same since it was created in the sixteenth century by a humble Franciscan monk. Fra Pasquale de Baylon tended to a small parish in the city of Turin in Piedmont. He decided that a frothy mixture of eggs, sugar, and wine would improve the health of his parishioners, providing both energy and nutrition. After he was canonized in the seventeenth century, his dish gained popularity in other parts of Italy. Saint Pasquale de Baylon became known in the local dialect as San Bajon, and his recipe became renowned as *l'Sanbajon*, which eventually morphed into *zabaione*. Saint Pasquale is one of several patron saints of cooks and cooking, and every year on May 17 his feast day is still celebrated at the church of his original parish of San Tomas in Turin. *Zabaione* is a favorite dessert in local restaurants.

Basic *zabaione* consists of just three ingredients: egg yolks whipped with sugar and wine over heat. Much, if not all, of the alcohol is cooked off, leaving behind the lingering flavor of the wine. Most chefs use a double boiler, but many of my Italian friends fondly remember their mothers whipping up *zabaione* directly over an open fire. It is best when served warm, and it doesn't hold very well, so to extend its life a bit, you can beat it until it is cool and then fold it into some whipped heavy cream, turning it into *crema zabaione*. I prefer to enjoy *zabaione* immediately after it is made, along with some perfectly ripe fruit or *biscotti*. It also works well as a dessert sauce, spooned over a cake or tart or, for a real treat, a slice of *panettone*.

Zabaione is not at all difficult to make; the only caveats are to control the heat and avoid overcooking it. The best vehicle is a wide, deep mixing bowl placed over a similarly wide-mouthed saucepan that can comfortably hold a few inches of simmering water. There should be enough clearance so the surface of the water does not touch the bowl; otherwise your *zabaione* will cook too quickly and you may wind up with scrambled eggs. The weight of your mixing bowl also helps to control the heat; a copper bowl is the ideal vessel, because it will distribute the heat most evenly, allowing for a velvety texture. A good solid stainless steel bowl also works quite well.

The airiness of your *zabaione* is something you can determine with your choice of whisk and whisking method. A balloon-type whisk and a vigorous stroke will result in an ethereal, frothy texture by incorporating a great deal of air into the structure, while a flat whisk will result in a richer *zabaione* that is more like a creamy sauce.

It is important to get your *zabaione* started properly. Place the egg yolks in the mixing bowl and whisk in the sugar. Continue whisking until the yolks have lightened a bit in color, then drizzle in the wine and any other liquid in the recipe. Next, place the mixing bowl over the pan of simmering water. Once you do this, plan on continuing until the *zabaione* is done—no answering the telephone or taking a quick trip out of the kitchen! Continue whisking, keeping in mind that the action is in the wrist, not the arm. When I am teaching my assistants how to whisk *zabaione*, I make them hold a book under their arm while they whisk, to help them concentrate on the move-

ment. As mentioned, whisking vigorously over a slightly higher heat will result in very foamy and airy *zabaione*. Whisking slowly over gentle heat will give you a thicker, creamier *zabaione*.

To test for doneness, remove the bowl from the saucepan for a moment and pick up the whisk; if the *zabaione* mounds on top of itself and holds its shape for a few seconds, it is done. If you see any bits of cooked egg, remove the bowl from the saucepan and keep whisking to reduce the heat and prevent the *zabaione* from further overcooking. To cool the *zabaione* completely, keep whisking it constantly; you can then fold it into an equal volume of whipped heavy cream for *crema zabaione*.

Marsala is the most popular choice for making *zabaione*, but there are as many variations on this theme as there are Italian regions. I have made *zabaione* with rum and even grappa, and one of my favorite versions is to use a delicious *vin santo* from Tuscany or Umbria. I have also added a few teaspoons of *aceto balsamico tradizionale* for a luxurious twist; it makes the most delicious *crema zabaione*.

COOL RHUBARB SOUP WITH ORANGE AND MINT FIOR DI LATTE

Fruit soups have become just a bit passé in the post–nouvelle cuisine age, but they can be a refreshing change from the usual cake-and-pie routine. In the early spring, pink rhubarb grown in hothouses in Holland appears on the scene. It is tender and delicate and will give this soup a lovely shade of pale pink. Depending on where you live, local rhubarb is available in late April and May, extending into the summer months. Here in New York, it tends to be a bit green at the ends. In that case, I use the colorful red part for the soup and save the tart green sections for use in savory dishes. The fior di latte, *or "flower of the milk," is actually a dressed-up combination of ricotta and whipped cream, flavored with orange zest, fresh mint, and crunchy crushed* amaretti. MAKES 4 SERVINGS

FOR THE RHUBARB SOUP

4 cups thinly sliced rhubarb (about 1 pound)

¾ cup granulated sugar

3 cups water

One 3–4-inch-long strip freshly peeled orange zest

1–2 teaspoons freshly squeezed lemon juice

FOR THE ORANGE AND MINT *FIOR DI LATTE*

1 cup heavy cream

¼ cup granulated sugar

¾ cup fresh whole-milk ricotta

Freshly grated zest of 1 large orange

2 tablespoons freshly squeezed orange juice

¼ cup fresh mint leaves

½ cup crushed *amaretti*, plus more for garnish

To make the rhubarb soup: Place the rhubarb, sugar, water, and orange zest in a large saucepan. Bring to a simmer and cook over medium heat, stirring occasionally, until the rhubarb is soft and translucent and the liquid is pink, about 10 minutes. Remove from the heat and allow the soup to cool. Strain the soup through a chinois or a fine-meshed sieve and discard the solids. Chill the soup thoroughly, at least 4 hours, then add the lemon juice to taste.

To make the *fior di latte*: Place the heavy cream and sugar in the bowl of an electric mixer fitted with the whisk attachment and beat on medium speed until the cream is thick and almost peaking. Add the ricotta, orange zest, and orange juice and continue beating until soft peaks form.

Using a very sharp chef's knife, mince the mint leaves finely and immediately add them to the bowl along with the *amaretti* crumbs. Beat just to incorporate all the ingredients fully and allow the mixture to form firm peaks. Chill the *fior di latte* for at least 30 minutes and up to 2 hours before serving.

To serve: Ladle about ¾ cup soup into each of 4 chilled dessert or soup bowls. Using a large spoon dipped in very hot water, form a perfectly smooth scoop of *fior di latte* and place it in the center of each bowl. Sprinkle a few *amaretti* crumbs on top.

TARTS

crostate

N ITALIAN BAKERY THAT SELLS A SMALL SELECTION OF SWEETS IN addition to breads, rolls, and pizza is sometimes called a *forno,* which literally means "oven." Among its offerings you will often find a freshly baked fruit tart or two. The simplest version of an Italian *crostata* consists of just two components: *pasta frolla,* a sweet, eggy, short dough, and a superb jam or preserves made from the bounty of native stone fruits and berries. Known as *crostata marmellata,* it is perhaps the most common dessert among all the diverse regions of Italy, the final punctuation of family meals that is enjoyed from the Alps to the toe of the boot.

When it comes to making a good *crostata,* I find that the ingredients are once again the defining factor and the stars of the show. If fruit preserves are not used, perfectly fresh and ripe fruits themselves are, sometimes complemented with a bit of pastry cream (*crema pasticceria*) or a simple custard made from fresh ricotta or farmer's cheese. Citrus fruits, nuts, and honey also provide classic fillings, which are always in ideal proportion to the amount of crust. The concept of a deep-dish pie or a mile-high mound of cream or meringue has no equivalent in Italy, where the crust is meant to be an equal partner to the filling rather than a mere vehicle.

I adore making tarts and have a collection of fluted tart pans made of heavy black steel with removable bottoms so I can indulge myself in this activity as often as possible. A walk through the morning market in the summer or fall always inspires me to run home and make a quick batch of tart dough, and I fall into a familiar quiet and relaxed state while I am making *pasta frolla.* The nature of this classic Italian pastry dough makes it quite easy to handle; you can chill it for rolling thinly or press it into the pan with your floured fingers for a more rustic style. Leftover slices of *crostata* make a great breakfast or a midafternoon snack to stem the tide of hunger before a late, lingering Italian dinner.

PASTRY CRUST 101

Pastry dough can be daunting—this I admit. If you have ever wound up with a wet, sticky mass that has affixed itself to your countertop or your rolling pin, I understand your trepidation completely. It takes a bit of practice, kind of like riding a bike, or like dog-paddling without your floaties for the first time. You may wind up with a few less-than-perfect attempts at first, but once you master the basic techniques of making tart dough, you'll be off and running. Here are my basic rules for achieving the perfect crust.

Think cold. The butter should be cold, straight out of the refrigerator. Measure it out first, then cut it into ¼-inch cubes, then put it straight back into the refrigerator. Any wet ingredients, such as eggs and cream, should be cold as well, and tap water should always be iced.

Use a food processor or your hands. If you don't have a food processor, making perfect tart dough is a good reason to get one. Flaky tart or pie dough comes from the layering of tiny pieces of butter with the flour; the butter melts and its moisture evaporates, creating a little pocket of air—that's the flakiness. To achieve this, you need to integrate the butter into the flour so that it resembles coarse bread crumbs. A food processor does this effortlessly and evenly. Your hands can do an equally fine job. It takes longer, but by using your fingertips to rub the butter into the flour, you can achieve a uniform consistency that you can actually feel. Using your fingers also has the advantage of making it nearly impossible to

break the butter down so much that it makes the flour wet. It is important to remember that if you work with your hands, your kitchen needs to be cool and you need to work quickly so the butter does not get too soft.

Hold back on the liquid sometimes. On a humid day your flour will already contain moisture, so you may not need all the wet ingredients for the dough to come together. It is hard to judge this right off the bat, but in time you will become more attuned to the atmosphere where you do your baking. If your dough becomes too wet, you will invariably need to add more flour to it, and that will make your crust tough rather than tender and flaky. On a similar note, don't be alarmed if you need to add a few more drops of moisture, whether in the form of cream, milk, or water. In very dry climates, this is often necessary.

Work it, but not too much. If you are using a food processor, pulse the wet ingredients into the butter and flour mixture with a few short, quick pulses. The dough may appear dry, but before adding any more liquid, pick up some of the dough and try to press it into a ball in the palm of your hand. If it comes together easily, you may need only a few more dribbles of wet ingredients worked in by hand to finish off the dough and form it into a disk. If you are using your hands, toss in the wet ingredients with a fork first, then use your fingers to work them into the dry spots.

Press it or chill it. Once you reach an even

(continued on next page)

consistency, you can press the dough directly into a tart pan with your fingers, which will give you a thick, more rustic consistency that is a good complement to fresh fruit. Chill the dough in the tart pan for about an hour. If you want to roll the dough thin for a more refined texture and presentation, form it into a flat disk, not a square; when you roll the dough out, it is much easier to achieve a circle if you begin with a circle! Wrap the dough in plastic and chill it for at least 1 hour; it should be firm, but not hard, for rolling. Whether you have pressed it into the pan or plan to roll it later, give the dough a rest; it needs time in order to even itself out in terms of consistency. The liquid you just added to the flour will distribute throughout the dough, and any random dry spots will glean moisture from the wetter spots. Do not skip this step; a bit of "alone time" is important for the dough to be optimal for baking.

Let's roll. Flour your work surface, flour your rolling pin, dust the surface of the dough, and go for it. How much flour is enough? Just enough so that the dough moves easily; it should not stick to the counter or to the rolling pin. No more, no less. Apply even pressure and try to roll in one direction only, moving the dough in a circular pattern. Slide your hands under the dough and feel around a bit—it's the only way to really judge the thickness. Once you are happy with the size and thickness of your dough circle, dust the surface with a little flour and quickly roll it up around the pin. Position the pin at the edge of the tart pan and unroll the dough like a carpet onto the pan. Press the dough into the bottom and sides of the pan, then roll the pin across the top of the pan to trim it flush. Chill the lined tart pan until the dough is completely firm.

Blindly forge ahead. Some recipes require you to prebake the crust, otherwise known as "blind baking." This is most necessary in the case of jam tarts and tarts with fillings that cook more quickly than the crust. Blind baking is not difficult; it is simply another step on the way to perfection. After lining and trimming the tart shell, chill it in the refrigerator for 15 minutes to firm it up. Tear off a large sheet of aluminum foil and fit it inside the dough-lined tart pan; it should be large enough to fold over and protect the edges of the pan. Parchment paper will also work, but it may cause the dough to brown more; plus, it won't fold over the edge of the crust and stay in place as aluminum foil does.

The next step is to line the bottom of the pan with something to weigh down the crust, preventing it from puffing up and bubbling as it cooks. It is easiest to use some loose dried beans or lentils. I use them and then store them in a container in my cupboard exclusively for use as dough weights. You can also purchase pie weights, which are made of metal. As a bonus, they help conduct heat to cook the dough.

Recipes should state how long to blind-bake your tart shell. Sometimes you will only partially bake the shell, which will continue to cook as the filling bakes. In other cases you will bake the shell completely, possibly even removing the foil or paper and weights to let the crust turn golden brown. This is most common in the case of tarts that are filled with cooked pastry cream, or *crema pasticceria*, and topped with fruit.

Pat yourself on the back. And pat the scraps of leftover dough into another disk. You can save it in the freezer for up to 2 months, wrapped tightly in plastic wrap and sealed in a freezer bag. Now make yourself a cup of coffee and relax before you make your filling. You just made a great pastry crust!

SWEET TART CRUST
pasta frolla

Pasta frolla *is the short, moist, sweet pastry dough used for most tarts, or crostate, in Italian homes as well as pastry shops. I think you will love this version, which I have worked hard to develop. I am always pleased when a customer comments on the tastiness of my tart dough—it is a compliment I take very highly.*

Pasta frolla *is a simple dough to make and easy to roll, flaky yet substantial and flavorful. This recipe makes slightly more dough than you need for a 10-inch tart. After rolling out and trimming your tart shell, you can gather the scraps together and freeze them for up to 2 months; combining the scraps from two batches will give you enough dough for another tart shell.* MAKES ONE 10-INCH TART SHELL

2⅓ cups unbleached all-purpose flour

⅓ cup granulated sugar

½ teaspoon kosher salt

½ teaspoon baking powder

Freshly grated zest of 1 lemon or 1 small
 orange

¾ cup (1½ sticks/6 ounces) unsalted butter,
 cold, cut into ¼-inch cubes

1 large egg

1 large egg yolk

½ teaspoon pure vanilla extract

¼ cup heavy cream

A few drops ice water, if necessary

Place the flour, sugar, salt, baking powder, and citrus zest in the bowl of a food processor and pulse several times to combine the dry ingredients. Add all of the cold, cubed butter to the bowl and pulse to process the mixture until it is sandy and there are no visible lumps of butter.

In a small bowl, whisk together the egg, egg yolk, vanilla extract, and heavy cream. Add the wet ingredients to the food processor and pulse 3 or 4 times, or until the dough comes together. If necessary, add some ice water, a few drops at a time, to make the dough come together.

Remove the dough from the food processor and work it with your hands to even out any dry and wet spots. Form the dough into a ball, flatten into a disk, wrap in plastic, and chill until firm, 1 to 2 hours, before rolling it out. You can also freeze the dough, well wrapped, for up to 2 months.

SOUR CHERRY CUSTARD TART, PAGE 164

BLUEBERRY AND COCONUT TART,
PAGE 150

WHITE PEACH AND PROSECCO
GELATINA, PAGE 222

CHOCOLATE AND TANGERINE SEMIFREDDO,
PAGE 192

CAPPUCCINO WITH FOAM ART AND
FLORENTINE DOUGHNUTS, PAGE 208

A PLATE OF SWEET FRIED DOUGH WITH *VIN SANTO*,
PAGE 204

CHOCOLATE AND NUT TART CRUST
pasta di cioccolato e mandorle

A chocolate crust can be a perfect accent for cheese tarts as well as some fruit tarts, providing a subtle touch of chocolate in an unexpected way. This crust is ideal (and it makes an excellent cookie, too—just roll and cut into your favorite shapes). The technique is different from that for the Sweet Tart Crust on page 142; the butter is creamed together with the sugar, as if you were making a cookie dough. Once the dough is chilled, however, it is easy to roll out. Be sure to use a well-floured board and rolling pin. MAKES ONE 10-INCH TART SHELL

1 cup unbleached all-purpose flour	½ teaspoon kosher salt
¼ cup plus 3 tablespoons Dutch-processed cocoa powder	½ cup (1 stick/4 ounces) unsalted butter, softened
½ cup sliced almonds, toasted and finely ground	½ cup granulated sugar
	1 large egg
½ teaspoon baking powder	2 teaspoons pure vanilla extract

In a medium bowl, whisk together the flour, cocoa powder, ground toasted almonds, baking powder, and salt and set aside.

In an electric mixer fitted with the paddle attachment, cream together the butter and sugar on medium speed until light and fluffy, about 1 minute. Beat in the egg and vanilla extract and scrape down the sides of the bowl. Beat in the dry ingredients just enough to form a soft dough.

Scrape the dough onto a large sheet of plastic wrap, press it into a disk, and wrap it tightly. Chill the dough until it is firm enough to roll, about 2 hours or overnight.

POLENTA TART CRUST
pasta di polenta

This dough is perfect for fruit crostate; *I often use it as an alternative to* pasta frolla. *It is especially good with berries, cherries, and plums, as the chewy texture and yellow hue provide a colorful contrast to soft, succulent fruits.*

MAKES ONE 10-INCH TART SHELL

1¼ cups unbleached all-purpose flour

½ cup instant or fine polenta

¾ cup sugar

1 teaspoon kosher salt

Freshly grated zest of 1 lemon

½ cup (1 stick/4 ounces) unsalted butter, cold, cut into ¼-inch cubes

1 large egg

2 tablespoons extra-virgin olive oil

1 teaspoon pure vanilla extract

Place the flour, polenta, sugar, salt, and lemon zest in the bowl of a food processor and pulse to combine them. Add the cold, cubed butter to the bowl and pulse until the mixture resembles coarse sand and no large lumps of butter are visible.

In a small bowl, whisk together the egg, olive oil, and vanilla extract. Add the wet ingredients to the food processor and pulse just until a ball of dough forms.

Form the dough into a disk and wrap tightly in plastic. Chill the dough until it is firm enough to roll, at least 1 to 2 hours.

HONEY AND PINE NUT TART
crostata di miele e pignoli

This tart is one of my most-requested desserts at Babbo. The filling is sweet and slightly salty, rich with butter and cream, aromatic with honey and pine nuts. I recommend a mild honey, such as acacia, orange blossom, eucalyptus, or millifiore ("a thousand flowers"); buckwheat and sage are also fine choices. The recipe may make just slightly more liquid custard than you need to fill the 10-inch tart shell; simply discard the extra custard rather than trying to overfill the shell.

This tart begs for a scoop of vanilla gelato; if you really want to gild the lily, drizzle it with a spoonful of Aceto Balsamico Tradizionale di Modena (see page 122).

MAKES ONE 10-INCH TART, 8 SERVINGS

Sweet Tart Crust (page 142)
⅔ cup honey
½ cup granulated sugar
1 teaspoon kosher salt
1 cup (2 sticks/8 ounces) unsalted butter
½ cup heavy cream
1 large egg
1 large egg yolk
1¼ cups pine nuts

On a floured board, roll the tart dough into an 11-inch circle ⅛-inch thick. Transfer the dough to a 10-inch tart pan with fluted sides and a removable bottom by rolling the dough around the pin like a carpet and then unrolling it onto the pan. Press the dough into the bottom and sides of the pan, then trim it so it is flush with the top of the pan. Chill the tart shell while you make the filling.

Preheat the oven to 325°F and position a rack in the center.

To make the custard: Place the honey, sugar, and salt in a medium saucepan and stir to combine them. Add the butter, place the saucepan over medium-high heat, and bring the mixture to a boil, stirring often. Remove the saucepan from the heat and transfer the mixture to a large mixing bowl; allow it to cool for 20 minutes. Whisk in the heavy cream, followed by the egg and egg yolk.

Distribute the pine nuts evenly over the bottom of the tart shell and pour the custard into the shell until it reaches the top of the crust. Place the tart on a baking sheet to catch any drips and bake for 30 to 55 minutes, or until both the crust and the filling have turned light golden brown and the custard is set but still jiggly. Allow the tart to cool completely on a rack before carefully removing the sides of the pan.

Serve the tart while still slightly warm, or cool it and serve at room temperature. Wrapped in plastic, leftovers will keep in the refrigerator for a few days.

THREE-CHEESE TART WITH CHOCOLATE AND ORANGE

crostata di tre formaggi con cioccolato e arancia

This tart pairs a chocolatey, nutty crust with a rich, creamy-sweet cheese filling and a shimmery glaze of orange marmalade. The combination of flavors, textures, and colors is unique, and the presentation is understated and elegant. The ingredients are easily acquired and not restricted by the seasons, and the tart works perfectly for any occasion. It's the dessert equivalent of your favorite little black dress.

MAKES ONE 10-INCH TART, 8 SERVINGS

FOR THE TART

Chocolate and Nut Tart Crust (page 143)

3 ounces cream cheese

½ cup mascarpone

1 cup fresh whole-milk ricotta

⅓ cup granulated sugar

1 large egg

1 teaspoon pure vanilla extract

¼ cup heavy cream

FOR THE ORANGE MARMALADE GLAZE

¼ cup orange marmalade

¼ cup orange juice

2 teaspoons freshly squeezed lemon juice

2 tablespoons granulated sugar

To make the tart: On a floured board, roll the tart dough into an 11-inch circle ⅛-inch thick. Transfer the dough to a 10-inch tart pan with fluted sides and a removable bottom by rolling the dough around the pin like a carpet and then unrolling it onto the pan. Press the dough into the bottom and sides of the pan, then trim it so it is flush with the top of the pan. Chill the tart shell while you make the filling.

Preheat the oven to 325°F and position a rack in the center.

In an electric mixer fitted with the paddle attachment, beat together the cream cheese, mascarpone, ricotta, and sugar on medium speed until smooth and creamy, about 2 minutes. Beat in the egg, vanilla, and heavy cream, scraping down the sides of the bowl after each addition.

Remove the prepared shell from the refrigerator and pour the filling into it, smoothing the top with a spatula. Bake the tart for 25 to 30 minutes, or until the filling is firm in the center. Allow the tart to cool completely on a rack before carefully removing the sides of the tart pan.

While the tart is cooling, prepare the glaze: Place the marmalade, orange juice, lemon juice, and sugar in a saucepan and cook over medium heat, stirring occasionally, until

CROSTATA MARMELLATA

A popular *crostata* found in most Italian pastry shops as well as homes is the jam tart, or *crostata marmellata*. Nothing could be easier, since all you need to make is the dough for the pastry crust. The jam is the star of the show, so I suggest you get your hands on the best jam or preserves possible. I like brands imported from Italy, France, Germany, and Switzerland, because the quality of the fruit is impeccable. My favorite flavor is peach, but strawberry, cherry, plum, apricot, and raspberry preserves make equally fantastic tarts.

Begin with a recipe of *pasta frolla* (page 142). Roll out the pastry dough as you would for any other tart and line a 9- or 10-inch fluted tart pan. Save the scraps for the lattice top; wrap and refrigerate them. Conventional pie pans are too deep for this kind of tart, since filling the shell with jam would result in a disproportionate amount of jam in relation to the shell. Blind-bake the shell for about 10 minutes in a preheated 350°F oven, remove it, and allow it to cool. Fill the shell with enough jam to come just below the top of the pastry; a 13-ounce jar should be plenty, but for a larger tart, you may want to make sure you have two jars on hand.

Roll out the dough scraps to a 10-inch circle and cut into ¾-inch strips. Twist the strips at both ends to make twists and lay them in a lattice pattern over the jam. Using a pastry brush, glaze the pastry dough with a little beaten egg and bake the tart until the pastry is golden, 20 to 25 minutes.

Jam tarts are perfect for unexpected company and in the dead of winter, when summer's fruit is unavailable. If you have small tart pans, individual jam tartlets are wonderful treats for afternoon tea. They will keep for a few days in the refrigerator if well wrapped in plastic.

the mixture boils. Remove the pan from the heat and allow the glaze to cool to room temperature. Brush the top and sides of the tart generously with the glaze. Chill the tart for 2 hours before serving; it may be served cold or brought to room temperature before serving. Store any leftovers in the refrigerator, wrapped in plastic; they will keep for a few days.

NONNA'S TART
torta della nonna

Even if you don't speak Italian, you can probably figure out that this is Grand-mother's tart, and there are just as many variations as there are grandmas. This version, made with pastry cream, is commonly found in Tuscany, but plenty of recipes come from other regions of Italy. Some grandmas seem to like a top crust; I prefer a scattering of pine nuts. This recipe is my best attempt to duplicate the Torta della Nonna served at Café Rivoire in the beautiful Piazza della Signoria in Florence, overlooking the magnificent tower of the Palazzo Vecchio. On a visit to Florence, I shared a slice with my mother—perfectly fitting for a dessert that symbolizes the bond between generations of mothers and children.

MAKES ONE 9-INCH TART, 8 TO 10 SERVINGS

Sweet Tart Crust, made with lemon zest
   (page 142)
2 cups whole milk
Two 3-inch-long strips freshly peeled
   lemon zest
½ vanilla bean
5 tablespoons granulated sugar

4 large egg yolks
Pinch of kosher salt
¼ cup unbleached all-purpose flour
1 tablespoon unsalted butter, softened
½ cup pine nuts, toasted and cooled
Bittersweet chocolate, for grating

Roll the tart dough on a floured surface to a thickness of ⅛ inch. Place a 9-inch spring-form pan on top of the dough. Using a small knife, trace a circle around the outside of the pan, leaving an extra ¾ inch all around. Place the circle of dough inside the spring-form pan and press it onto the bottom and sides. (Save the scraps for another use, if desired.) The dough should come up about ¾ inch around the sides. Place the pan in the refrigerator to chill for 20 minutes.

Preheat the oven to 350°F and position a rack in the center.

While the tart shell is chilling, prepare the filling. Place the milk and lemon zest in a medium saucepan. Scrape the seeds from the ½ vanilla bean with the flat side of a small knife and add the seeds and the bean to the pan. Stir in 3 tablespoons granulated sugar and place the saucepan over medium heat.

Meanwhile, place the egg yolks in a medium bowl and whisk them with the remaining 2 tablespoons sugar and the salt. When the milk mixture begins to boil, remove it from the heat. Quickly whisk the flour into the yolks, then whisk in a few splashes of the milk mixture. Gradually add more milk mixture, whisking constantly to remove any lumps.

Return the mixture to the saucepan and cook over low heat, whisking constantly, until it has thickened enough to mound when it falls from the whisk. Remove the saucepan from the heat and strain it through a chinois or fine-meshed sieve to remove the zest, vanilla bean, and any lumps of cooked egg. Transfer the pastry cream to a large, shallow bowl and whisk in the butter, then press a piece of plastic wrap to the surface to prevent a skin from forming.

After the tart shell has chilled for 20 minutes, tear a large sheet of aluminum foil or parchment paper and press it against the entire surface of the shell. Fill the shell with metal weights or enough dried beans or lentils to cover the surface of the foil or paper. Blind-bake the tart shell for 15 minutes. Carefully remove the foil or paper and the weights and return the shell to the oven, baking it for an additional 5 to 7 minutes, or until it is light golden brown.

Remove the tart shell from the oven and allow it to cool for 10 minutes. Pour the pastry cream into the still-warm shell, smoothing the top with a spatula. Allow the pastry cream and the shell to cool completely so the cream sets into the shell, then transfer the tart to the refrigerator to chill.

To serve, carefully remove the sides of the springform pan and transfer the tart to an attractive serving plate. Scatter the toasted pine nuts across the top and garnish with finely grated bittersweet chocolate. Serve cold or at room temperature. Wrapped in plastic, leftovers will keep in the refrigerator for a few days.

BLUEBERRY AND COCONUT TART
crostata di mirtillo e cocco

Coconut is one of my very favorite ingredients to bake with, and I am always in search of a way to depart from the tired pairing of pineapple with it, otherwise known as the piña colada treatment. Maybe it was the color palette here that inspired me—picturing plump, purple-blue berries against a backdrop of snowy coconut. This tart remains one of my favorites; the crumbly, buttery topping is an exciting contrast against the soft, bursting berries. Be sure to use only unsweetened dried coconut, which can be found in any health-food store or upscale market.

MAKES ONE 10-INCH TART, APPROXIMATELY 10 SERVINGS

Sweet Tart Crust (page 142)

FOR THE TOPPING

¼ cup (½ stick/2 ounces) unsalted butter

¾ cup unbleached all-purpose flour

½ cup granulated sugar

¼ teaspoon kosher salt

½ cup unsweetened shredded dried coconut

1 teaspoon pure vanilla extract

FOR THE FILLING

¼ cup (½ stick/2 ounces) unsalted butter, softened

½ cup confectioners' sugar

2 large egg yolks

Freshly grated zest of 1 lemon

Pinch of kosher salt

¾ cup unsweetened shredded dried coconut

FOR THE ASSEMBLY

About 3 cups fresh blueberries

2 tablespoons freshly squeezed lemon juice

¼ cup granulated sugar

2 teaspoons cornstarch

Confectioners' sugar, for dusting (optional)

To prepare the crust: On a floured board, roll the tart dough into an 11-inch circle ⅛-inch thick. Transfer the dough to a 10-inch tart pan with fluted sides and a removable bottom by rolling the dough around the pin like a carpet and then unrolling it onto the pan. Press the dough into the bottom and sides of the pan, then trim it so it is flush with the top of the pan. Chill the tart shell while you make the topping and filling.

To make the topping: Melt the butter in a small saucepan over low heat and let it cool. Place the flour, sugar, salt, and coconut in a large bowl and whisk together to combine well. Add the vanilla extract to the melted butter, then add the butter mixture to the dry ingredients, stirring with a fork to combine well. Spread the topping in an even layer on a baking sheet lined with parchment or wax paper and chill for 30 minutes, or until firm.

Remove the topping from the refrigerator and place it in the bowl of a food processor. Pulse the mixture several times to make tiny crumbs. Set aside.

To make the filling: Place the butter and confectioners' sugar in the bowl of an electric mixer and, using the paddle attachment on medium speed, beat together until smooth and creamy, about 2 minutes. Beat in the egg yolks, one at a time, scraping down the sides. Beat in the lemon zest and salt, followed by the coconut.

Preheat the oven to 350°F and position a rack in the center.

To assemble the tart: Place the blueberries in a large bowl. Add the lemon juice, sugar, and cornstarch and stir together to combine, thoroughly coating the berries.

Remove the tart shell from the refrigerator and, using a spatula or the back of a spoon, evenly spread the filling in the shell. Top with the blueberries, drizzling any liquid from the bottom of the bowl on top. Evenly cover the surface with the topping crumbs. Bake until the topping is lightly golden and the blueberries are bubbling, 45 to 50 minutes.

Serve the tart while still slightly warm, or cool and serve it at room temperature. If desired, garnish with a dusting of confectioners' sugar. Wrapped in plastic, the tart will keep in the refrigerator for a few days.

HOW WELL DO YOU KNOW YOUR OVEN?

I moved in and out of a number of apartments during my postcollegiate life and consequently formed relationships with a number of ovens. Since I bake for a living, it is important for me to get to know this appliance on a somewhat intimate level. The best way to discover the quirks of your oven is to get an oven thermometer, and with the aid of a timer or watch and some good oven mitts, you can really become familiar with your oven.

To begin with, try to determine how long your oven takes to preheat, an important piece of knowledge to have, since your baking times entirely depend on having your oven at the required temperature before you slide anything into it. Most baking is best accomplished in the center of the oven, so position your racks properly, then set the thermometer dead center. Set your oven to 350°F and then set a count-up timer or take a look at your watch. When the thermometer reaches 350°F, you have arrived at your required preheating time. If it never reaches 350°F or if the temperature soars past that number, then you know

that the calibration of the oven is slightly off. You can either dial it up or down a few notches or have it repaired, but at least you know how much to adjust your temperature dial before starting to bake.

Once I know the oven is stabilized at a particular temperature, I begin moving the thermometer around, from front to back as well as up and down between the racks. All ovens have hot spots and cold spots, and it is important to know where they are so you can position your treasures properly. I once had an oven that singed cookies if they were on the bottom rack but baked them perfectly on the top rack. It wasn't an ideal situation, but at least I learned how to avoid winding up with a sheet of cookies fit for the trash can.

It is also important to remember that your oven loses heat when you open and close the door and place more foods in it. Try to keep the thermometer off to the side as you bake, so you can keep an eye on the rate at which the temperature "catches up" and adjust your baking times accordingly.

CRANBERRY TART

Let's be honest here: cranberries haven't made it to Italy, and this tart is a slice of Americana more than anything else. I first put this on my menu at Babbo with some trepidation; after all, why would someone want to end a beautiful Italian meal with a decidedly non-Italian dessert? Well, our customers proved my fears to be needless, and this tart goes on the books as one of my all-time best sellers. The combination of the sweet polenta crust and the tart cranberries is absolutely divine. I'll state the obvious here: this tart is perfect for the holidays. **MAKES ONE 10-INCH TART, 8 TO 10 SERVINGS**

Polenta Tart Crust (page 144)

3 cups fresh cranberries

1 cup granulated sugar

½ cup light corn syrup

½ cup heavy cream

3 large egg yolks

1 teaspoon pure vanilla extract

2 tablespoons unbleached all-purpose flour

¼ teaspoon kosher salt

Preheat the oven to 350°F and position a rack in the center.

On a floured board, roll the tart dough into an 11-inch circle ⅛-inch thick. Transfer the dough to a 10-inch tart pan with fluted sides and a removable bottom by rolling the dough around the pin like a carpet and then unrolling it onto the pan. Press the dough into the bottom and sides of the pan, then trim it so it is flush with the top of the pan. Chill the tart shell while you make the filling.

Sort through the fresh cranberries to make sure there are no stems or bruised or soft berries. In a medium saucepan, stir together the sugar and corn syrup. Place over medium heat and bring to a boil, stirring constantly. Add the cranberries and continue to cook over medium heat until the berries just begin to soften and pop, about 2 minutes. Pour the mixture into a shallow bowl to cool for about 20 minutes, stirring occasionally to dissipate the heat.

In another bowl, whisk together the cream, egg yolks, vanilla extract, flour, and salt. Pour this mixture over the cranberries and stir gently.

Pour the filling into the prepared tart shell. Place the tart on a large baking sheet to catch any drips and bake for 40 to 45 minutes, or until the crust has turned golden brown and the filling is set; it may jiggle slightly but should not be liquid. Allow the tart to cool completely on a rack before carefully removing the sides of the tart pan.

Serve at room temperature or slightly reheated. Wrapped in plastic, the tart will keep in the refrigerator for a few days.

CHOCOLATE AND POLENTA TART
crostata di cioccolato e polenta

The texture of this tart, which combines smooth, silky chocolate with the chewy bite of polenta, is irresistible. Be sure to use the finest bittersweet chocolate you can find, as it truly makes a difference in the taste of the tart. Serve it warm, with a scoop of vanilla gelato or some lightly sweetened whipped cream.

MAKES ONE 10-INCH TART, 8 TO 10 SERVINGS

Polenta Tart Crust (page 144)

4 ounces bittersweet or semisweet chocolate

½ cup (1 stick/4 ounces) unsalted butter, softened

2 large eggs

½ cup granulated sugar

Pinch of kosher salt

1 teaspoon pure vanilla extract

3 tablespoons instant or fine polenta

1 tablespoon unbleached all-purpose flour

Confectioners' sugar, for dusting

Preheat the oven to 350°F and position a rack in the center.

On a floured board, roll the tart dough into an 11-inch circle ⅛-inch thick. Transfer the dough to a 10-inch tart pan with fluted sides and a removable bottom by rolling the dough around the pin like a carpet and then unrolling it onto the pan. Press the dough into the bottom and sides of the pan, then trim it so it is flush with the top of the pan. Chill the tart shell while you make the filling.

Place the chocolate and butter in a large, heatproof bowl and set the bowl over a pan of simmering water, whisking occasionally to combine the chocolate and butter while they melt. Remove the bowl from the pan of water and set it aside.

Place the eggs, sugar, and salt in the bowl of an electric mixer fitted with the whisk attachment and beat together on high speed until they are thick and tripled in volume, about 3 minutes. Beat in the vanilla extract.

Add the egg mixture to the bowl with the melted chocolate mixture and fold the two mixtures together with a rubber spatula until they are mostly combined. Sift the polenta and flour over the batter and continue folding until no streaks appear and the dry ingredients have been completely incorporated.

Pour the filling into the prepared shell and place it on a baking sheet to catch any drips. Bake the tart for 25 minutes, or until the filling is puffed and cracking and the crust is lightly golden brown. Allow the tart to cool on a rack for 20 minutes before carefully removing the sides of the tart pan.

Dust the top with confectioners' sugar and serve the tart warm. Wrapped in plastic, it will keep in the refrigerator for a few days.

A BIT ABOUT CHOCOLATE

What can I possibly say about chocolate that has not been said before? For true chocophiles—and you know who you are—a bite of chocolate results in a sensory zenith: chocolate simultaneously calms, excites, soothes, comforts, invigorates, and, as hardcore chocolate addicts will attest, transcends. The creamy feel of melting chocolate on the tongue makes not only our hearts swoon, but our minds as well; chemically speaking, eating chocolate triggers the release of seratonin in the brain, a powerful signal to your body that all is well. Chocolate has legendary qualities as an aphrodisiac, a theory tested every Valentine's Day by countless suitors yearning to impress their sweethearts with a gift of assorted chocolates tucked inside a big heart-shaped box.

But what exactly is this magical substance that holds so many of us firmly within its grasp?

Solid chocolate as we know it today is produced in a multistep process that begins with the harvesting of cocoa beans, the fruit of the cacao tree. Cacao trees are indigenous to Central America and Mexico, and today they are cultivated in their native lands as well as along the Ivory Coast of Africa. The original way to enjoy chocolate was as a drink; there is evidence that the ancient Mayans of Central America were drinking chocolate 2,600 years ago. The Aztecs, who flourished in Mexico during the fourteenth through the sixteenth centuries, associated cacao with their goddess of fertility and drank chocolate that they flavored with vanilla, chile pepper, and achiote.

Christopher Columbus and Hernán Cortés both took cacao back to Europe from their explorations in the New World, and by the sixteenth century cacao was being imported to Europe regularly, albeit in small amounts. Chocolate was introduced to Europeans as a beverage, and while the addition of vanilla was embraced, sugar and milk were added instead of chile and achiote to make it more palatable. As the flavoring of chocolate improved, so did its popularity, and by the seventeenth century drinking chocolate was a symbol of status, wealth, and luxury among European nobility.

Italians can be justly proud that solid chocolate was discovered in Turin, the capital of the northern region of Piedmont, towards the very end of the eighteenth century. The credit, however, goes to a Frenchman by the name of Doret, who was living in the city at the time. Further advancements in chocolate making continued through the beginning of the nineteenth century, such as the extraction of fat from cocoa beans to make cocoa butter and cocoa powder and the addition of alkali to cocoa powder to reduce its bitterness. These developments led to the creation of the first chocolate candy bar in 1847.

The process of making chocolate is arduous, involving many time-consuming steps that must be undertaken with great care and attention to detail. First and foremost is the selection of the *cabosse*, or the cacao pod. Three varieties of cacao trees are harvested today: Criollo, Forastero, and Trinitario. Criollo cacao is primarily grown in Venezuela and is considered the finest, producing cocoa beans that are complex in flavor yet delicate and aromatic. Criollo cacao is very rare, constituting only about 1 percent of the world crop. The Forastero variety is the most widely cultivated, especially in Africa; most of the chocolate we consume, whether for eating or for cooking, is made from this variety. Trinitario, born in Trinidad, is a hybrid of Criollo and Forastero trees that is gaining popularity in the areas of Central and South America that used to be home to the rare Criollo trees.

Cacao trees have a particularly long flowering period, almost year-round; the trees become most productive when they have matured for ten to twelve years. Harvesting the pods is still done by hand, as is removing the cocoa beans inside, along with their mucous-like surrounding membrane. The beans are placed in specially constructed crates with open bottoms and subjected to a closely monitored period of fermentation, which typically lasts for two to four days. During the fermentation period, acids are leached out, the beans separate from their sugary membranes, and their germ becomes inactive. It is also during this time that the eventual flavor profile of the beans is determined. Fermentation is a painstaking task, full of peril. The beans are carefully stirred, aerating them to ensure that they ferment evenly and at the proper pace. After fermentation, they are quickly laid out to dry, preventing the growth of mold and further developing their aromatic qualities. This is another laborious phase; the beans may be dried only naturally, under the heat of the tropical sun, for one to two weeks. Needless to say, a sudden rainstorm can be disastrous.

Chocolate makers emphatically insist that it is their skill at roasting the beans that is the most crucial component of their final product—and what sets them apart from their competitors. During the careful and sometimes secretive roasting phase, whatever moisture is left in the beans after drying is removed and the beans are brought to their fullest flavor.

After roasting, the beans are ground, often in a stone mill. The heat and pressure of the mill creates a liquid paste known as chocolate liquor, which is then separated from the natural fat, or cocoa butter, that was contained inside each bean. The residue eventually becomes cocoa powder, which may or may not be treated with an alkali that alters its flavor (see page 55).

After further refining, the cocoa liquor is ready to be recombined with cocoa butter and other ingredients to create a specific kind of chocolate. This is where all those mysterious percentages that you see on chocolate in stores come into play. Typically, the percentage that categorizies chocolate refers to the amount of cocoa liquor present; the remaining ingredients are generally cocoa butter and sugar. Some chocolate manufacturers also add lecithin or other ingredients that act as

(continued on next page)

emulsifiers, creating a pleasant mouthfeel when you eat the chocolate. The finest chocolate, known as couverture, contains little or no emulsifier; the silky mouth feel is entirely due to the richness and purity of the cocoa butter. This is the chocolate used by professional pastry chefs, and thankfully, it is now available to consumers on an ever-increasing basis.

During the next step of chocolate production, the conching, we arrive at the make-or-break stage of the game. The refined and blended chocolate is placed inside tanks known as conchs, which contain tiny metal beads. At a controlled temperature, the chocolate is mixed for up to seventy-two hours. This is another step that depends on the skill and desire of the chocolate maker and is often shrouded in secrecy. During the careful and precisely timed conching period, excess moisture and volatile acids are eliminated, the chocolate is homogenized and thoroughly united with the cocoa butter and other ingredients, and the desired result is achieved—a soft, velvety feel along with fully developed, complex flavor and aroma.

The final stage is tempering, which essentially brings the liquid chocolate to a solid state that is molecularly stable, allowing for optimal appearance and mouthfeel as well as storage. Tempering chocolate requires it to be melted, cooled, and then reheated, each at a specific temperature. When chocolate is melted, it is considered "out of temper"; professional pastry chefs and chocolatiers must always retemper it in order to create molded, filled, or shaped chocolate.

To use chocolate in recipes, you usually do not have to temper it, but it should always be treated with care. Too much heat will cause it to scorch or separate; always melt it gradually and allow it to cool to lukewarm before adding it as an ingredient, unless the recipe notes otherwise. I prefer to melt chocolate in a stainless steel or glass bowl fitted over a saucepan of gently simmering water. Stir the chocolate often and remove it from the heat as soon as it is melted. It should always be perfectly smooth, with an unmistakable sheen. When melting chocolate in the microwave, be sure to do so in 10- to 15-second intervals, stirring in between to ensure that the chocolate does not overheat in any one spot.

Chocolate is very sensitive to drastic changes in temperature and humidity. Store it in a cool, dry place, preferably between 55°F and 65°F, well wrapped or in an airtight container and away from strong-smelling foods. It does not have an infinite shelf life and should be used within six months of purchase. After that, it begins to break down, compromising the texture, flavor, and aroma.

I must admit that I am a fan of dark, bittersweet chocolate. When shopping for couverture, I look for a brand with 66 to 72 percent cocoa liquor. Semisweet chocolate has a higher sugar content and a lower percentage of cocoa liquor, usually 55 to 60 percent. Milk chocolate has an even higher amount of sugar and has been blended with milk or milk powder and usually vanilla. White chocolate isn't really chocolate at all, since it contains no chocolate liquor, only cocoa butter, lecithin, sugar, and vanilla.

Are you seated? Here is the big whammy. There are actually some wonderful Italian chocolate producers you have never heard of! It is a sad fact that most Italian chocolate does not even make it out of Italy; the Swiss, Belgians, and French have been far more successful in sending their chocolate to our shores, in the form of both chocolate for eat-

ing and the couverture used by professionals. Italian chocolate producers, such as Amadei, based in Pisa, Domori, from Genoa, and Slitti, outside of Florence, are gaining ground on their European competitors, making fine couvertures for professionals and consumers alike. Whenever I visit Italy, I make sure to tuck a few bars of these chocolates into my suitcase; in the meantime, I use the best couvertures I can find for my recipes, at work and at home.

Wholly admitting that I am a fan of French chocolate, I offer you the following recommendations. I adore the complex flavor and bright acidity of Valrhona chocolate from France; Extra-Bitter 66% is my favorite, and I like the Manjari 64%. E. Guittard, a California firm, was founded by a French immigrant; it carries a complete line of excellent couverture chocolates that are available in many specialty stores and online. Michel Cluizel is another French chocolatier from Paris who makes just about the richest, creamiest couverture I have ever had the pleasure of melting on my tongue; the milk chocolate is absolutely to die for. See Sources, pages 285–87, for online suppliers of fine chocolate.

ALL-OF-THE-LEMON TART
crostata "tutto il limone"

I love the idea of using all of the lemon, including the skin, in this dessert. This is the concept behind Shaker lemon pie, and I think Italian cooks would embrace it with a kiss on both cheeks. The one drawback of this recipe is that you do need to plan ahead, because it's important for the sliced lemons to soak in the sugar overnight (the sugar removes the bitterness from the pithy part of the rind). Once this step is done, the tart comes together easily and quickly with the aid of a blender. The resulting texture is soft and creamy, with the finely chopped bits of lemon rind providing a pleasing chewiness. Be sure to use lemons that are not coated with a thick layer of wax (see page 22), since the rind is a key ingredient.

MAKES ONE 10-INCH TART, 8 TO 10 SERVINGS

2 large lemons (see headnote)

1½ cups granulated sugar

Sweet Tart Crust, made with lemon zest
   (page 142)

⅓ cup freshly squeezed lemon juice

3 large eggs

2 large egg yolks

2 tablespoons *limoncello*

½ cup heavy cream

½ teaspoon pure vanilla extract

Pinch of kosher salt

Confectioners' sugar, for dusting (optional)

The day before you plan to make the tart, wash the lemons well, then slice them as thinly as possible, using a sharp knife. Remove the seeds from the lemon slices and place the slices in a medium nonreactive bowl (glass, ceramic, plastic, or stainless steel). Add the sugar and toss to coat the lemon slices. Cover the bowl and refrigerate overnight.

The following day, preheat the oven to 325°F and position a rack in the center.

On a floured board, roll the tart dough into an 11-inch circle ⅛-inch thick. Transfer the dough to a 10-inch tart pan with fluted sides and a removable bottom by rolling the dough around the pin like a carpet and then unrolling it onto the pan. Press the dough into the bottom and sides of the pan, then trim it so it is flush with the top of the pan. Chill the tart shell while you make the filling.

Remove the bowl of lemon slices from the refrigerator and place the entire mixture in a blender. Add the lemon juice and blend the ingredients on high speed until the lemon rinds are finely chopped. Transfer the contents of the blender to a medium nonreactive bowl.

In a separate bowl, whisk together the eggs, egg yolks, *limoncello,* heavy cream, vanilla extract, and salt. Add the egg mixture to the lemon mixture, whisking well to combine thoroughly.

Remove the tart shell from the refrigerator and place it on a baking sheet to catch any drips. Pour the filling into the shell and bake the tart for 20 minutes, then rotate the pan so the tart cooks evenly. Bake for an additional 20 to 25 minutes, or until the filling is set but still pale and the crust is lightly golden. Allow the tart to cool completely on a rack before carefully removing the sides of the pan.

Before serving, dust the surface of the tart lightly with confectioners' sugar, if desired. Serve the tart at room temperature or chilled. Wrapped in plastic, it will keep in the refrigerator for a few days.

FRESH FIG TART
crostata di fichi

Fresh figs are a treat, and thankfully, I see them more and more in markets. I like to think of figs as a very elegant fruit, so I regard this tart as a very elegant dessert, worthy of a special occasion or fancy dinner party. A dollop of fresh mascarpone is an elegant adornment. MAKES ONE 10-INCH TART, 8 TO 10 SERVINGS

Sweet Tart Crust (page 142)

¼ cup (½ stick/2 ounces) unsalted butter, softened

¼ cup confectioners' sugar

1 large egg yolk

1 tablespoon honey

¼ cup sliced almonds, toasted and finely ground

12–15 medium fresh Black Mission figs or brown, green, or purple Turkish figs

1 tablespoon freshly squeezed lemon juice

¼ cup granulated sugar

On a floured board, roll the tart dough into an 11-inch circle ⅛-inch thick. Transfer the dough to a 10-inch tart pan with fluted sides and a removable bottom by rolling the dough around the pin like a carpet and then unrolling it onto the pan. Press the dough into the bottom and sides of the pan, then trim it so it is flush with the top of the pan. Chill the tart shell while you make the filling.

Preheat the oven to 350°F and position a rack in the center.

In the bowl of an electric mixer, use the paddle attachment on medium speed to cream together the butter and confectioners' sugar. Beat in the egg yolks one at a time, followed by the honey, scraping down the sides of the bowl after each addition. Beat in the ground almonds. Remove the tart shell from the refrigerator and spread the filling evenly on the bottom with a spatula or the back of a large spoon.

Trim the stems off the figs and cut the figs into lengthwise quarters. Place them in a large bowl and sprinkle the lemon juice and granulated sugar over them, tossing to coat the figs evenly.

Arrange the figs on top of the tart filling, skin side down, flesh side up, in a circular pattern. Bake the tart for 35 to 40 minutes, rotating it after about 15 minutes to ensure even browning. The figs will be soft and collapsing and the filling should be lightly golden brown. Allow the tart to cool for at least 30 minutes on a rack before carefully removing the sides of the pan.

The tart is wonderful served warm or at room temperature, with a dollop of mascarpone, if desired. Wrapped in plastic, it will keep in the refrigerator for a few days.

IN PRAISE OF THE FIG

The truth is, along with being exotic and sophisticated, figs are also just a bit sexy. Having been around for thousands of years, figs are also significant from historical, mythological, and religious perspectives. Many believe that the forbidden fruit given to Adam by Eve was a fig rather than an apple. Romulus and Remus, the founders of Rome, were suckled by the she-wolf under a fig tree, and Siddhartha is said to have experienced the revelations that were to become the foundation of Buddhism while resting beneath a fig tree. The Greek King Mithridates believed figs to be an antidote for all ailments and ordered his physicians to use them medicinally. Pliny the Elder of Rome heralded figs as restorative, advising that they be fed to the weak and sick in order to forge a path to recovery and touting them as a food to reverse the effects of aging. The original Olympians were crowned with wreaths of fig leaves as well as olive leaves and feasted on figs in celebration of their victories.

Pliny wasn't too far from the truth: figs are rich in iron, potassium, calcium, and phosphorus, as well as being low in fat. There are several varieties, all belonging to the family Moraceae, or mulberry family. They come in a rainbow of colors: purple, pink, green, black, and brown, to name a few. In Italy, they grow rampantly throughout the southern regions, and it is not at all uncommon to be able to pull up to an obliging fig tree growing beside the road and steal a warm, sweet treat. In the United States, California produces a lovely fig crop; my favorites are the large, plump brown Turkey figs and the smaller, purple Black Mission variety. Kadota figs are a beautiful shade of pale green, with contrasting pink interiors. Fresh figs are available from early summer into the fall; if you see them, don't miss out on a single sweet bite.

SOUR CHERRY CUSTARD TART
crostata di ciliegie con crema

I am very lucky to live in a part of the country that produces succulent fresh cherries. In New York State, the harvest begins in July, when piles of red, white, and sour cherries appear at the greenmarkets in New York City. My favorite way to enjoy sweet cherries is completely unadorned, with a bowl to catch the pits. Sour cherries, though, are perfect for baking and cooking. This tart is fantastic; the cherries, coddled in the sweet custard, retain their shape and just enough of their pucker quotient for a nice contrast. Try serving this with some pana montata, *or whipped cream, but for a unique twist, infuse the cream with some torn mint leaves before whipping it with just a bit of sugar.* MAKES ONE 10-INCH TART, 8 TO 10 SERVINGS

Sweet Tart Crust (page 142)

4 large egg yolks

½ cup granulated sugar, plus more for
   sprinkling

1 tablespoon cornstarch

Pinch of kosher salt

1 vanilla bean

1 cup heavy cream

1 tablespoon grappa

2½–3 cups sour cherries (about 1 pound),
   pitted and drained

Confectioners' sugar, for dusting (optional)

On a floured board, roll the tart dough into an 11-inch circle ⅛-inch thick. Transfer the dough to a 10-inch tart pan with fluted sides and a removable bottom by rolling the dough around the pin like a carpet and then unrolling it onto the pan. Press the dough into the bottom and sides of the pan, then trim it so it is flush with the top of the tart pan. Chill the tart shell until firm, about 1 hour.

Preheat the oven to 325°F and position a rack in the center.

In a medium bowl, whisk the egg yolks with the granulated sugar, cornstarch, and salt. Split the vanilla bean lengthwise, scrape out the seeds with the blunt side of a small knife, and add the seeds to the egg yolk mixture. Beat in the heavy cream and the grappa.

Arrange the cherries attractively in a circular pattern in the tart shell, with the stem side down and the rounded side up. The cherries should fit snugly next to each other in one layer. Pour the custard over the cherries and sprinkle the entire surface with a tablespoon or so of granulated sugar.

Place the tart pan on a large baking sheet to prevent any drips. Bake the tart for 30 to 35 minutes, or until the custard is set and the crust is lightly golden brown. Allow the tart to cool for 30 minutes on a rack before carefully removing the sides of the pan.

Serve the tart slightly warm or cooled to room temperature. If desired, lightly dust the surface with confectioners' sugar. Wrapped in plastic, the tart will keep in the refrigerator for a few days.

ITALIAN APPLE CRUMB TART
crostata di mele

The dual inspiration for this tart comes from my own, wholly American apple crumb pie and an apple cake recipe I found in an Italian cookbook Mario gave me as a gift a few years ago. Here we would categorize it as a deep-dish pie, but in Italy I wouldn't be surprised to see it labeled as a torta. *It is made in a springform pan rather than a shallow tart pan, and the depth provides more of the soft, spiced apples in every bite. The topping goes on crumbly, then bakes soft and cakelike. Feel free to experiment with your favorite apples; I tend to favor New York's own hybrid, the Empire, but any good baking apple will be fine. A scoop of gelato or softly whipped heavy cream is a nice accompaniment.*

MAKES ONE 10-INCH TART, 10 TO 12 SERVINGS

FOR THE CRUST

1½ cups unbleached all-purpose flour

½ cup cake flour

1 tablespoon plus 1 teaspoon granulated sugar

½ teaspoon kosher salt

¾ cup (1½ sticks/6 ounces) unsalted butter, cold and cut into ¼-inch cubes

1 large egg yolk

¼ cup ice water, plus a few tablespoons if needed

FOR THE TOPPING

1 cup plus 2 tablespoons unbleached all-purpose flour

½ cup packed light brown sugar

1 tablespoon granulated sugar

½ teaspoon ground ginger

¼ teaspoon ground nutmeg

¼ teaspoon kosher salt

6 tablespoons (¾ stick/3 ounces) unsalted butter, cold and cut into ¼-inch cubes

3 tablespoons sour cream or crème fraîche

1 teaspoon pure vanilla extract

FOR THE FILLING

¾ cup granulated sugar

3 large egg yolks

1 tablespoon all-purpose flour

5 tablespoons sour cream or crème fraîche

1 teaspoon pure vanilla extract

3–4 large baking apples, such as Rome, Cortland, Macintosh, Golden Delicious, or Empire

2 tablespoons freshly squeezed lemon juice

Confectioners' sugar, for dusting

To make the crust: Place the all-purpose flour, cake flour, sugar, and salt in the bowl of a food processor, and pulse several times to combine. Add the cold, cubed butter and pulse until the butter is in tiny granular bits. In a small bowl, whisk together the egg yolk and ice water, then add it to the flour mixture, pulsing until the dough begins to gather. If necessary, add a bit more water, a teaspoonful or two at a time, until the dough comes together. Form the dough into a ball, flatten the ball into a disk, and wrap tightly in plastic. Chill the dough for at least 1 hour or overnight.

When the dough is chilled, roll it out on a floured surface to a thickness of ⅛ inch. Place a 10-inch springform pan on top of the dough and using a small knife, trace a circle around the outside of the pan, leaving a 1-inch border of dough. Place the circle of dough inside the springform pan and press it onto the bottom and sides of the pan. (Save the scraps for another use, if desired.) The dough should come up the sides about 1½ inches. Place the shell in the refrigerator to chill while you make the topping and filling.

To make the topping: Place the flour, brown sugar, granulated sugar, ginger, nutmeg, and salt in the bowl of a food processor. Process briefly to combine, then add the cold, cubed butter and process until the butter disappears into the dry ingredients. Add the sour cream and vanilla extract and pulse to form a crumbly texture. Set the topping aside while you make the filling.

To make the filling: Reserve 2 tablespoons of the granulated sugar for the apples. Fit an electric mixer with the paddle attachment and beat the egg yolks and remaining sugar on medium speed until light and fluffy, about 2 minutes. Switch to low speed and beat in the flour, followed by the sour cream and vanilla extract. Set the filling aside.

Preheat the oven to 350°F and position a rack in the center.

To assemble the tart: Peel, quarter, core, and thinly slice the apples. You should have about 4 cups sliced apples. Place the slices in a large bowl and sprinkle the lemon juice over them, tossing to coat them evenly, then sprinkle over the reserved 2 tablespoons granulated sugar and toss to coat. Place the apple slices in the tart shell in an even layer. Pour the filling over them and sprinkle the entire surface with the topping. If any of the crust is visible, gently fold it over the surface of the tart.

Place the springform pan on a baking sheet to catch any drips and bake the tart for 45 to 55 minutes, rotating the pan halfway through the baking time to ensure that it browns evenly. The tart is done when the topping is deep golden brown and the bubbling juices have thickened. Remove the tart from the oven and allow it to cool on a wire rack for about 25 minutes, then carefully remove the sides of the pan.

Serve the tart slightly warm or cool and serve at room temperature. To garnish, dust the top with confectioners' sugar. Wrapped in plastic, the tart will keep in the refrigerator for a few days.

HAZELNUT AND GRAPE TART
crostata di nocciole e uve

Sweet, juicy grapes and rich, toasty hazelnuts are an unusual combination that works surprisingly well. Seedless grapes are easiest, but if you don't mind picking out the seeds, large purple or red globe grapes are delightful here. This tart is light and delicate, perfect for afternoon tea or a Sunday brunch.

MAKES ONE 10-INCH TART, 10 TO 12 SERVINGS

Sweet Tart Crust (page 142), made with
    orange zest

3 large eggs, separated

⅓ cup plus 4 tablespoons granulated sugar

Freshly grated zest of 1 small orange

Several pinches of kosher salt

½ teaspoon pure vanilla extract

1¼ cups hazelnuts

About 1 pound large red or purple grapes,
    preferably seedless

1 tablespoon grappa

On a floured board, roll the tart dough into an 11-inch circle ⅛-inch thick. Transfer the dough to a 10-inch tart pan with fluted sides and a removable bottom by rolling the dough around the pin like a carpet and then unrolling it onto the pan. Press the dough into the bottom and sides of the pan, then trim it so it is flush with the top of the tart pan. Chill the tart shell until firm, about 1 hour.

Preheat the oven to 325°F and position a rack in the center.

In the bowl of an electric mixer, use the paddle attachment on medium speed to beat the egg yolks, ⅓ cup sugar, orange zest, and pinch of salt together until light and pale yellow, 2 to 3 minutes. Beat in the vanilla extract.

Place the hazelnuts in a food processor with 2 tablespoons sugar and grind them finely. Fold the ground hazelnuts into the egg yolk mixture.

In a clean bowl, use the whisk attachment on high speed to whip the egg whites with a pinch of salt until foamy and light. Gradually whip in 1 tablespoon granulated sugar and continue beating until the whites are softly peaked. Gently fold the whites into the hazelnut mixture in 3 batches. The hazelnut mixture will be stiff—do not be afraid to use vigorous strokes to fold in the whites.

Pour the filling into the prepared tart shell, spreading it evenly on the bottom. Cut the grapes in half; if seeded, carefully remove the seeds. Place the grapes in a medium bowl and sprinkle them with the grappa and the remaining 1 tablespoon sugar, tossing to coat them. Arrange the grapes, cut side down, in concentric circles on top of the filling until you have completely covered the surface. You may need to cut more grapes as you go.

Bake the tart for 35 to 40 minutes, or until the crust is golden and the filling is puffed and lightly browned. Remove it from the oven and allow to cool on a wire rack for about 25 minutes, then carefully remove the sides of the pan.

Serve the tart slightly warm or cool and serve at room temperature. Wrapped in plastic, it will keep in the refrigerator for a few days.

ICE CREAMS, SORBETS, AND SEMIFREDDOS

gelati, sorbetti, e semifreddi

I LOVE ASKING FIRST-TIME VISITORS TO ITALY WHICH FOODS THEY LONG FOR the most upon their return. With a few exceptions, the answer is usually a dramatic roll of the eyes along with the heartfelt moan of a single word: "*Gelatooooo.*" Italian *gelato* is the best form of ice cream on the planet, and without question eating it is a national pastime. The local ice cream shop, or *gelateria*, is as much a beloved meeting point as the local café, and the indulgence of a daily cone or cup is not considered the least bit excessive. In Sicily and other southern regions, Italians sandwich fresh *gelato* in a split brioche roll and eat it as a refreshing breakfast before facing the intense heat of a summer day; even on the coldest winter days in northern cities like Turin and Milan, the neighborhood *gelaterie* are filled with customers. Along with sipping espresso and drinking wine, eating *gelato* is deeply woven into the fabric of Italian life.

Nowadays nearly every department store, discount retailer, and upscale cookware shop in America carries at least one model of countertop ice cream machine, making it easy for you to experience this bit of Italy at home. It is important to remember that fresh, homemade *gelato* lives a very short life in your freezer; it should be enjoyed as soon as possible after it is churned. The texture of most commercial ice cream is the result of added stabilizers and preservatives, which enable it to remain frozen for an extended time before it turns icy. Homemade ice cream, in chemical terms, is unstable; there are no additives to delay the formation of ice crystals. I hardly think that enjoying your *gelato* quickly will be much of a problem, as you will soon discover that freshly made *gelato* is irresistible. Busy cooks can get a head start by making the base a day or two in advance if necessary and then churning the *gelato* the same day it is to be served.

Achieving the perfect *gelato*, whether it is custard-based or fruit-based, is less about technique and more about the ingredients. Italians insist on the freshest eggs, milk, and cream, perfectly ripe fruits, and the best chocolate and nuts. It is the ingredients that elevate Italian *gelato* above all competitors, and it will be your choice of ingredients that determines the greatness of your *gelato* at home. It is also important to follow the directions of the manufacturer of your ice cream machine carefully and to keep it pristinely clean. Since you'll want to consume your homemade *gelato* the same day it is made, the recipes in this chapter yield 3 to 4 liquid cups of unfrozen *gelato* or sorbet, which equals 2 or 3 cups of frozen *gelato* or one batch, depending on the capacity of your machine. To make a larger amount of base, simply double the quantities of the ingredients.

Gelato is a sweet treat that adapts itself to any situation; it is elegant and refined when served in a porcelain cup or stemmed glass, casual and relaxed when eaten in your bathrobe in front of the television. My advice is to immerse yourself in the sensual pleasures of eating *gelato* slowly, letting the intense flavors melt over your tongue as it slips down your throat, all the while savoring *il dolce far niente,* or the sweetness of doing nothing.

SIMPLE SYRUP

Sugar syrup, or simple syrup, as we call it in the professional realm, is integral in making fruit-based sorbetti *and* gelati. *Every chef has her or his own preferred ratio of sugar to water; this happens to be mine, and it works well for sweetening fruit sorbets. It may seem overly cautious to be careful about boiling sugar and water together, but it is important to make sure the syrup comes to a full boil; otherwise the sugar may not fully dissolve and will recrystallize. On the other hand, do not let the syrup boil too much, or you may run the risk of evaporating too much of the water, which will make your syrup too thick. Once the mixture reaches a full boil, it is done. I find that simple syrup is always good to have on hand for sweetening cocktails or iced tea; in the summertime I make a double batch, and it keeps well in a tightly covered plastic container for up to 3 weeks.* **MAKES ABOUT 3 1/2 CUPS**

3¼ cups plus 1 tablespoon granulated sugar
2 cups water

Place the sugar and water in a 3-quart saucepan. Stir the two together well to ensure that all of the sugar crystals are wet.

Place the pan over medium heat and cook until the mixture comes to a rolling boil. Remove the pan from the heat and allow the syrup to cool completely to room temperature before refrigerating.

SWEET GRAPE FOCACCIA, PAGE 248

PANFORTE DI SIENA, PAGE 254

GUBANA, PAGE 264

SAINT JOSEPH'S DAY CREAM PUFFS,
PAGE 243

CASSATA ALLA SICILIANA,
PAGE 261

BABBO BREADSTICKS WITH
HONEYDEW PROSECCO, PAGE 270

TARALLI WITH RED PEPPER AND
OREGANO, PAGE 272

A TRAY OF ITALIAN CHEESES
CLOCKWISE FROM TOP RIGHT: CASTELMAGNO,
PIAVE VECCHIO, PECORINO DOLCE, ROBIOLA
"LA TUR," ROBIOLA "ROCHETTA," *STRACCHINO,*
BURRATA, GORGONZOLA DOLCE

STRAWBERRY GELATO
gelato di fragole

Some desserts need no accompaniment other than a bowl and a spoon, and this gelato is one of them. I think it has just the right balance of custard and fruit and is both refreshing and luxurious. I make no apologies for the following rule: only the best strawberries can be used for this recipe, and they should be at the height of their harvest season. So, depending on where you live, you should attempt this recipe only during the summer. I also insist on the exact proportions of cream, milk, and egg yolks here, so please, no attempts at skimping on the fat with this one. Freeze this gelato immediately after making it, to lock in the bright, fresh flavor of the berries. MAKES ABOUT 3 1/2 CUPS

1 cup heavy cream	½ vanilla bean
1 cup whole milk	6 large egg yolks
1 cup granulated sugar	½ pound cleaned, sliced strawberries

Place the heavy cream, milk, and ½ cup sugar in a heavy-bottomed saucepan. Split the vanilla bean, scrape out the seeds with the blunt side of a small knife, add the seeds and bean to the pan, and place over medium heat.

Meanwhile, whisk the egg yolks well with 1 tablespoon sugar in a large bowl. When the cream mixture comes to a boil, remove the pan from the heat. Add a splash of the hot liquid to the bowl with the yolks and immediately begin to whisk vigorously. Slowly whisk in the remaining cream mixture, then return the liquid to the saucepan and continue to whisk for about 1 minute.

Strain the custard through a chinois or fine-meshed sieve to remove any bits of cooked egg. Allow the *gelato* base to cool completely in the refrigerator, whisking occasionally so it will cool evenly.

After the base has cooled, place the cleaned strawberries in a blender or food processor along with the remaining 3 tablespoons sugar. Pulse to achieve a chunky puree, but do not overprocess, or the strawberries will liquefy.

Stir the strawberry puree into the cold *gelato* base to combine them thoroughly. Immediately transfer the *gelato* to an ice cream maker and freeze according to the manufacturer's instructions.

BERRY AMORE

There is a bittersweet Greek myth about the origin of the strawberry: it is said that Venus wept uncontrollably when her lover Adonis died, and her tears, falling to the earth from her cheeks, formed heart-shaped strawberries. Ready-made for romance, strawberries have symbolized love and lust for centuries. Health-conscious Americans can herald their nutritional attributes, since strawberries are packed with vitamin C, folic acid, fiber, and potassium. But I would venture a guess that Italians really dig the *amore* factor.

Italy is a leader when it comes to exporting strawberries to other parts of Europe, though in recent years producers have struggled with a reduction in the acreage devoted to strawberry cultivation as well as with increased competition from producers in neighboring Austria and Switzerland. Within Italy, strawberries are grown in the southern regions of Basilicata, Campania, and Sicily and in Emilia-Romagna, Piedmont, and the Veneto in the north. In Lazio, around the Lago di Nemi, the wild strawberry is revered. Nestled in the Alban hills surrounding Rome, the town of Nemi holds an annual Sagra delle Fragola, a festival that lasts almost two months and celebrates the harvest of the tiny *fragolini di bosco*, fragrant wild strawberries

that grow in the woods around the volcanic lake. Wild strawberries are also found in Emilia-Romagna, outside the city of Ferrara, providing the perfect complement to the sublime *aceto balsamico* from the neighboring city of Modena.

Here in America we have a strawberry that is truly worthy of high praise, the Tri-Star. These fragrant berries are classified as a "day-neutral" strain, meaning that they grow unaffected by the length of the day, producing up to four full crops per season. Tri-Stars have it all: they are small, sweet, juicy, bursting with flavor, and red, red, red all the way through. Luckily, several local farmers provide me with a steady supply throughout the summer months, even up to the first frost of autumn. I can't imagine a summer season without featuring them prominently on my menu at Babbo.

One of the simplest ways to enjoy strawberries in Italy is known as *fragole al vino*. Hull the berries and cut them in halves or quarters (slices will break down a bit too far and fall apart), then toss them in a bowl with a little sugar and a few splashes of good wine, red or white. Let the berries sit in the refrigerator for a few hours, then enjoy. The wine-spiked juices are wonderful, especially spooned over *gelato* or mascarpone.

TOASTED ALMOND GELATO
gelato di mandorle

In a word, de-li-cious. My staff and I can't seem to get enough of this creamy, nutty, and sweet gelato, *which has no egg yolks yet is still rich and luxurient. The most important step is toasting the almonds until they are nicely golden brown, for the toastier they are, the more intensely flavored your* gelato *will be. Seek out* millifiori, *or "a thousand flowers," honey for this recipe. The subtle floral notes are sublime with the almond flavor.* **MAKES ABOUT 2 CUPS**

1 cup sliced blanched almonds

1 cup heavy cream

1½ cups whole milk

¼ cup plus 1 tablespoon granulated sugar

1 heaping tablespoon flavorful honey, such as
    clover or *millifiori*

Pinch of kosher salt

2 teaspoons amaretto

¼ teaspoon pure almond extract

Preheat the oven to 375°F. Spread the almonds in a single layer on a clean baking sheet and toast them for 12 to 14 minutes, or until they are golden brown and aromatic.

Remove the almonds from the oven and place them in a medium saucepan. Add the heavy cream, milk, sugar, and honey and place over medium heat, stirring occasionally.

When the mixture comes to a boil, remove the saucepan from the heat and set aside to infuse the liquid with the flavor of the almonds.

Allow the mixture to cool to room temperature, then strain it through a chinois or fine-meshed sieve and discard the almonds. Stir in the salt, amaretto, and almond extract.

Chill the *gelato* thoroughly in a covered container, at least 3 to 4 hours. Freeze it in an ice cream maker according to the manufacturer's instructions.

FIG AND RICOTTA GELATO
gelato di fichi e ricotta

This is a terrific gelato, full of the flavor of juicy figs and creamy ricotta. You can substitute freshly squeezed orange juice for the vin santo if you like. It is important to use ripe figs, since underripe figs are virtually flavorless and simply not worth the effort. Like the Strawberry Gelato on page 175, you should freeze this as soon as you make it, to preserve the flavor and color of the figs. MAKES ABOUT 3 1/2 CUPS

½ pound fresh ripe Black Mission or Turkish figs

1¼ cups granulated sugar

½ cup *vin santo*

2 cinnamon sticks

2 wide strips freshly peeled orange zest

1¾ cups whole milk

¾ cup heavy cream

4 large egg yolks

¾ cup fresh whole-milk ricotta

Wash the figs, then trim off the stems and cut the figs into quarters. Place them in a small saucepan with ¼ cup sugar, the *vin santo*, 1 cinnamon stick, and the orange zest; stir the ingredients around a bit to wet the sugar. Place the pan over low to medium heat and cook the mixture, stirring often to ensure that it does not scorch. Simmer the mixture until the figs break down and become soft and mushy, 3 to 5 minutes. Set aside the fig compote to cool.

Meanwhile, place the milk, heavy cream, the remaining cinnamon stick, and ½ cup sugar in a medium saucepan and bring to a boil over medium heat, stirring occasionally. While the milk is coming to a boil, whisk the egg yolks and the remaining ½ cup sugar together in a large bowl. When the milk mixture has come to a boil, remove it from the heat. Add a splash of the hot liquid to the bowl with the yolks and immediately begin to whisk vigorously. Slowly whisk in the remaining milk mixture, then return the liquid to the saucepan and continue to whisk for about 1 minute.

Strain the custard through a chinois or fine-meshed sieve to remove the cinnamon stick and any bits of cooked egg. Allow the *gelato* base to cool completely in the refrigerator, whisking occasionally so it will cool evenly.

Place the ricotta in a large bowl and whisk it to break down the curds and soften the texture. Remove the cinnamon stick and orange zest from the fig compote and place the compote in a food processor or blender. Pulse a few times to create a slightly chunky puree. Gradually whisk the cooled *gelato* base into the ricotta, taking care to make sure there are no lumps of ricotta. Whisk in the pureed fig compote.

Immediately transfer the *gelato* to an ice cream maker and freeze according to the manufacturer's instructions.

GELATO **THEN AND NOW**

The history of *gelato* is about as crystal clear as a waffle cone, with about as many versions of the story as there are flavors. We do know that precursors of modern ice cream have been traced back as far as ancient Greek, Roman, and Chinese civilizations, and Turkish and Arab empires both had versions of sweet, icy concoctions a little farther along the time-line. These early examples usually involved snow or chipped ice flavored with locally available embellishments such as almond milk, honey, and grape must. The result was a pleasant, slushy beverage that was enjoyed only by the upper echelons of society. It was not until the mid-sixteenth century that solid historical evidence of refined chilled desserts began to appear. Florentines proudly state that ice cream was invented by a chef from Florence, assigned to accompany Catherine de Médici when she married Henry II of France in 1533. Sicilians claim that Arab conquerors passed on the skill to them centuries before. Ice cream history, it seems, is highly subjective and entirely dependent on where you are from.

The common theme woven through the various versions of *gelato* history is that frozen desserts have their roots as cordials, intensely flavored drinks derived from the essences of fruits, herbs, and aromatics. A French confectioner by the name of Audiger traveled to Italy in the latter half of the seventeenth century to learn the secrets of Italian chefs, who he felt were the undisputed mas-

ters of making "flavored waters." In 1692 he published his steward's handbook, *La Maison Réglée*, singing the praises of Italian chefs and describing how they skillfully chilled their flavored waters to make *sorbetti*. By the time *La Maison Réglée* was published, *sorbetti* carts were commonplace in major Italian cities such as Venice, Florence, Naples, and Palermo, as were exclusive shops that sold *sorbetti* to a privileged clientele. Sometime between 1692 and 1694, Antonio Latini, a steward at the royal court in Naples, wrote an essay on the skills of Italian *sorbetti* makers titled "Treatise on Various Kinds of *Sorbetti* or Water Ices," which contained the first written recipes for making *sorbetti* from fresh, abundant local fruits, lemon juice, and sugar water.

It was an Italian medical professor by the name of Filippo Baldini who wrote the first complete book about *sorbetti*, simply entitled *De'sorbetti*, which was published in Naples in 1775. Baldini was especially excited about making *sorbetti* with pineapple, a new fruit that had arrived in Italy from the Americas, along with traditional flavors such as lemon, orange, cherry, and strawberry. The so-called aromatic sorbets were made with fragrant aniseed, cinnamon, coffee, and the wildly popular chocolate. Baldini also included a chapter on "milky" *sorbetti*, which eventually gave birth to—you guessed it—ice cream. His greatest contribution, however, was in detailing the chemical process of using specific proportions of sea salt and ice to facilitate the freezing of the *sorbetti*. Baldini's method, which was both easy and economical, spread quickly among Neapolitan *sorbetti* makers, sparking the Italian obsession with *gelato* and *sorbetti* and contributing to the eventual development of modern refrigeration in Italy.

The word *gelato* derives from the Italian verb *gelare*, which means "to freeze." *Gelato* may be used to describe a range of frozen delights, both milk- and water-based, but in the most general terms it is used to identify milk- or custard-based ice cream, while *sorbetti* are usually fruit-based. Nonetheless, it is quite common to find *gelati* that contain no dairy or eggs and *sorbetti* that contain milk or cream. *Semifreddo*, which means "partly frozen," is similar to *gelato*, with the addition of whipped cream to lighten it further before it is frozen.

The regions of Italy where *gelato* is produced account for further variation; in the north, the addition of cream is more common, while in the south, vegetable starch or soft, fresh cheese are sometimes added instead of eggs to thicken the base. Regardless of the name used, both *gelati* and *sorbetti* deliver a flavor-packed punch that is hard to forget and impossible to resist. The flavor impact is a result of the unique way in which they are frozen. The machinery incorporates a minimum of air into the base mixture, resulting in a dense, creamy texture that coats the tongue with the vivid flavors of the ingredients.

It is important to distinguish between *gelato artiginale*, or *gelato* that is artisan-produced, and *gelato* that is industrially produced, which is certainly not awful but nowhere near as special. One needs merely a supply of powdered *gelato* base, water, some freezing equipment, and a neon sign to serve *gelato industriale*. True *gelato* professionals make *gelato artiginale* with passion and dedication, using only the finest ingredients available; they know that the best *gelato* is produced daily and in small batches, with no preservatives or stabilizers to increase freezer life. It is the exacting level of care with which such *gelato* is made that makes it so unforgettable. *Produzione in Casa* or *Nostra Produzione*—which basically translates to "made on the premises"—are important words to look for on the storefront when sizing up a *gelateria*.

Gelaterie are social hubs; a stop at the *gelateria* is a way to catch up with friends and share some local gossip. The *passeggiata*, or slow evening stroll when members of the community come out to enjoy each other's company, is the perfect excuse to have a cone piled high with a few of your favorite flavors. The local *gelato* shop is often a family-owned and -operated business, serving *gelato* made from recipes that have been handed down from generation to generation. This daily practice of families serving families makes *gelato* a part of the unbroken chain of Italian tradition.

GINGER HONEY GELATO
gelato di zenzero e miele

Ginger and honey is one of my favorite flavor combinations. Fresh ginger provides zing, which contrasts with the mellow sweetness of the honey. Make sure you purchase ginger that is moist and plump; avoid any "hands" that look wrinkled and dry. A sharp peeler or paring knife will easily remove the woody skin. This recipe was inspired by the fresh ginger gelato from San Crispino, one of the finest gelaterie in Rome. MAKES ABOUT 3 CUPS

3 ounces fresh ginger, peeled

1½ cups whole milk

1½ cups heavy cream

¼ cup granulated sugar

4 large egg yolks

½ cup flavorful honey, such as eucalyptus, sage, or *millifiori*

Finely grate the ginger using a microplane grater, or slice it thinly, and place it in a large saucepan. Add the milk and cream, then stir in the sugar. Place the pan over medium heat and bring the mixture to a boil, stirring occasionally to prevent any scorching. Remove the pan from the heat and allow it to sit for 30 minutes to infuse the milk mixture with the flavor of the ginger.

Place the saucepan over the heat again to bring the mixture just to a boil. As it reheats, whisk the egg yolks with the honey in a large bowl. When the milk mixture has come to a boil, remove it from the heat. Add a splash of the hot mixture to the bowl with the yolks and immediately begin to whisk vigorously. Slowly whisk in the remaining liquid, then return the mixture to the saucepan and continue to whisk for 1 minute.

Strain the *gelato* base through a chinois or fine-meshed sieve to remove the ginger and any bits of cooked egg. Allow the base to cool completely in the refrigerator, whisking occasionally so it will cool evenly.

If you are storing the *gelato* to freeze later, keep it in an airtight container.

Freeze it in an ice cream maker according to the manufacturer's instructions.

ESPRESSO CINNAMON GELATO
gelato di caffe e cannella

Some people like their cappuccino with a dash of cinnamon; if so, this gelato *will fit the bill. Italians don't sprinkle their cappuccino with cinnamon, so if you wish to remain on the purist side of the fence, omit the cinnamon sticks and orange zest for a more direct espresso experience. The one thing that is most important is to start with whole coffee beans and chop them in the food processor, not a coffee grinder. Finely ground espresso will make the* gelato *too strong. You may use decaffeinated, of course, but I rather like the idea of getting a jolt from a scoop of* gelato.

MAKES ABOUT 3 CUPS

1¼ cups whole milk

1 cup heavy cream

½ cup plus 2 tablespoons granulated sugar

½ cup whole espresso beans

2 cinnamon sticks

Two 4-inch-long strips freshly peeled orange zest

5 large egg yolks

Pinch of kosher salt

Place the milk, heavy cream, and ½ cup sugar in a medium saucepan. Place the espresso beans in a food processor and process to chop them roughly. Add them to the saucepan with the cinnamon sticks and orange peel. Bring the ingredients to a boil over medium heat, stirring occasionally. Turn off the heat and allow the milk and cream to infuse for 30 minutes.

Place the saucepan back on the heat and bring the mixture to a boil. Meanwhile, place the egg yolks in a large bowl with the salt. Add the remaining 2 tablespoons sugar and whisk well. When the milk mixture has come to a boil, remove it from the heat. Add a splash of the mixture to the bowl with yolks and immediately begin to whisk vigorously. Slowly whisk in the remaining liquid, then return the mixture to the saucepan and continue to whisk for about 1 minute.

Strain the *gelato* base through a chinois or fine-meshed sieve to remove any bits of cooked egg and the cinnamon sticks, espresso beans, and orange peel. Allow the base to cool completely in the refrigerator, whisking occasionally so it will cool evenly.

If you are storing the *gelato* to freeze later, keep it in an airtight container. Freeze the *gelato* in an ice cream maker according to the manufacturer's instructions.

MILK CHOCOLATE GELATO
gelato di cioccolato al latte

I am not as big a fan of straight chocolate as I should be, considering my profession. The exception is this divine gelato, *which accentuates the creaminess of milk chocolate. I find that adding a bit of bittersweet chocolate tames the cloying nature of milk chocolate and balances the flavor perfectly. For a real treat, try dribbling some* vincotto *over a few scoops. This* gelato *is probably the ultimate justification for investing in an ice cream machine.* **MAKES ABOUT 3 1/2 CUPS**

4 ounces milk chocolate

3 ounces semisweet or bittersweet chocolate

1¾ cups whole milk

1 cup heavy cream

½ cup granulated sugar

6 large egg yolks

Pinch of kosher salt

Using a serrated knife or chef's knife, finely chop the two chocolates and set aside.

Place the milk, heavy cream, and ¼ cup sugar in a medium saucepan and bring to a boil over medium heat, whisking occasionally.

Meanwhile, in a large bowl, whisk the egg yolks with the remaining ¼ cup sugar and the salt. When the milk mixture has reached a boil, remove from the heat and add the chopped chocolates, whisking to melt them thoroughly.

Add a splash of the hot chocolate mixture to the bowl with the yolks and immediately begin to whisk vigorously. Gradually whisk in the remaining liquid, then return the mixture to the saucepan and continue to whisk for about 1 minute or so.

Strain the *gelato* base through a chinois or fine-meshed sieve to remove any bits of cooked egg. Allow the base to cool completely in the refrigerator, whisking occasionally so it will cool evenly.

If you are storing the *gelato* to freeze later, keep it in an airtight container. Freeze the *gelato* in an ice cream maker according to the manufacturer's instructions.

EGGS OF MANY SIZES

The size of an egg is determined by several factors, the primary one being the age of the hen: the older the hen, the larger the eggs. Other factors include the hen's breed as well as the environmental conditions, such as heat, overcrowding, stress, and poor nutrition, all of which decrease the size of eggs.

The American system of sizing eggs classifies them as peewee, small, medium, large, extra-large, and jumbo. (Personally, I have never seen a peewee egg, and it has been years since I saw a carton of small eggs at the grocery store.) Most recipes are written with a middle-of-the-road approach, calling for large eggs. Nonetheless, you shouldn't feel limited in your cooking if all you happen to have in the house is eggs of a different size.

Among medium, large, extra-large, and jumbo eggs, the size begins to matter only when you are dealing with more than two eggs in a recipe. According to the American

Egg Board, you can use the following substitutions:

Jumbo	X-Large	Large	Medium
2	3	3	3
3	4	4	5
4	4	5	6
5	5	6	7

I have never had any hugely adverse effects when I have used large or extra-large eggs in a recipe; it is only when the two extremes are in play (say, medium eggs as opposed to jumbo eggs) that I have run into noticeable differences in my recipes. If the eggs in your refrigerator are too large and the recipe calls for only one egg, it is a bit trickier than if they are too small. In that case, simply crack the egg into a small bowl, lightly beat it to combine the white and the yolk, then add most of it to the recipe, holding back just a bit.

HONEYDEW MINT SORBET
sorbetto di melone e menthe

This is a simple and very refreshing frozen treat for hot summer days. Leaving the mint and honeydew to combine for several hours or even overnight enables the mint to infuse the fruit with flavor. This sorbetto *is wonderful with fresh blackberries.*

MAKES ABOUT 3 CUPS

½ large ripe honeydew (about 2½ pounds)

¼ cup packed fresh mint leaves

Freshly squeezed juice of ½ lime, plus more
   if needed

1–1½ cups Simple Syrup (page 174)

Remove the seeds and pare the skin from the honeydew and cut it into 1½-inch chunks. You should have about 4 cups. Place the chunks in a large bowl. Crush the mint leaves slightly by rubbing them between your palms to release the oils, then mix them into the honeydew. Cover the bowl with plastic wrap and refrigerate for 6 to 8 hours or overnight.

Transfer the honeydew and mint to a blender. Add the lime juice along with 1 cup simple syrup. (You can do this step in batches if your blender container is small.) Blend the ingredients until the honeydew is completely liquefied.

Strain the *sorbetto* through a chinois or fine-meshed sieve to remove all the mint and the pulp. Taste the *sorbetto* and add lime juice and/or simple syrup if necessary to suit your taste.

If you are storing the *sorbetto* to freeze later, keep it in an airtight container; it can be held for 1 day before freezing. Freeze the *sorbetto* in an ice cream maker according to the manufacturer's instructions.

CREAMY LEMON SORBET
sorbetto di limone

I find straight-up lemon sorbet to be overpowering, and I am a self-proclaimed lemon lover. I prefer to mellow out the sharp acidity of fresh lemons with some dairy, and in this case, my sorbet gets its creaminess from thick, Greek-style yogurt. The brand known as Total Greek yogurt is sweeping the nation and is perfect for this recipe—it is made with cow's milk and is super-creamy and mild. Sheep's or goat's yogurt will work fine too but can be sharply tangy. Ultimately, this sorbetto can have whatever level of sour or sweet you like—feel free to experiment.

I like to leave little pieces of lemon zest in the sorbet, but you can strain the mixture to remove the zest if you prefer. Limoncello, *the sweet lemon liqueur from Italy, contributes floral notes from the oils in the lemon skin and a bit of extra sweetness; it can be omitted without a problem, but you may wish to add a tablespoon or so of simple syrup to compensate.* MAKES ABOUT 3 CUPS

2 medium lemons

1 cup plain Greek-style yogurt, such as Total, classic or 2%

¾ cup granulated sugar

½ cup Simple Syrup (page 174)

½ cup water

2 tablespoons *limoncello* (optional)

Grate the zest of one of the lemons. Squeeze the juice of both lemons into a small bowl and strain it to remove any seeds or pulp. You should have ½ cup lemon juice.

Place the juice and grated zest in a blender. Add the yogurt and sugar and blend on medium speed to liquefy the yogurt, about 20 seconds. Add the syrup, water, and, if desired, *limoncello* and blend to combine thoroughly.

Freeze the sorbet immediately in an ice cream machine according to the manufacturer's instructions.

RASPBERRY SORBET
sorbetto di lampone

If I had to pick one berry to make a fantastic sorbet, it would be il lampone, *the raspberry. The general rule of thumb for raspberries is that the smaller they are, the more intense their flavor is, and if you have access to local berries grown on small farms, you are in for a real treat. I like to use champagne vinegar rather than lemon juice to balance the sweetness, because it enhances the fruitiness of the berries. This* sorbetto *is a wonderful finish to a summer meal or a nice afternoon treat on a sweltering day. Try dousing a scoop with a splash of prosecco—fantastico!* MAKES ABOUT 2 1/2 CUPS

4 cups fresh raspberries (2 pints)

1 cup Simple Syrup (page 174)

½ cup water

1 tablespoon champagne vinegar

Place the raspberries in a medium saucepan and add the simple syrup. Place the pan over medium heat and bring the mixture to a boil. Simmer the berries gently for 2 minutes, then remove the pan from the heat and allow the mixture to cool completely. Use an immersion blender to puree the mixture until it is smooth, or transfer the contents to a canister blender to create a smooth puree.

Strain the sorbet through a chinois or fine-meshed sieve to remove the seeds, then whisk in the water and vinegar.

If you are storing the sorbet to freeze later, keep it in an airtight container. Freeze the sorbet in an ice cream maker according to the manufacturer's instructions.

TOASTED SESAME SEMIFREDDO
semifreddo di sesamo tostato

I adore biscotti di Regina, *the quasi-savory cookies studded with sesame seeds found in most southern Italian pastry shops. While munching on a bag of them one day, I was inspired to create a frozen sesame dessert. This variation on* semifreddo *is a snap to put together. Try serving it garnished with sections of blood orange, or douse a scoop with a double shot of espresso.* MAKES 6 TO 8 SERVINGS

¼ cup sesame seeds

1½ cups heavy cream

4 large egg yolks

½ cup pure tahini

Pinch of kosher salt

¼ cup plus 1 tablespoon sugar

3 tablespoons honey

1 tablespoon warm water

½ teaspoon pure vanilla extract

Preheat the oven to 350°F. Place the sesame seeds in a single layer on a small baking sheet or dish and toast until they are lightly golden and aromatic, about 15 minutes. Transfer the seeds to a plate or a sheet of parchment paper and set them aside to cool.

In an electric mixer fitted with the whisk attachment, whip the heavy cream on medium speed until firm peaks form. Transfer the cream to a large bowl and place it in the refrigerator to chill.

Place the egg yolks, tahini, and salt in the bowl of an electric mixer, and with the whisk attachment beat them together on medium speed until thick and creamy, about 2 minutes. Switch the mixer to low speed and keep it running.

Place the sugar, honey, and water in a small saucepan, stir them together, place the pan over low heat, and bring the mixture to a boil. When it reaches a boil, set a timer for 45 seconds. After the 45 seconds have passed, remove the saucepan from the heat and, with the mixer still on low speed, slowly add the hot sugar-and-honey mixture to the egg mixture, keeping the stream of hot liquid running down the side of the bowl. Try to avoid letting the hot liquid touch the whisk attachment, which will make it fly onto the sides of the mixing bowl rather than incorporating it into the yolks. After all the hot liquid has been added, switch the mixer to medium speed and beat the mixture until it is cool. Beat in the vanilla extract and sesame seeds.

Gently fold the sesame mixture into the chilled whipped cream, using a whisk if necessary to remove any lumps or streaks of cream. Transfer the *semifreddo* to a loaf pan or another freezable container and cover it by pressing a sheet of plastic wrap against the surface. Freeze the *semifreddo* for 4 to 6 hours, or until it is firm enough to scoop.

GELATO IS A STATE OF MIND

On my first trip to Italy, I vowed to try as much *gelato* as I possibly could in fourteen days. I was an Italian American, after all, and all my life I had only heard of the wonders of real Italian *gelato*. I was determined to set right this huge injustice. I did a prodigious amount of research, consulting with native Italians and digging through guidebooks for information on the best *gelato* in each of the cities I was visiting. Each day I would pull out my maps and navigate my way through the ancient streets to arrive at yet another gleaming *gelato* boutique and order a double cone of the most interesting and exotic flavors offered. It was all good—incredibly, amazingly good, in fact. Yet somehow I felt I was missing that gush of excitement, a euphoric sense of the heavens parting and the earth moving under my blistered feet as I worked my way through one brain freeze after another. What was wrong with me? I questioned my emotional capacity. I was in Italy, eating *gelato*, for goodness' sake; it was not supposed to get better than this. I

counted on meeting up with some portion of my destiny with all of this *gelato*. Perhaps I had overplanned, or set my expectations too high for my own good.

After Florence and Rome, I lost the necessary enthusiasm to continue my search. It was November, not the optimal weather for *gelato* as I moved farther north. In Venice, I abandoned my quest altogether. Although there are a number of fine *gelaterie* in Venice, I decided to concentrate on spider crabs, sardines, and creamy polenta while I was there. I needed a *gelato* time-out.

On my last day in Venice, I decided to take a *vaporetto* ride to the opposite side of Canareggio, the *sestiere*, or district, where my hotel was located. Most of Venice is a tangle of small canals and tiny *campos*, or squares, and since Canareggio is a particularly vast area, I promptly became lost on my way back to the hotel. It was an inconvenience more than anything else, but I was feeling inappropriately sorry for myself. The autumn sun was setting as I wound my way bit by bit toward what I hoped was my hotel. Along the way, my initial feelings of uneasiness began to fade as I began to notice exactly what was going on around me. The crush of tourists had disappeared. On the park benches of a quiet, residential *campo* sat a mother watching her children play. An elderly woman made her way home from the produce market, which was closing for the day, and a young, handsome Venetian couple strolled by, hand in hand. The buildings around me were in varying shades of amber, red, yellow, and sand. Flowerboxes still overflowed from open shutters, despite the November chill. I could hear the sounds of dinner being prepared, and the streetlights fickered on one by one. I was in Venice. I was surrounded by magic.

I crossed a tiny bridge, rounded a narrow corner, and finally recognized a main thoroughfare that would lead me right to my hotel. Relief set in, followed by a triumphant sense of accomplishment. As I passed a side street, a small *gelateria* suddenly leapt into my line of sight—not a fancy boutique, but a neighborhood *gelateria* serving a small assortment of beautiful flavors, which looked extremely appealing in my now giddy mood. I stepped up to the counter, manned by an awkward, skinny teenage boy. One flavor caught my eye: *gelato di Doge*, or the Doge's *gelato*. To this day I am not entirely sure what was in it, but it was creamy and white, with bits of caramelized candy and nuts in it. I got a double cone and stepped back out into the dusk of a serene Venetian evening. As I walked, I savored that double cone of the Doge's *gelato* from a tiny *gelateria* in a residential area of a real Italian city. I crunched the last bite of the cone, licking my fingers, knowing I had just finished the best *gelato* of my trip. And I came to understand what I have come to think of as my own *gelato* philosophy. *Gelato* is always very, very good. Sometimes it is utterly fantastic. And every now and again, *gelato* is truly a state of mind.

CHOCOLATE AND TANGERINE SEMIFREDDO
semifreddo di cioccolato e mandarino

I love the combination of chocolate and citrus, and tangerines have a particularly spicy sweetness that marries perfectly with dark chocolate. The crumbs from the chocolate wafer cookies absorb the moisture from the cream and provide a soft, almost cakey texture. In Italy cooks would use plain chocolate "biscuits," but here in the States, chocolate wafer cookies, such as Nabisco's Famous Chocolate Wafers, are a fine substitute. I like to garnish this dessert with some chopped pistachios for a crunchy and colorful finishing touch. **MAKES 6 TO 8 SERVINGS**

FOR THE SEMIFREDDO

2 tangerines

4 ounces bittersweet or semisweet chocolate

1 tablespoon Dutch-processed cocoa powder

¼ cup plus 2 tablespoons granulated sugar

2 teaspoons amaretto

4 large egg yolks

4 ounces chocolate wafer cookies, ground

1 cup heavy cream

¾ cup mascarpone

Chopped pistachios, for garnish

FOR THE CHOCOLATE TANGERINE SAUCE

1 tangerine

6 ounces bittersweet or semisweet chocolate, finely chopped

1 tablespoon unsalted butter

½ cup boiling water

3 tablespoons heavy cream

2 teaspoons light corn syrup

2 teaspoons Triple Sec or other orange-flavored liqueur

To make the *semifreddo:* Zest the tangerines and squeeze them. Reserve ¾ cup juice and set the zest aside.

Place the chocolate, cocoa powder, 2 tablespoons sugar, and tangerine juice in small saucepan and cook over medium heat, stirring constantly. The mixture will bubble and then begin to thicken; continue cooking until it is almost the consistency of pudding, about 2 minutes. Remove from the heat and stir in the tangerine zest and amaretto. Allow the mixture to cool for 15 minutes and transfer it to a large mixing bowl.

In the bowl of an electric mixer, use the whisk attachment to beat together the egg yolks and the remaining ¼ cup sugar on medium speed until light-colored and thick, about 2 minutes. Fold the egg yolk mixture into the cooled chocolate mixture. Fold in the chocolate wafer crumbs.

Clean the bowl and the whisk attachment and whip the heavy cream with the mascarpone at high speed until it is thick and softly peaking. Gently fold the cream mixture into the chocolate mixture.

Pour the *semifreddo* into a loaf pan or another freezable container and press plastic wrap on the surface. Freeze for at least 6 hours, or until firm.

Before serving, make the chocolate tangerine sauce: Zest the tangerine and squeeze it until you have 1 teaspoon zest and 2 tablespoons juice.

Place the chocolate and butter in a medium bowl. Pour in the boiling water and allow the ingredients to sit for 30 seconds, then whisk them together until smooth. Whisk in the heavy cream, corn syrup, tangerine zest, Triple Sec, and tangerine juice.

To serve: Scoop the *semifreddo* into individual bowls, or unmold the whole *semifreddo* by dipping the pan in hot water and inverting it over a plate and then slice it into portions with a hot thin-bladed knife. Drizzle each serving with some of the warm sauce and sprinkle with chopped pistachios.

The sauce can be made ahead of time and kept in a covered container in the refrigerator for 3 days. Before serving, heat in the microwave or the top of a double boiler.

ALL THINGS FRIED

tutti fritti

LONG WITH CHEESE, OLIVE OIL, CURED PORK PRODUCTS, PASTA, *gelato*, and chocolate, Italians love fried foods. It is confusing when you travel there and see how slim and trim Italians are, a fact that continues to vex us calorie-counting and carbohydrate-abstaining Americans. I am convinced that their collective secret is portion control and an almost complete absence of the concept of deprivation and dieting. For the most part, Italians are not afraid of the occasional doughnut. So while I do not advocate a steady diet of fried dough, I think a warm fritter every now and then is an indulgent treat that can be enjoyed today and worked off on the treadmill tomorrow. I dare you to try a square of crispy *crema fritta* or a warm *bomboloni* and not come to the same conclusion.

You may be surprised to find a few savory treats tucked into this chapter. I simply could not resist including them. The Pumpkin Fritters are a cherished recipe from my mother's powerful arsenal of family classics, and my Herbed Goat Cheese Fritters are a popular favorite with our customers at Babbo; with a drizzle of honey, they perfectly walk that line between sweet and savory.

Frying is easier than ever these days, thanks to improvements in countertop electric fryers, which are essentially miniature versions of their larger restaurant cousins. My favorite models are made by (no coincidence) the DeLonghi company of Italy and are available in many fine cookware stores. You can achieve the same fantastic results with a well-made, heavy stockpot and a deep-fry thermometer, which is the way I fry at home. With some good olive oil and my trusty tongs, I am set to go—but I must admit that the breeze from an open kitchen window is a welcome companion in the absence of a kitchen ventilator.

MOM'S PUMPKIN FRITTERS
frittelle di zucca

Every year my mother would faithfully clean and roast our carved Halloween pumpkins on November 1 for her pumpkin puree, which she later used for our Thanksgiving pumpkin pie. Before freezing it, she would always make a batch of these fritters for us. I can't remember what I loved more about trick-or-treating, the orgy of candy on Halloween night or having Mom's frittelle the next day, warm, soft, and cheesy. Don't be afraid to substitute canned pumpkin here; one of its virtues is that it is consistent, as well as convenient. MAKES 15 TO 20 FRITTERS

1½ cups fresh pumpkin or butternut squash puree, or canned pumpkin

2 large eggs

½ cup unbleached all-purpose flour

½ teaspoon baking powder

1 teaspoon kosher salt

¾ cup grated Grana Padano or Parmigiano-Reggiano

¼ cup finely chopped fresh flat-leaf parsley

Finely ground black pepper, to taste

Olive oil for frying

Place the pumpkin puree in a medium bowl. Lightly beat the eggs with a fork and stir them into the pumpkin with a wooden spoon or spatula. In another bowl, whisk together the flour, baking powder, and salt. Add the dry ingredients to the puree mixture, along with the grated cheese, the parsley, and a pinch of black pepper. Use the wooden spoon or a fork to combine all the ingredients into a light batter; be careful not to overmix it.

Heat ½ inch olive oil in a heavy sauté pan. Drop heaping tablespoonfuls of the batter into the oil, flattening them slightly and turning them when they are golden brown. Fry in batches, cooking for about 2 minutes per side.

Drain the fritters on paper towels and serve hot.

HERBED GOAT CHEESE FRITTERS

This recipe is one of my favorite uses for Coach Farm's fresh, tangy goat cheese, which you will find in individually wrapped logs in the dairy case of many super-markets and specialty shops. If Coach Farm's aged grating stick is hard to find, you can use grated Pecorino Romano instead. Either way, these little fritters make a wonderful warm cheese course, drizzled with some warm honey, or they're great as part of a selection of passed hors d'oeuvres. They are fun to make, and since they fry up nicely in a sauté pan, they're quick, too! MAKES ABOUT 20 FRITTERS

12 ounces fresh goat cheese

1 cup "00" flour, plus more for forming the
    fritters

1 teaspoon baking powder

½ teaspoon kosher salt

2 large eggs

½ cup finely grated aged goat cheese (see
    headnote)

2 teaspoons fresh thyme leaves, finely
    chopped

½ cup fresh flat leaf Italian parsley, finely
    chopped

Freshly ground black pepper, to taste

Olive oil, for frying

Place the fresh goat cheese in a medium bowl and break it up with your hands. In another bowl, stir together the flour, baking powder, and salt, then add it to the fresh goat cheese, followed by the eggs, grated goat cheese, thyme, parsley, and pepper. Use your hands to mix the ingredients together just to combine them and form a soft dough.

Dipping your fingers into a bit of flour to prevent the dough from sticking, break off pieces of dough and form them into 1½-inch disks. You can form the fritters several hours ahead of time and store them in the refrigerator, lightly covered with plastic wrap.

In a medium or large sauté pan, heat about ½ inch olive oil over medium heat. When the oil is hot, add 5 or 6 fritters to the pan, taking care not to overcrowd them. Fry the fritters on both sides until they are golden brown and crispy, turning them with a spatula.

Drain the fritters on paper towels and repeat with the remaining fritters. Serve the fritters hot. They are wonderful plain or drizzled with a bit of honey.

LEMON RICOTTA FRITTERS
fritelle di limone e ricotta

Flecked with lemon zest, bits of chocolate, and amaretti *crumbs and spiked with a little rum, these fritters speak for themselves. Serve them quickly after they have been fried, while they are still warm and soft, accompanied by some lemon* sorbetto, *chocolate* gelato, *or both. Be sure not to grind the* amaretti *into a fine powder in a food processor. Instead, crush them gently into coarse crumbs with a rolling pin.*
MAKES ABOUT 15 FRITTERS

1 cup unbleached all-purpose flour

¾ cup granulated sugar

½ cup coarsely crushed *amaretti* crumbs

1½ teaspoons baking powder

½ teaspoon kosher salt

¼ teaspoon freshly grated nutmeg

1½ cups fresh whole-milk ricotta

Finely grated zest of 1 medium lemon

2 large eggs

1 tablespoon dark rum

1 teaspoon pure vanilla extract

½ cup finely chopped semisweet or bittersweet chocolate, or mini chocolate chips

Olive oil, for frying

Confectioners' sugar, for dusting

In a medium bowl, stir together the flour, sugar, *amaretti* crumbs, baking powder, salt, and nutmeg until thoroughly combined.

Place the ricotta and lemon zest in another bowl. In a small bowl, use a fork to beat the eggs lightly with the rum and vanilla extract. Add the egg mixture to the ricotta mixture and whisk to combine them well. Add the dry ingredients and the chopped chocolate and use a fork to mix all the ingredients together thoroughly. Do not over-mix; a few lumps of ricotta are fine.

Heat about 2 inches (4 cups) olive oil in a large, heavy-bottomed saucepan or a deep fryer until it reaches 360°F. Working in batches, drop the batter by heaping teaspoonfuls into the oil and fry them until they are a deep golden brown on both sides. Use a skimmer or slotted spoon to remove them from the oil, and drain them on paper towels.

Serve the fritters warm, with a generous dredging of confectioners' sugar.

FRIED DOUGH: WHAT'S IN A NAME?

By now you've probably picked up on the fact that in Italy, the same foods can have many names, depending on which region or even which town you're in. It can be more than mildly confusing. The best way around it is simply to apply the rule that there are no rules and proceed with a sense of humor and a hunger for knowledge. History certainly plays a role; the name of a dish may have been handed down from centuries past, evolving along with the local dialect, or come from a quirky source that defies modern logic.

Italians enjoy doughy, fried treats during Carnevale, or Mardi Gras, when each town seems to have a specialty. They fall easily into general categories, under which there are literally endless variations. From town to town—or even house to house—you find specific ingredients and flavorings, and of course names. The most important thing to remember is that in all circumstances, your mama's version is absolutely the correct one. Uniting them all is one constant factor: Italians fry everything, even sweet treats, in good olive oil (see page 19).

Frittelle are fritters, a mercifully easy translation to comprehend. They are sometimes made from a very soft dough that can be rolled out or shaped, but most often *frittelle* are simply spoonfuls of batter dropped directly into the hot oil. In the case of fruit fritters, slices of fruit are dipped into the batter and then fried. In Friuli and Alto Adige these are quite popular and may be made with apples, pears, peaches, or plums. Some fritters consist of dough that is rolled, cut, filled, and folded like ravioli or covered with another round of dough. In America we are very familiar with funnel cakes, another sort of a fritter—batter that is poured into the oil through a funnel or squeezed through a pastry bag into thin spirals. You may see them referred to as *spiralli*, but in Italy this is a pretty broad category, with numerous local versions and specific recipes.

Cenci literally translates as "rags," and most often they are irregularly cut, twisty strips of a rolled dough that are fried until golden brown and then sprinkled with powdered sugar. There are a number of labels for this crispy treat, a Carnevale favorite throughout Italy, including *frappe* ("fringes"), *zacarette* ("shavings"), *nastrini* ("ribbons"), and *bugie* ("lies"). My favorite name for them has to be *chiacchiere della nonna*, or "grandmother's chatter," and the alternative *chiacchiere di suora*, or "nun's gossip." Go and figure that one out.

Everybody loves *zeppole*, which means "zeppelins." A specialty of Naples, they are made from an eggy batter similar to cream puff or pâte à choux dough, piped into rings and served hot with sugar. They are sometimes served with custard or *zabaione* to dip them into. They puff up, big and airy, and when they are fried in good olive oil the flavor is especially wonderful. The name variations usually involve their size; *zeppollini* are smaller and *zeppollone* are a more substantial serving. The other common name is *sfinci*, such as the beloved *sfinci di San Giuseppe*, filled with pastry cream and served on Saint Joseph's feast day.

Bomboloni are yeast doughnuts, shaped into balls instead of rings and sometimes filled with custard or fruit. They are most common in Tuscany, and since I adore soft, breadlike doughnuts, they are my favorites. In the Veneto, Alto Adige, and Friuli you see doughnuts labeled *krapfen* or *crafen*, indicative of the Austrian and German influences on the cuisine of those regions. *Krapfen* are likely to be filled, and they can be quite large—a perfect afternoon treat while people-watching in a Venetian café.

APPLE FRITTERS
frittelle di mela

If you happen to be in Italy and find yourself strolling through the outdoor market of a hill town, or past the corner frutte e verdure *of a large city, you will probably see wooden cases of gorgeous apples bearing the sweet name of Melinda on the side. Melinda is the name used to market the DOP apples produced by the farmers of the Val di Non, a valley nestled just south of the city of Bolzano. Apples are deeply interwoven into the history of the valley; the names of the towns Malè and Malosco are said to derive from the Latin* maletum, *meaning, "place of the apples." For nearly two hundred years, the apple crop has been a vital part of the region's economy, and the farmers of Val di Non tend to their orchards with the care of a nervous father. The apples thrive in the mineral-rich soil of the dolomitic rock formations that dominate the terrain and in the temperate Alpine air. The names of the specific varieties roll off the tongue like an Italian poem:* Rosa Gentile, Mantovano, Napoleone, Rosso Nobile, Bianco d'Inverno. . . .

These scrumptious apple fritters, or frittelle di mela, *are a favorite dessert in Trentino–Alto Adige as well as the Veneto and Friuli–Venezia Giulia, where apples also abound. Don't be tempted to gussy up the batter; let the flavor of the apples shine through. Also, remember that fritters are meant to be served at once. They are best enjoyed straight out of the fryer, perhaps with a scoop of* gelato *on the side.*

MAKES 16 FRITTERS

6 cups olive oil, for frying

1 large egg

½ cup whole milk

1 teaspoon pure vanilla extract

1 cup plus 1 tablespoon unbleached
    all-purpose flour

1 teaspoon baking powder

½ teaspoon baking soda

½ teaspoon kosher salt

2 large Golden Delicious apples

Freshly squeezed juice of ½ lemon

Confectioners' sugar, for dusting

Place the oil in a 5-quart, heavy-bottomed stockpot or Dutch oven and clip a candy or deep-fry thermometer to the side. Heat the oil over low heat while you prepare the fritter ingredients. It is ready when the thermometer reaches 360°F.

In a medium bowl, whisk the egg and milk together with the vanilla extract. In another bowl, stir the flour, baking powder, baking soda, and salt together. Using a fork or small whisk, stir the dry ingredients into the wet ingredients to form a batter. Let the batter sit for a few moments while you prepare the apples.

Peel and core the apples, cut them in half, and then cut each half into 3 or 4 slices. Sprinkle the apple slices with a few drops of lemon juice to keep them from turning brown.

Working in batches, dip the apple slices into the batter, heavily coating them, then quickly and gently place them in the oil, one at a time. Fry 3 to 4 fritters at once, turning them until they are nicely golden brown on both sides, then remove them to paper towels to drain briefly.

Sprinkle the fritters generously with confectioners' sugar and serve immediately, while they are still warm.

SWEET FRIED DOUGH

cenci

Depending on which region of Italy you are in, this treat has any number of names. It is a soft, slightly sweet dough that is cut into strips or ribbons, deep-fried, and eaten hot. A traditional way to eat these crispy sweets is to dip them in vincotto, *but I also enjoy* cenci *with a bit of warm honey and some fresh sheep's-milk ricotta.*

MAKES ABOUT 24 *CENCI*

1½ cups unbleached all-purpose flour, plus about ½ cup more for kneading and rolling

2 teaspoons baking powder

½ teaspoon kosher salt

3 large eggs

4 tablespoons (½ stick/2 ounces) unsalted butter, softened

1 tablespoon granulated sugar

2 tablespoons confectioners' sugar, plus more for dusting

2 teaspoons pure vanilla extract

Olive oil, for frying

In a medium bowl, whisk together the 1½ cups flour, baking powder, and salt.

In the bowl of an electric mixer, use the paddle attachment on medium speed to beat the eggs with the butter, granulated sugar, 2 tablespoons confectioners' sugar, and vanilla extract until combined; the mixture will appear somewhat curdled. Add the dry ingredients and beat to form a soft dough. Turn the mixture onto a floured board and, using up to ½ cup additional flour, knead until the dough is smooth and just firm enough to roll, about 1 minute. Do not allow the dough to become elastic; it should remain very soft and smooth.

Divide the dough into 3 pieces. Work with 1 piece at a time, keeping the other 2 pieces wrapped in plastic in the refrigerator. Have ready a parchment-lined baking sheet lightly dusted with flour.

Lightly dust your work surface, rolling pin, and the dough with flour. Roll the dough to a thickness of about ¹⁄₁₆ inch. Using a fluted pastry wheel, cut the dough into strips 6 to 8 inches long and ¾ inch wide. Lay the strips on the flour-dusted baking sheet, keeping them covered with plastic wrap as you continue to roll out and cut the dough.

When all of the dough has been cut, heat 6 inches olive oil (4 to 6 cups) in a heavy-bottomed stockpot or a countertop fryer to 360°F. Fry the strips, 4 or 5 at a time,

taking care not to overcrowd the pot. The *cenci* should be puffed and lightly golden brown on each side.

Drain the *cenci* briefly on paper towels, then sprinkly them generously with confectioners' sugar on both sides. They are best served immediately.

ORANGE "FRIED CREAM"
crema fritta al'arancia

I don't know about you, but the mere pairing of the word "fried" with the word "cream" makes me happy. Granted, it sounds a bit odd, but it is really quite simple: make a thick pastry cream with milk, sugar, egg yolks, flour, and some flavorings, cool it, cut it into shapes, roll it in bread crumbs, and fry it golden brown and crispy. (You can make your own untoasted bread crumbs by processing cubes of slightly stale Italian bread, crusts trimmed, in a food processor or blender.) This treat is a specialty of the Veneto region, but as with so many other dishes, you will find versions of it in the southern regions of Italy as well. Kids love it; not only can they help roll it in bread crumbs, but it is completely transportable.

The key to the ultimate enjoyment of crema fritta *is not to overthink it or inject it with fancy ingredients or methodology. Like so many other traditional Italian dishes, it has withstood the test of time because it was fine to begin with. About the only liberty I have taken is to use some orange zest and vanilla. Make this for your family as a surprise treat on a lazy Saturday afternoon and you will send them to a little corner of heaven.* MAKES 20 TO 24 PIECES

2 cups whole milk	4 large eggs, separated
¼ cup plus 2 tablespoons granulated sugar	About 2 cups fine, untoasted, unflavored
Pinch of kosher salt	bread crumbs, preferably made from sturdy
Finely grated zest of 1 large orange	Italian bread
1 teaspoon pure vanilla extract	Olive oil, for frying
1 cup unbleached all-purpose flour	Confectioners' sugar, for dusting

Place the milk, ¼ cup sugar, salt, orange zest, and vanilla extract in a medium saucepan and place over low heat. Measure the flour into a medium bowl and set aside. In another bowl, whisk the egg yolks with the remaining 2 tablespoons sugar.

When the milk comes to a boil, remove it from the heat. Slowly and carefully whisk half of it into the egg yolks, then add that mixture to the pan and whisk well. Add the flour, whisking vigorously and thoroughly to remove any lumps. Place the pan over low heat again and simmer, whisking, until the mixture thickens to the consistency of stiff pudding, 2 to 3 minutes.

If you have a marble countertop, pour the *crema* directly onto it. Or pour it onto a baking sheet that has been lightly greased with butter or olive oil. Use a spatula to spread it into an even layer about 1 inch thick. Immediately press some plastic wrap onto the surface of the *crema* to prevent a skin from forming, and allow the *crema* to cool on the marble counter or place the baking sheet in the refrigerator to chill. In the meantime, place the bread crumbs in a shallow dish.

When the *crema* is completely cool, use a sharp knife to cut it into shapes, such as diamonds, circles, triangles, or finger-length rectangles. In a medium bowl, lightly beat the egg whites with a fork until they are foamy. Dip the *crema* shapes into the whites to coat, then roll them in the bread crumbs to coat evenly.

Heat about 1 inch (3 cups) olive oil in a heavy skillet and fry the *crema* shapes in batches until golden brown on both sides, about 1 minute per side.

Drain on paper towels and dust with confectioners' sugar. Serve the *crema fritta* warm but not piping hot.

FLORENTINE DOUGHNUTS WITH VANILLA CUSTARD
bomboloni con crema di vaniglia

I dedicate this recipe to my good friends German and Leah Casati. German grew up in Florence and met his American wife, Leah, when she was studying there during college. Needless to say, they learned a thing or two about bomboloni, *the yeast doughnuts found in many a Florentine café. When I featured these on the menu at Babbo, German and Leah pronounced them the best* bomboloni *they had ever had.*

MAKES 20 TO 25 *BOMBOLONI*

½ cup warm water

5 teaspoons (2 packages) active dry yeast (not fast-rising)

1¼ cups plus ½ teaspoon granulated sugar

¾ cup whole milk

4½ cups unbleached all-purpose flour, plus more for kneading

1½ cups cake flour

1 tablespoon kosher salt

1 teaspoon ground cinnamon

½ teaspoon ground nutmeg

4 large eggs

8 tablespoons (1 stick/4 ounces) unsalted butter, well softened

Olive oil, for frying

Confectioners' sugar, for dusting

Vanilla Custard (recipe follows), for dipping

Place the warm water in a small bowl and sprinkle the yeast over it. Add ½ teaspoon granulated sugar and stir to dissolve the yeast. Set the bowl aside and allow the yeast to proof until foamy, about 4 minutes. Place the milk in a small saucepan or a microwaveable container and heat until warm to the touch.

Place the all-purpose flour, cake flour, remaining 1¼ cups granulated sugar, salt, and spices in the bowl of an electric mixer and use the paddle attachment to combine them thoroughly. Make a well in the center of the bowl and add the yeast mixture, warm milk, and eggs. Beat on medium until a smooth dough forms. Beat in the butter, then remove the paddle and beat in enough additional flour on low speed to make a smooth, soft, somewhat elastic dough. Switch to medium speed and mix for 2 to 3 minutes. Turn the dough into a greased bowl and cover with plastic wrap. Place the bowl in a warm, draft-free spot and allow the dough to rise until doubled, about 2 hours.

Gently deflate the dough by pulling it from the sides of the bowl and turn it onto a floured surface. Pat or roll the dough to a thickness of about ½ inch. Using a fluted or plain-edged round cutter 1 to 1½ inches in diameter, cut the doughnuts. Place them on a baking sheet dusted with flour and cover them with plastic wrap. Allow them to proof while you heat the oil.

Heat 6 inches (4 to 6 cups) olive oil to 360°F in a large, heavy-bottomed pot. Fry the doughnuts in batches, 4 or 5 at a time, in the hot oil, gently turning them until they are golden brown on both sides and cooked in the center.

Drain the doughnuts on paper towels. While they are still warm, sprinkle them generously with confectioners' sugar on both sides. The *bomboloni* are best served warm, with vanilla custard alongside for dipping.

VANILLA CUSTARD

crema di vaniglia

MAKES ABOUT 2 CUPS

1½ cups whole milk
1½ cups heavy cream
1 vanilla bean
1 teaspoon pure vanilla extract
¾ cup plus 1 tablespoon granulated sugar
12 large egg yolks
Pinch of kosher salt
1 tablespoon cornstarch

Pour the milk and cream into a medium saucepan. Split the vanilla bean lengthwise, scrape the seeds with the blunt side of a small knife, and add them to the pan along with the bean and vanilla extract. Add ½ cup sugar and place the pan over medium heat.

Meanwhile, place the egg yolks in a large bowl. Whisk in the remaining ¼ cup and 1 tablespoon sugar, followed by the salt and cornstarch. When the milk mixture comes to a boil, remove the pan from the heat. Slowly pour some of the mixture into the egg yolks, whisking constantly. Add the rest of the hot liquid to the eggs, whisking constantly, then transfer the mixture back to the saucepan and place it over low heat. Keep whisking it to prevent the custard from scorching or overcooking.

When the custard has thickened somewhat, remove it from the heat and strain it through a chinois or fine-meshed sieve into a bowl. Place the bowl in a larger bowl of ice water to chill it, whisking occasionally as the custard cools. Press a piece of plastic wrap onto the surface of the custard to prevent a skin from forming. Refrigerate the custard in an airtight container until ready to serve.

NEAPOLITAN DOUGHNUTS WITH
WARM CHOCOLATE SAUCE
zeppollini

These little ring shaped doughnuts will be familiar to anyone who has strolled through an Italian street fair. Zeppole are the fried dough of southern Italy, especially associated with the city of Naples. The batter is similar to that of cream puffs, but it is piped into small rings and chilled before being plunged into the hot oil. The doughnuts are light and crispy and pair perfectly with a puddle of warm bittersweet chocolate. It is important to pipe the doughnuts onto a baking sheet that has been greased, lined with parchment, and then generously greased again, so they will slide off easily with the assistance of an offset spatula or butter knife. I think of this as a buddy project—one person to do the frying and one to do the sugar-dusting. There is a brief window of opportunity to reheat the doughnuts if necessary, but they are best enjoyed as soon as possible after they come out of the oil. Since you fry them in batches, you can place all the zeppollini on a baking sheet in a hot (375°F) oven for 2 to 3 minutes before serving. **MAKES 35 ZEPPOLLINI**

¾ cups water

6 tablespoons (¾ stick/3 ounces) unsalted butter, cut into 1-inch pieces

3 tablespoons granulated sugar

½ teaspoon kosher salt

1¼ cups unbleached all-purpose flour

4 large eggs, cold

½ teaspoon ground cinnamon

¼ teaspoon ground nutmeg

2 teaspoons pure vanilla extract

Finely grated zest of 1 medium lemon

Olive oil, for frying

Confectioners' sugar, for dusting

Warm Chocolate Sauce (recipe follows), for dipping

In a small saucepan, combine the water, butter, 1 tablespoon granulated sugar, and salt. Bring the mixture to a full rolling boil over medium heat, then remove the pan from the heat and dump the flour in all at once. Stir the mixture quickly with a heatproof spatula to form a thick pastelike dough. Return the pan to the heat and continue to cook the dough over medium heat for 2 minutes, constantly spreading it, regathering it, and turning it over the surface of the pan with the spatula.

Transfer the dough to the bowl of an electric mixer fitted with the paddle attachment. Beat on medium speed to release some of the heat. When the steam dissipates, beat the cold eggs into the dough, one at a time; do not add another egg until the previous one has been completely beaten into the dough. When the last egg has been incorporated, add the remaining 2 tablespoons of granulated sugar and the spices, vanilla extract, and lemon zest. Continue beating on medium speed until the dough becomes glossy and thick, about 1½ to 2 minutes.

Scrape the dough into a piping bag fitted with a large round tip. Prepare two large baking sheets by greasing them lightly with olive oil, lining them with parchment paper, and brushing them generously with more olive oil. Pipe the dough into 2- to 2½-inch rings on the lined baking sheet, spacing the rings about ½ inch apart. Place the baking sheets in the refrigerator to chill the *zeppollini* for at least 2 hours. They should be firm enough to retain their shape when lifted off the baking sheet with a butter knife or offset spatula; they will be soft but manageable.

While the *zeppollini* are chilling make the chocolate sauce.

In a medium-sized, heavy-bottomed saucepan, heat 8 inches (about 2 quarts) of olive oil to 360°F. Working in batches, drop 4 to 6 *zeppollini* into the hot oil carefully and quickly; they will sink at first and then rise quickly to the surface. When they are pale golden brown on the bottom side, gently flip them with a pair of tongs or a slotted spoon. Continue turning them in the oil until they are a rich golden brown and crispy, then remove them to drain on layers of paper towels.

Quickly and generously dust the *zeppollini* with confectioners' sugar and serve hot with warm chocolate sauce.

WARM CHOCOLATE SAUCE

MAKES ABOUT 1 1/2 CUPS
8 ounces bittersweet or semisweet chocolate, chopped
½ cup (1 stick/4 oz.) unsalted butter
½ cup warm water
1 tablespoon corn syrup
1 tablespoon rum, brandy or grappa (optional)

Place the chopped chocolate and butter in a medium heatproof bowl and place it over a pan of simmering water, whisking the ingredients together until smooth. Whisk in the water and the corn syrup, then the rum, brandy or grappa, if desired.

Serve warm. The chocolate sauce may be refrigerated, covered, and reheated.

FRYING BASICS

There aren't a lot of rules to follow for great frying, nor is there any particularly fancy equipment to buy. All you need is a heavy, deep pot. Cast iron is a particularly good choice, since it retains its heat better than anything else I have tried. Le Creuset makes cast-iron cookware coated in enamel; it is attractive and the most functional cookware you will ever use, and it's available in a range of sizes. I like their Dutch ovens for frying. Lodge brand cast-iron cookware is another great choice; the pieces are inexpensive and will last a lifetime. I have a deep cast-iron frying pan I inherited from my grandmother, and I can't imagine my kitchen without it. It is older than I am and still the most versatile and useful pan I own, always reliable, consistent, and easy to clean.

The other indispensable tool for frying is a good candy or deep-fry thermometer. I prefer the kind that clips onto the side of the pot, which is suitable for candy making as well as deep-frying. A good thermometer makes it possible to monitor the heat of the oil as you fry and turn the heat up or down as needed. Never crowd the pan when frying, especially doughy items like doughnuts and fritters. Crowding will cause the temperature of the oil to drop, and the food will absorb too much oil and taste greasy.

A Chinese skimmer with a wooden handle is handy for removing delicate foods from the oil. I've seen some of those ingenious little countertop fryers, and if I had more than 6 inches of available counter space in my apartment, I would surely own one.

The golden rule to follow is always to fry in good olive oil. It doesn't necessarily have to be extra-virgin, though this is certainly my preference; a good, mild virgin oil works just fine for frying. As in cooking only with wine you would happily drink, never fry with an oil that you would not be willing to toss into a salad or sop up with a piece of bread. Remember the mantra of safety first: never try to drain or dispose of oil while it is still hot; allow it to cool completely first.

Turn your foods often while frying, using tongs or a long-handled slotted spoon; if you allow them to cook too much on one side without flipping them, soft things like fritters become misshapen. Drain fried sweets on absorbent paper or cloth towels as soon as you remove them from the oil, and though some doughnuts and fritters reheat nicely, it's best to eat them as soon as possible, dusted with plenty of confectioners' sugar.

CREAM PUFFS WITH RUM ZABAIONE
bigne al rhum

Bigne *are puffs of eggy dough, the Italian equivalent of pâte à choux, or what we know as cream puffs. In this case they are filled with a chilled* crema zabaione *made with rum and* vin santo *in place of the traditional marsala. The components may require a number of steps, but they are not at all complicated. You can make the dough up to 2 hours before frying the cream puffs; simply store it in an airtight container in the refrigerator. The zabaione also holds nicely in the refrigerator for several hours. Fry and fill the* bigne *no more than 1 hour before you want to serve them—if they are made earlier, they will become soggy (but they will still be delicious). The* bigne *are also wonderful baked, as in the variation on page 215. An elegant dessert, these* bigne *deserve a delicate china plate and a pretty, lacy doily.*
MAKES APPROXIMATELY 15 *BIGNE*

FOR THE RUM *ZABAIONE*

1 cup heavy cream

4 large egg yolks

¼ cup granulated sugar

1 tablespoon *vin santo*

1 tablespoon dark rum

FOR THE *BIGNE*

½ cup water

4 tablespoons (½ stick/2 ounces) unsalted
   butter, cut into pieces

2 tablespoons granulated sugar

¼ teaspoon kosher salt

¾ cup unbleached all-purpose flour

3 large eggs, cold

¼ teaspoon baking powder

½ teaspoon pure vanilla extract

Olive oil, for frying

Confectioners' sugar, for dusting

To make the rum *zabaione:* In an electric mixer fitted with the whisk attachment, whip the heavy cream on medium speed until stiff peaks form. Place the bowl in the refrigerator to chill the cream.

Bring several inches of water to a simmer in a saucepan big enough to hold a stainless steel or copper mixing bowl. In the mixing bowl, whisk the egg yolks very well with the sugar, *vin santo,* and rum. Place the bowl over the simmering water; the water should not touch the bottom of the bowl. Whisk the mixture constantly, keeping the water at a low simmer. The egg yolk mixture will increase in volume and lighten in color as you whisk. If it seems that the egg yolks are cooking, causing small bits of cooked egg to appear, remove the bowl from the pan of water and continue whisking

(continued on next page)

for a minute or so off the heat, then replace it and continue whisking. The *zabaione* is cooked when it mounds and holds its shape when dropped from the whisk, 5 to 7 minutes.

Remove the bowl from the saucepan and continue to whisk the *zabaione* until it is completely cool. Transfer the *zabaione* to the clean bowl of an electric mixer with a whisk attachment and whip it at medium-high speed until it is completely cool.

Using a whisk, fold one-third of the cooled *zabaione* into the chilled whipped cream until thoroughly combined. Fold the remaining *zabaione* into the cream mixture and combine thoroughly. Cover the *crema zabaione* with plastic wrap and chill it thoroughly in the refrigerator while you make the *bigne*.

To make the *bigne*: In a large saucepan, heat the water, butter, 1 tablespoon granulated sugar, and salt over medium heat until the butter is melted and the water is simmering. Add the flour all at once and use a heat-resistant spatula to combine the flour and water into a thick paste. Lower the heat and cook the paste, spreading it along the bottom of the pan and gathering it up into a ball. Repeat this procedure for 1 minute, until the paste appears dull and dry and has begun to stick to the bottom of the pan. Turn off the heat.

Immediately transfer the paste to a bowl. Using an electric mixer fitted with the whisk attachment, beat the cold eggs into the paste on medium speed, one at a time. Incorporate each egg fully into the dough before adding the next. Scrape down the sides of the bowl after each addition. Beat in the remaining 1 tablespoon granulated sugar, the baking powder, and the vanilla extract on low speed until they are incorporated, then switch to medium-high speed and continue to beat the dough until it is cool and glossy, about 2 minutes.

In a medium heavy-bottomed saucepan, heat 8 inches (about 2 quarts) of olive oil to 360°F. Working carefully and quickly, drop 4 or 5 rounded teaspoonfuls of the dough into the hot oil. They will sink at first and then rise rapidly to the surface. When they are pale golden brown on the bottom, gently flip them with a pair of tongs or a slotted spoon. Continue turning them in the oil until they are a rich golden brown and crispy, then remove them to drain on paper towels. Immediately poke each puff with the tip of a sharp knife to allow the steam inside to escape. Repeat with the remaining dough, working in batches.

To serve the *bigne*: Split each puff in half, making a top and a bottom. Place a generous dollop of the rum *zabaione* on the bottom of each one, then replace the top. Dust the cream puffs with confectioners' sugar. Chill the filled puffs for up to 30 minutes before serving.

VARIATION: You can bake the cream puffs instead of frying them. After you have beaten the dough until it is cool, transfer it to a pastry bag fitted with a large (no. 6 or higher) plain round tip. Pipe ¾-inch mounds of the dough 1 inch apart onto a baking sheet lined with parchment paper. You may also drop the mixture by rounded teaspoonfuls onto a greased baking sheet, 1 inch apart. Sprinkle the tops with pinches of raw sugar.

Bake the cream puffs at 400°F until they are puffed and golden brown, about 18 minutes, rotating the baking sheet after 10 minutes to ensure that they brown evenly. Turn off the oven and prop open the door to release some of the heat. Leave the cream puffs in the oven for 10 minutes more. Remove the baking sheet from the oven and immediately pierce each cream puff with the tip of a small knife to allow the steam to escape. Serve as directed above.

WAYS WITH FRUIT
con frutta

T HE DESSERTS I REMEMBER MOST FROM MY CHILDHOOD ARE NOT desserts at all but heaping platters of fresh fruit that were presented at the end of every meal. There was always a selection of fruits to choose from— melons and grapes, apples, pears, peaches or nectarines. Every now and again, a whole pineapple would appear as a special surprise. At the end of family dinners with my grandparents, fruit would be a segue to whatever sweet *biscotti* my grandmother had made for me, my brother, my sister, and our cousins. No matter what, my grandfather insisted that we have fruit after every meal; he firmly believed it helped us digest. Since it was Grandpa that stood between us and our cookies, we quickly learned that it was in our best interest to eat our fruit with gusto and smiles planted firmly on our faces. Some of my fondest memories of my grandfather are of watching him precisely and methodically carve a fresh pear at the dinner table, divide it in to wedges, and stab them one by one, with the tip of his paring knife to hand across to each of his grandchildren. There was often a bowl of nuts and a nut-cracker at the table as well, along with some imported Italian cheeses, perhaps some *caciocavallo* or *Pecorino Pepato*.

It is with those memories in mind that I have created some of my favorite recipes featuring fresh or dried fruits. They span the seasons, making it easy for you to serve them when the time is exactly right and the fruit is at its peak of availability. Feel free to experiment where it is appropriate, substituting whatever local fruits are outstanding where you live or catch your eye at the market. Be mindful of which fruits are most interchangeable: berries can usually be mixed with ease, and stone fruits, such as peaches, plums, apricots, and cherries, can trade places with intriguing and tasty results. The same concept applies to citrus fruits, although it may be necessary to adjust the sugar in the recipe.

Wine and fruit can often be used to enhance each other, especially bubbly and fizzy wines such as prosecco and Moscato d'Asti. Nothing is more refreshing on a warm day than slicing some fresh peaches, nectarines, or plums, tossing them in a large bowl with a touch of sugar, and dousing it all with a bottle of sparkling wine. Serve with toothpicks for fishing out the slices of fruit, plenty of napkins to catch the drips, and glasses for the fruit-infused wine. Indulgence was never simpler.

STRAWBERRIES IN CHIANTI WITH BLACK PEPPER RICOTTA CREAM
fragole al vino con ricotta e pepe

This is a fantastic summer dessert; make it when the strawberries are in their peak season, from June through August. The sweet ricotta cream spiked with crushed black peppercorns is a recipe that I first contributed to The Babbo Cookbook, *and it is an especially good partner for the wine-infused berries. The sweetness of the strawberries, the zing of the black pepper, and the full, fruity taste of a good Chianti come together in perfect unison. Be sure to crack whole peppercorns for this recipe; pepper becomes spicier the more finely it is ground, and ground pepper would be far too strong. You can easily crack peppercorns by smashing them with the bottom of a small, heavy sauté pan. The ricotta cream may be made 3 to 4 hours in advance. Keep it chilled in the refrigerator, covered with a sheet of plastic wrap.*

MAKES 6 SERVINGS

2 pints ripe, fragrant strawberries
   (about 1 pound)
½ cup granulated sugar
1 cup Chianti Classico

1 cup heavy cream
1¼ cups fresh whole-milk ricotta
2 teaspoons black peppercorns, cracked

About 2 hours before serving the dessert, lightly rinse the strawberries if they are sandy and place them in a single layer on a clean dish towel to dry. Remove the hulls, then cut the berries in quarters or in half lengthwise, according to size, and place them in a large bowl. Sprinkle 2 tablespoons sugar over the berries and toss them to distribute. Pour the Chianti Classico over them. Using a large spoon, gently turn the berries to coat them with the wine. Place the bowl in the refrigerator to chill, giving them a gentle toss every so often.

Place the heavy cream and the remaining 6 tablespoons sugar in the bowl of an electric mixer and use the whisk attachment on medium speed to beat the cream until soft peaks form. Add the ricotta and black pepper and briefly beat until the mixture is combined and makes firm peaks.

To serve, place a generous spoonful of the ricotta cream in each of six dessert glasses and spoon some of the berries and their juices alongside and over the top.

BALATON CHERRIES WITH GRAPPA
AND MASCARPONE
ciliege con grappa e mascarpone

Balatons are a sweet-tart cherry native to Hungary; they made their debut in America in the mid-1980s. They are firmer and sweeter than the sour cherries widely grown in Michigan, the Pacific Northwest, and New York State. Balatons are generously sized and plump, with a deep, pink-red, translucent hue; their flavor is fuller than that of a sour cherry and more delicate than that of Bing cherries. When Balaton cherries ripen, they naturally separate from their stems, forming a cellular layer at the stem end that seals off the fruit and protects it from air. If you live in Michigan or the Upper Midwest, you are lucky; there, more and more family-run orchards growing Balaton cherries appear every year, and in the summer you can find the fruits in local farmers' markets. Elsewhere, you can order them directly from some of the growers.

I adore this simple and elegant dessert. When I unexpectedly received a case of Balaton cherries, I came up with this preparation on the fly and offered it as a special one evening at Babbo. It sold out within an hour. In the absence of Balatons, sweet dark cherries are a fine substitute. When mint leaves are chopped with a knife, they will oxidize and turn black quickly, so tear them with your fingers to keep the color and release the flavor simultaneously. MAKES 6 SERVINGS

1½ pints Balaton cherries or sweet dark
    cherries, pitted
¼ cup plus 2 tablespoons granulated sugar
½ cup grappa

10–12 fresh mint leaves
1 cup mascarpone
½ cup heavy cream
1 vanilla bean

Place the pitted cherries in a large bowl. Sprinkle ¼ cup sugar on them and pour on the grappa, using a large slotted spoon to toss the ingredients together. Tear the mint leaves in half and add them to the bowl, tossing again to coat the cherries with the mint. Place the bowl in a cool place or in the refrigerator for 2 hours, stirring now and again to distribute the juices evenly.

About 35 minutes before serving the cherries, place the mascarpone, heavy cream, and remaining 2 tablespoons sugar in the bowl of an electric mixer. Split the vanilla bean lengthwise, scrape out the seeds with the blunt side of a small knife, and add them to the cream. Whip the ingredients together on medium speed until firm peaks form. Chill the mascarpone cream for 30 minutes.

To serve, spoon a portion of the cherries into each of six dessert glasses. Top with a dollop of the mascarpone cream and spoon on some of the juices. Serve with *biscotti* alongside, if desired.

WHITE PEACH AND PROSECCO GELATINA
gelatina di prosecco con pesche

My mother loved making fruity gelatin molds, and I can't help but smile and remember some of her concoctions whenever I make this. My take on Jell-O elevates it a notch or two: delicate white peaches are suspended in a pale golden gelatina *made with a dry, crisp prosecco. This echoes the flavors of the classic Bellini cocktail, a blissful marriage of fresh peach nectar and prosecco that was invented at Harry's Bar in Venice.* **MAKES 6 SERVINGS**

1½ cups granulated sugar

1¼ cups water

1 750ml bottle prosecco

8 sheets gelatin (see page 127)

2 large, ripe white peaches

2 teaspoons freshly squeezed lemon juice

In a medium saucepan, stir together the sugar and water until the sugar has dissolved. Add the prosecco. Bring the mixture to a boil over medium heat, then lower the heat to a simmer. Continue simmering for 10 minutes to boil off all the alcohol. Remove the pan from the heat and allow the mixture to cool for 15 minutes.

In the meantime, in a medium bowl, immerse the gelatin sheets in cold water to soften them. When they are soft, remove from the water, gently pat them dry, and whisk them into the warm prosecco mixture. Transfer the mixture to a bowl. Refrigerate the *gelatina* until it is cold and beginning to thicken 1½ to 2 hours; it should be wobbly when shaken, not fully set, but strong enough to suspend the peaches.

While the *gelatina* is chilling, peel and pit the peaches. Cut them into halves and then into quarters. Slice the quarters across the length to make small triangles. Place them in a bowl and toss them with the lemon juice to prevent discoloration.

As soon as the *gelatina* has begun to thicken, add the peaches and divide the mixture evenly among 6 dessert or juice glasses. Refrigerate until fully set, at least 2 hours.

DREAMING-OF-SUMMER ORANGES

I crave this presentation of oranges, usually in January. It cannot be merely a coincidence that the dead of winter is the height of citrus season. When snow is on the ground and winter winds are whipping, I need to get away, even if only in my imagination. I want to pretend I am on a beach in sun-drenched Sicily, or on a veranda overlooking the Amalfi Coast, relaxing with a dark-haired, handsome Italian soccer player. A large platter of orange wedges drizzled with a fruity green olive oil and sprinkled with sea salt is ultimately transporting. Cara Cara oranges are a navel variety that have pink-hued flesh, a low acid content, and bright sweetness; ask for them in your local specialty produce store. If you can't find them, be sure to use the sweetest oranges you can get your hands on; otherwise the sea salt will be too dominant. MAKES 2 TO 4 SERVINGS

3–4 sweet navel oranges, preferably Cara Cara

1–2 tablespoons granulated sugar

Highest-quality extra-virgin olive oil, for drizzling

Generous pinch of large-crystal sea salt

Cut the oranges into thick wedges, leaving the skin on. Place the wedges in a large bowl and sprinkle them with sugar to taste, tossing them to distribute and dissolve the sugar. Let the oranges sit for 5 to 10 minutes to release their juices.

Transfer the orange wedges and their juices to a shallow serving platter. Drizzle the oranges with extra-virgin olive oil. Just before eating them, sprinkle the orange sections with sea salt.

PALACINCHE WITH SUGAR PLUM JAM

These delicate pancakes are enjoyed not only in Friuli–Venezia Giulia but in neighboring Austria, Hungary, Istria, and Romania as well. One good way to eat them is filled with slightly sweetened ricotta or the finest fruit preserves. At Babbo, I fill them with sugar plum jam and top with a slivovitz-perfumed mascarpone cream. Slivovitz is a plum brandy; if you can't find it, try using Friulian grappa.

Do not attempt to make these crepes without using a blender, since it is nearly impossible to whisk the batter enough by hand to remove all the lumps. Also be sure to use a nonstick crepe pan for your palacinche—*they should be whisper-thin and lacy. You can make the jam, the crepe batter, and the mascarpone cream a day before cooking and serving the crepes.* **MAKES 4 TO 6 SERVINGS, WITH LEFTOVERS**

FOR THE SUGAR PLUM JAM
½ vanilla bean
1½ pounds ripe, pitted sugar plums or other small red-fleshed plums
¾ cup granulated sugar
2 tablespoons freshly squeezed lemon juice
½ cup water

FOR THE CREPES
½ cup whole milk
2 tablespoons cold water
2 large eggs
½ teaspoon pure vanilla extract
2 tablespoons granulated sugar

¼ teaspoon kosher salt
¼ teaspoon ground cinnamon
1 tablespoon slivowitz
¾ cup all-purpose flour
4 tablespoons (½ stick/2 ounces) unsalted butter, melted
Confectioners' sugar, for dusting

FOR THE PLUM-SCENTED MASCARPONE CREAM
1 cup mascarpone
¼ cup granulated sugar
½ cup heavy cream
2 tablespoons slivowitz

To make the sugar plum jam: Split the ½ vanilla bean and scrape out the seeds with the blunt edge of a small knife. Place the plums, sugar, lemon juice, water, and the vanilla seeds and bean in a medium saucepan. Cook over low heat until the fruit is soft and the juices have thickened somewhat, about 25 minutes. Remove from the heat and allow the jam to cool completely. The jam may be made up to 2 days in advance; store it in the refrigerator in an airtight container.

To make the crepes: Place all the ingredients except the melted butter in a blender and blend on high speed until lump-free and smooth, about 1 minute. Add the melted butter and blend for another 20 seconds to incorporate it thoroughly. Allow the batter to sit at room temperature for about 30 minutes before making the crepes.

In the meantime, make the mascarpone cream: Place all the ingredients in the bowl of an electric mixer and use the whisk attachment to beat them together on medium speed until soft peaks form. Chill the cream while you cook the crepes.

To cook the crepes: Heat an 8- or 10-inch nonstick sauté pan or crepe pan over medium heat until very hot and spray it lightly with vegetable cooking spray. Pour in only enough batter to coat the bottom of the pan when it is swirled around; the batter should not pool in the center, or the crepe will be too thick and gummy. When the edges turn golden brown, carefully loosen the crepe with a heatproof rubber spatula, grab the edges with your fingers, and quickly flip it to cook on the other side. When it is a pale golden brown, remove it from the pan and lay it on a parchment-lined baking sheet. Continue with the remaining batter, slightly overlapping the crepes on the parchment paper and layering additional crepes with another sheet of parchment.

To serve: Lightly dust the serving plates with confectioners' sugar. Lay a warm crepe off-center on each plate and spread about 1 tablespoon sugar plum jam on it, then fold it over to create an attractive appearance. Dust with additional confectioners' sugar and serve with a dollop of mascarpone cream.

HONEY-BAKED FIGS STUFFED WITH WALNUTS
fichi ripieni

When I was growing up, there was always an aluminum foil–lined coffee can full of these baked figs in our pantry. My mom would bring them out after dinner on Sundays, to enjoy with sliced raw fennel, caciocavallo cheese, and fresh fruit. Sometimes I would sneak to the coffee can and swipe one of the stuffed figs, always thinking that I had put one over on my unsuspecting mom. She definitely knew what I was up to, and that I loved those figs, because we never seemed to run out of them. MAKES 12 STUFFED FIGS

12 large dried Calimyrna figs

¾–1 cup walnut halves

1 cup *vin santo* or other slightly sweet Italian dessert wine

2 tablespoons honey

Two 3–4-inch-long freshly peeled strips orange zest

Preheat the oven to 325°F and position a rack in the center.

Make sure the figs are whole and intact. Starting at the top of one fig, near the stem, make a vertical slit in the side with a paring knife, ending at the bottom. Repeat with the other figs. Insert 3 or 4 walnut halves into each fig; the trick is to stuff the fig with enough nuts to fill it but not puncture the skin on the opposite side from the slit. Close the slit over the nuts, encasing them.

Place the figs in a baking dish that will just comfortably accommodate them, such as a 9-inch square or round cake pan. Pour the *vin santo* into the dish and drizzle the honey over the top of the figs. Add the orange zest strips to the pan.

Bake the figs, uncovered, for 20 to 25 minutes, turning them once and basting them with the bubbling juices, which should reduce by half. Remove the figs from the oven and allow the pan to cool completely on a wire rack.

When they have cooled completely, you may store them in an airtight container at room temperature for up to 2 weeks. They may also be gently reheated and served slightly warm. The stuffed figs are excellent served as an accompaniment to an assortment of cheeses and fresh fruit.

SWEET FRIULI

From the Alps in the west to the sea in the east, Friuli–Venezia Giulia is a tiny region with a huge identity, marked by an uneasy history and a culture that borrows from its borders with Slovenia, Austria, and Croatia. The cuisine reflects these diverse influences and terrain.

Stone fruits are a source of particular pride among Friulian farmers and are an integral part of the local cooking. Fruits often appear in savory dishes, as Friulian cooks have long recognized the endless possibilities presented by the abundance of peaches, plums, and figs, cherries and apricots, apples and pears.

Native farmers of Friuli–Venezia Giulia are acutely aware of the particular climate and topography of individual microregions and how those characteristics are perfectly suited to cultivating a variety of magnificent fruits. The Italian-Slovenian border region of Collio originally produced cherries that were prized throughout Europe. As viticulture began to dominate the area, the cherry trees were cut down to make room for grapes, a crop of higher value to farmers as world-class winemaking began to prosper in the latter half of

the 20th century. Cherry trees are still present in smaller numbers, producing their exquisite crop for local consumption in hotels, restaurants, and, most important, homes. Cormons is another microregion known for producing some of the finest stone fruits grown in Europe. Succulent apricots and plums as well as cherries, grapes, and figs from Cormons are prized for their complexity and uniquely fragrant sweetness. In Carnia, apples and pears are abundant and appear in desserts such as the Austro-Hungarian–influenced *strucolo*, or strudel, in sweet omelets, and softly cooked alongside gnocchi, polenta, and risotto. Local berries are used in sauces and made into intense fruit preserves and heady vinegars.

Friuli–Venezia Giulia exports many of its products to the rest of the world—wonderful prosciutto San Daniele, the finest roasted espresso beans from Illy and Cremcaffé, rich and nutty Montasio DOP cheese, not to mention some of the finest white wines produced in Italy. The bounty of the fruit harvest, however, is harder to find on this side of the world. All the more reason to visit Friuli–Venezia Giulia someday.

SWEET APPLE OMELET
omelet con mele

If you have never tried a sweet omelet, you are in for a treat. This kind of omelet is common in the northernmost regions of Italy, such as Trentino Alto Adige and Friuli–Venezia Guilia, which both have cuisines that have been greatly influenced by their Slavic, Austrian, and Swiss neighbors. The combination of fluffy soft eggs, tender spiced apples, and warm honey butter is a winner. The Sugar Plum Jam on page 224 would also be a wonderful filling, as would any excellent store-bought or homemade jam. The obvious choice is to serve this sweet, tender omelet for break-fast or as part of a brunch menu, but I would not hesitate to enjoy it for lunch or dinner. MAKES 2 TO 4 SERVINGS

2 medium Golden Delicious, Rome, or Empire apples	1 tablespoon grappa
3 tablespoons extra-virgin olive oil	2 tablespoons unsalted butter
2 tablespoons granulated sugar	1 tablespoon honey
¼ teaspoon ground cinnamon	4–5 large eggs
	Confectioners' sugar, for dusting

Peel and core the apples, cut them into quarters, then cut the quarters into slices. Heat a large sauté pan over medium heat and add the olive oil, followed by the apples. Sauté the apples until they just begin to turn soft, translucent, and tender, about 5 minutes. Add the sugar and cinnamon to the pan, shaking to coat the apples. Remove the pan from the heat and slowly add the grappa, then return the pan to low heat and let the apple mixture simmer for 2 to 3 minutes to cook off the alcohol and tender-ize the apples.

In a small saucepan, melt 1 tablespoon butter over low heat; do not allow it to bubble. Add the honey and swirl the pan to combine the butter and honey thoroughly. Set the pan aside, off the heat. Have ready a serving plate dusted with confectioners' sugar.

Crack the eggs into a medium bowl and whisk them until the yolks and whites are combined. In a nonstick 10-inch omelet pan, melt the remaining 1 tablespoon butter over medium heat, swirling it around to coat the bottom completely. When the butter begins to bubble, add the eggs. Use a fork or spatula to pull any cooked egg toward the center of the pan while tilting the pan to move uncooked egg to the edges. Continue moving the eggs around gently until all the eggs are cooked, 2 to 3 minutes. Very quickly, spoon some of the cooked apples into the center of the omelet in a straight line spanning the diameter of the omelet. Shake the pan to loosen the omelet completely, then fold one side of the omelet over the apples.

Quickly slide the omelet onto the sugar-dusted serving plate, folding it over on top of itself with the edge of the pan or a spatula. Immediately drizzle the warm honey-butter mixture evenly over the surface of the omelet, then dust it with confectioners' sugar.

Serve immediately, cutting the omelet into 2 large halves or 4 smaller quarters.

MEYER LEMON MARMALADE
marmellata di limone

Rounder than a lemon, Meyer lemons have a smooth, shiny, deep golden skin. The first thing you will notice when you slice into one is that the fruit has a deep, beguiling saffron hue, which is accompanied by complex flavor and a softer level of acidity than ordinary lemons have. Their flavor is distinctive—somewhat floral, evocative of a mandarin orange and a sweet lime.

Meyer lemons originated in China; they were discovered and brought to the United States by an American scientist of the same name working for the U.S. Department of Agriculture. Today they are primarily grown in Southern California, as well as in Florida and Texas, and their peak season is from late November to as late as April. When you can find them in season, treat yourself to a bagful and make this marmalade. If you are handy at canning, it makes a wonderful gift at Christmastime, packed in clear jars or glasses. I especially enjoy it with a young Pecorino or a soft, fresh goat cheese. **MAKES ABOUT 2 1/2 CUPS**

8 Meyer lemons

1 cup water

2 cups granulated sugar

Place 6 Meyer lemons in a large saucepan and add enough water to cover them. Place the saucepan over medium heat and bring the water and lemons to a boil. Lower the heat and simmer the lemons until they are fork-tender, about 20 minutes. Drain the water and allow the lemons to cool for about 20 minutes.

Squeeze the remaining 2 Meyer lemons and strain the juice of any seeds or pulp.

When the cooked lemons have cooled enough to handle, cut them in half. Scoop out the pulp and discard it. Cut the rinds in half, then into thin slices; cut the slices into ¼-inch dice.

Place the diced rinds, lemon juice, water, and sugar in a medium saucepan and stir to combine. Place the pan over low heat and bring the mixture to a simmer. Continue simmering until the rinds are soft and translucent and the liquid is thick and syrupy, about 15 minutes. Cool the marmalade completely before storing. In an airtight container, the marmalade will keep in the refrigerator for up to 2 weeks.

SPICED BLOOD ORANGE MARMALADE
marmellata di arancia rossa

I enjoy this brightly colored, tangy-sweet marmalade with both fresh and aged cheeses. If you happen to spot imported blood oranges from Sicily, snap them up; otherwise, blood oranges from California will work just fine (they appear in markets from December through March). The great thing about this marmalade is that it is so unbelievably easy to make. It is a good idea to chop the oranges by hand into small, even dice, but beyond that chore, all you do is throw the ingredients into a pan and let it simmer until the peel is translucent. The pink peppercorns and coriander add just the right spicy accent. MAKES ABOUT 2 CUPS

3 medium blood oranges	½ cup freshly squeezed lemon juice
2 cups granulated sugar	2 teaspoons whole coriander
½ cup water	1 tablespoon pink peppercorns

Slice the blood oranges with their skin into rounds, then cut the slices into small, even dice. Place the diced oranges in a large saucepan, then add the sugar, water, and lemon juice.

Finely grind the coriander and pink peppercorns in a spice mill or coffee grinder and stir them into the blood orange mixture. Place the saucepan over medium heat and bring the marmalade to a simmer, stirring occasionally to prevent the mixture from scorching.

Cook the marmalade until the peel of the blood oranges is tender and translucent and the liquid is thick and syrupy, about 20 minutes. Allow it to cool before storing. In an airtight container, the marmalade will keep in the refrigerator for up to 2 weeks.

CELEBRATIONS

feste

T O UNDERSTAND THE IMPORTANCE OF THE *SAGRA*, OR FESTIVAL, IN Italian life, you must first acknowledge a deeply rooted sense of community that lies within the heart of most Italians. Italy was unified as a country in 1861, but the notion of a single nation standing under a single flag has only partially crept into the consciousness of its people. The truth is that Italy is composed of thousands of individual communities, entities that have existed alongside each other for centuries within a relatively small geographic area.

These communities were established, destroyed, and reestablished by consecutive Etruscan, Greek, Roman, and Saracen civilizations. They have been subjected to the dominion of both close and distant neighbors as well as the invading armies of Turkish, Arabic, Norman, French, Spanish, and Austrian empires. Through all of this, the communities have survived, often in spite of their location in a topography that includes expansive beachfronts, snow-capped mountain peaks, gently rolling hills surrounding wide and open valleys, and deep, isolating gorges carved out of impenetrable rock and tufa. The bond of an Italian with his community is second only to that with his family, and it is with these two elements that Italians feel their deepest connections.

Festivals in Italy mark the rhythms of life, the seasons of the earth, the movements of the moon, stars, and sun; they commemorate political and social upheaval and express thanks for the gifts of divine intervention and blessings. The *sagra* is the festival of a country town or village, celebrating the wonders of nature and the bounty of the fertile earth. Other festivals celebrate the power and majesty of places that were once mighty city-states. The feast days of patron saints are celebrated in even the tiniest of villages, and political parties sponsor festivals to demonstrate their numbers and commitment to a common cause. Regardless of the theme or the size of the community, there is color, commotion, and of course an abundance of food. Flowerboxes are filled to overflowing, banners and flags are proudly flown, symbolic costumes from every time period imaginable are donned, and the *piazza* is transformed into a picnic site cum theatrical stage. There may be races, tournaments, parades, processions, and reenactments, and the mood can be raucous, solemn, and anything in between. The preparations may begin months beforehand, and the celebrations are not limited to a single day—some festivals last for weeks or even longer.

As a part of the rhythm of life in Italy, festivals are a way for people to make communal connections—with the past and with each other. I love making celebration foods for the very same reason: they help me connect with who I am, my cultural history, and the people I care for the most. This is probably my favorite chapter of this book, because it contains recipes that I turn to year after year with happy anticipation; they are my own way of celebrating the march of the seasons, the blessings of another year, and the precious connections that continue to sustain me.

SAFFRON

Saffron, or *zefferano*, was introduced to Italy through the spice trade with the Orient and, in a strange twist, was cultivated in certain areas for export back to the East. The most precious and expensive spice in the world, saffron threads are actually filaments—the dried stigmas, or female sex organs, of a particular crocus flower. Each flower contains only three of them, laden with the essential oils and pigments that give saffron its slightly bitter, metallic flavor and heady fragrance. The stigmas must be carefully harvested by hand, and to complicate matters further, harvesting can take place only in the morning, before the heat of the sun causes the flowers to wither. It takes a mind-boggling 75,000 flowers to make one pound of saffron threads.

The cultivation of saffron in San Gimignano in Tuscany can be traced as far back as A.D. 1200, when saffron exportation to eastern and African countries was documented. Saffron was used not only in cooking but also as a pigment to color paints for artists and as a dye for cloth merchants, and it was believed to have powerful medicinal properties. Saffron trade was so successful for several prominent families of San Gimignano that it helped finance the construction of their famous towers. During the height of the city's power as regional force, saffron was actually used as currency, reward, and even ransom. San Gimignano's decline came in the fourteenth century, when it was eventually brought under the rule of the duchy of Florence. The decline of the saffron trade came a bit later, around 1600.

An enterprising Dominican monk introduced saffron to the city-state of L'Aquila in Abruzzo. The priest returned to Italy from Spain after spending time there during the Inquisition, convinced that the precious flowers would survive in the rugged plains of his homeland. He adapted the Spanish growing methods to produce what became known as the finest saffron available in the world, the so-called hair of angels. As with San

Gimignano, saffron became part of the history of the city itself. Venetian merchants acted as intermediaries in the trade of L'Aquila's saffron to Germans, and eventually L'Aquila gained a considerable amount of economic clout via its production and trade of saffron. As with San Gimignano, too, invasion and eventual foreign domination led to the decline of the saffron trade in L'Aquila in the mid-seventeenth century.

Thanks to the current renaissance of Italian cooking, what was once a nearly extinct local product has literally blossomed (pardon the pun) into a healthy export for the province of San Gimignano. _Zafferano di San Gimignano_ is once again being used throughout Italy and is even slowly being exported in small quantities to other countries. In 2003 the consortium of growers applied to the European Union for DOP status, which was granted in February 2005. The producers are hopeful that the superiority of their harvest will be noted, allowing the world export market to accept San Gimignano's saffron at levels that will enable competition with the major producers of other countries.

Italian saffron is most widely cultivated on the rugged island of Sardinia, in the province of San Savino Monreale. As in San Gimignano and L'Aquila, there is a long history of saffron farming here, dating back to the fifteenth century. A significant portion of Sardinian land is still devoted to saffron production, and saffron is featured in many traditional Sardinian dishes, both sweet and savory. In the province of Cagliari, it is used to flavor Murgia Villacidro Giallo, a popular digestive liqueur.

Saffron is not difficult to incorporate into a recipe. To extract flavor from the threads, soak them in water or milk and then add the intensely flavored liquid to your recipe. If the dish includes a liquid such as milk or cream, simply infuse the saffron into all or a portion of the recipe's measurement.

SARDINIAN SAFFRON AND POTATO DOUGHNUTS
zippulas

We have our Mardi Gras celebration in New Orleans, but I think Italians take Martedi Grasso, or Fat Tuesday, to a new level, especially in terms of eating. This is a day to worship all things fried, and throughout Italy local, traditional recipes for fritters, dumplings, and twisty bits of dough are made, plunged into hot oil, and devoured, crispy, hot, and dusted with confectioners' sugar. On the island of Sardinia, people enjoy these potato and saffron yeast doughnuts during Carnivale. The potato gives the zippulas a silky texture, and the saffron provides a final salute of brilliant orange-yellow before the more austere mood of Lent takes hold. Sardinians are likely to use their own local saffron, cultivated in the region of Cagliari, for these unusual treats.

When making any dumpling recipe that calls for a boiled potato, be sure to use baking potatoes, which have a lighter, fluffier consistency than waxy potatoes, which hold their shape and are better for roasting. A ricer is essential for breaking down the cooked potato to a texture that will perfectly accept the wet ingredients without making the dough gummy. This is not an everyday sort of recipe, but a way to honor and participate in a distinct cultural celebration. Make zippulas when you have a crowd ready and waiting to enjoy them while they are hot and fresh.

MAKES 20 TO 25 SMALL DOUGHNUTS

1 large baking potato	2 teaspoons kosher salt
1 medium orange	1 large egg
1 cup whole milk	¾ cup granulated sugar
1 teaspoon saffron threads	¼ cup grappa
3 teaspoons (1½ packages) active dry yeast	6 cups olive oil, for frying
4 cups unbleached all-purpose flour, plus more for kneading	Confectioners' sugar, for dusting

Boil the potato in salted water until it is tender when pierced with a knife. Drain the water and allow the potato to cool slightly, then peel off the skin. While the potato is still warm, put it through a ricer and spread the riced potato on a plate to cool completely.

In the meantime, zest the orange and squeeze the juice into a small bowl, straining out any seeds. You should have ½ cup of orange juice. Scald the milk in a small saucepan over medium heat and add the saffron. Remove the pan from the heat and allow the saffron to infuse and color the milk, whisking occasionally, until the milk has cooled to lukewarm, about 105°F. Whisk the yeast into the milk to dissolve it and allow the mixture to proof for 5 minutes.

Place the flour in a large bowl and combine it with the salt. Add the potato to the bowl. In a medium bowl, whisk the egg together with the sugar, orange juice and zest, and grappa, then add this mixture to the flour and potato, along with the warm milk and yeast mixture. Work the ingredients together with a fork, then by hand, forming a ball of dough. Transfer the dough to a lightly floured board and knead it, adding more flour if necessary, until the dough is smooth and elastic, about 2 minutes.

Place the dough in a greased bowl, turn it once to coat it, and cover the bowl with plastic wrap or a damp towel. Place the bowl in a warm place to rise until the dough has doubled in bulk, about 2 hours.

In a heavy-bottomed stockpot or countertop fryer, heat the olive oil to 360°F. Using your fingers, break off 1-inch pieces of dough, and roll them into balls with your palms. Fry the doughnuts in batches, 3 or 4 at a time, until they are golden brown and crispy, turning them to brown evenly.

Drain the doughnuts on paper towels, dust them with confectioners' sugar, and serve while warm.

CARNEVALE

In the depths of chilly winter, when the days are short on light and the long stretch of Lenten abstinence lies directly ahead, Italian cities let out a collective whoop and celebrate Carnevale. Depending on the region, the celebration can last for months, beginning right after Epiphany in January. A more compact version is *la settimana grassa*, or "the fat week," which begins on Thursday of the week prior to Ash Wednesday and ends with *Martedì Grasso*—Fat Tuesday, also known as Shrove Tuesday.

Venice's Carnevale has centuries of history to draw upon. In the mid-1500s, a curious event became an unofficial kickoff to the Venetian carnival. The "Flight of the Turk" first occurred one day in the square of San Marco, when a young Turkish acrobat precariously walked the length of a rope suspended from a boat docked in the Grand Canal to the belfry of the Campanile, or bell tower. Venetians were so awestruck by his courage and skill that the feat became an annual ceremony to celebrate the start of Carnevale, performed in front of the Doge's Palace and a crowd of enthusiastic spectators. Acrobats would train year-round to perform the dazzling act, but in 1759, one young man met his untimely demise in an accidental fall. The Flight of the Turk turned into the Flight of the Dove; a wooden dove was suspended over the crowd instead, sprinkling them with confetti and flowers.

Carnevale was a time of indulgence, an opportunity to practice the art of illusion and to lose oneself completely in revelry and abandon. Venice was already a city of sensual pleasure, but during Carnevale the rules of state and social station were disregarded. The citizens of *La Serenissima* would don elaborate masks and cloaks, not only to maintain the magical air of illusion but also to guard their anonymity during the no-holds-barred celebrations. One's sex or social class was of no consequence; the *palazzi* were lit up every night and open to all comers, and the public square, or *campo*, of each neighborhood became a gathering place for revelry.

The Venetian Carnevale faded somewhat when the Republic of Venice ended in 1798, and the tradition of wearing masks was alternately forbidden and allowed in subsequent periods, according to the whims of whatever regime was controlling the state. In 1979 the city revived its Carnevale tradition in a very successful, albeit controversial, attempt to draw tourists to the area during the slow winter season. Once again enthusiastic revelers from all parts of the world gather in Venice to don elaborate costumes and fanciful masks for a week of partying and parading. Carnevale masks have become popular souvenirs for tourists year-round, creating a robust business for the Venetian artisans who make them.

Viareggio is located on the northern coast of Tuscany, just north of Pisa. Although its celebration is not as old as Venice's, it is in some ways more elaborate, featuring fantastic parades with majestic and dazzling floats. Carnevale festivities began in Viareggio in 1873, taking on a somewhat political slant when a group of citizens decided to use the celebration to protest unfair tax policies and wore masks to conceal their identities. Today the parades always include the traditional lampooning of political and popular figures.

The magnificent floats are made by skilled craftsmen, who work all year on their creations. Originally the floats were constructed of wood and iron by the city's shipbuilders, but in the 1920s local artisans discovered the use of papier-mâché and found it a much better medium for their creativity. Viareggio's grand Carnevale celebration has survived two World Wars as well as a huge fire in the hangars that house the floats, in 1960. Despite the setbacks, the city has persevered, and today the celebration consists of five huge, televised parades held on five consecutive weekends before Lent. Viareggio heaves with tourists, and hotels are booked almost a year in advance of the big party.

Farther north, Carnevale celebrations take a bit of an odd turn in Ivrea, which lies in a bucolic green valley along the border of Piedmont and Val d'Aosta. During the Middle Ages the city was ruled by a series of brutal tyrants; the people of Ivrea repeatedly rose up against the lords, destroying their castles in violent acts of defiance. These uprisings are faithfully reenacted in the Battle of the Oranges, which features costumed "rebels" on foot hurling oranges at "guards," representing the armed guards of the castles. The guards stand in carts that are pulled by horses through five different *piazzas* in the historical

center, or *centro storico*, of the city. Anyone brave enough to wander the streets during these epic battles must wear a red cap to signify his or her status as a noncombatant; lightning-fast reflexes and well-honed duck-and-cover skills come in pretty handy as well.

Ivrea is awash in color during Carnevale, from the costumed cast of characters to the smashed and spattered remains of tons of oranges that are shipped from Sicily for the intense week of battles. What makes Ivrea's carnival so unique is that it is rooted in actual historical events and features characters based on real people. Violetta the Miller's Daughter is one such figure. In the telling of her tale, the tyrants become one, and the unjust taxes become *jus primae noctis*, or the right of the first night, in which the local lord exercises his right to sleep with a bride on her wedding night. Violetta was taken to the evil lord's castle, but she hid a dagger beneath her skirts. She cut off the head of her captor and displayed it for all the people to see, sparking a rebellion during which the castle was burned and sacked.

Violetta's annual procession to the castle is faithfully reenacted, complete with her attendants and an additional player, the uniformed French General. This character represents the period of Napoleon's occupation of Piedmont, when the emperor appointed a French general to maintain peace in the five districts of Ivrea during Carnevale. The daily Battles of the Oranges continue, as does a

(continued on next page)

considerable amount of dancing, singing, drinking, and feasting on traditional foods. On the day before Ash Wednesday, one final, epic Battle of the Oranges takes place, with all the carts from all the districts participating in the main *piazza*. Carnevale ends with a solemn "funeral" and cortege, led by Violetta and the General, sounding a fittingly somber note for the beginning of Lent.

Sicily hosts two major Carnevale celebrations, in Sciacca, near Agrigento, and in Acireale, in the province of Catania. Both feature huge, colorful parades, and in Acireale, the festivities end with a huge bonfire in which Il Re Carnevale, or the King of Carnival, is set ablaze. Fano, a seaside town in Le Marche, features a Carnevale celebration with Musica Arabita, a motley band that parades through the streets banging on pots and pans, wine bottles, spoons, and the odd umbrella or two. In the Puglian city of Putignano, the central character of Carnevale is Farinella, a jester dressed in green and white who is named after the region's traditional dish, made with chickpea and barley flour. Cento, in the commune of Ferrara in Emilia-Romagna, boasts that its Carnevale celebration is the most important of its kind in Europe. Cento's carnival is the twin celebration to that of Rio de Janeiro, complete with a gorgeous cast of scantily clad beauties, which was probably not present when the celebration began there in the sixteenth century.

Of the many things Italians know how to do properly, throwing a communal party is certainly one, and these are just a few examples of the Carnevale festivities that are eagerly anticipated every year in Italian cities. Varied as they are, the common denominators are plenty of feasting, lots of good—if not always clean—fun, and the revival of traditions that reach back centuries.

SAINT JOSEPH'S DAY CREAM PUFFS
sfinci di san giuseppe

At Babbo, we like to celebrate the Feast of San Giuseppe, or Saint Joseph's Day, which falls on March 19. Mario invites his friends to visit the restaurant and have a sip of his homemade nocino, *a digestive liqueur made from green walnuts, accompanied by one of my cream-filled* sfinci. *To compliment the* nocino, *I make my pastry cream with aromatic toasted walnuts.*

Saint Joseph was the father of Jesus Christ, and he is the patron saint of both families and pastry cooks (one of several patron saints of my profession), so sweets abound on his feast day. If you want the puffs to remain as crisp as possible, fill them as soon as they have cooled and serve them right away. You may also fill them and keep them refrigerated until serving; the puffs will soften from the moisture in the cream and take on a comforting tenderness. **MAKES 16 TO 18** *SFINCI*

FOR THE TOASTED WALNUT PASTRY CREAM
2¼ cups whole milk
¼ cup plus 3 tablespoons granulated sugar
½ vanilla bean
½ cup walnut pieces, toasted, cooled, and finely chopped
4 large egg yolks
1 large egg
¼ teaspoon kosher salt
⅓ cup plus 1 tablespoon unbleached all-purpose flour
1 tablespoon unsalted butter
2 teaspoons *nocino* or 1 tablespoon dark rum

FOR THE *SFINCI*
½ cup water
4 tablespoons (½ stick/2 ounces) unsalted butter
½ teaspoon kosher salt
2 tablespoons granulated sugar
¾ cup unbleached all-purpose flour
4 large eggs, cold (taken straight from the refrigerator)
1 teaspoon pure vanilla extract
½ teaspoon baking powder

1½ cups heavy cream
Confectioners' sugar, for dusting

To make the toasted walnut pastry cream: Place the milk and ¼ cup sugar in a medium saucepan. Scrape the seeds from the ½ vanilla bean with the blunt side of a small knife and add them to the pan along with the bean. Add the walnuts and place the pan over low heat. Heat the milk to a boil, whisking occasionally, then remove the pan from the heat and allow the walnuts to infuse the milk for about 20 minutes.

(continued on next page)

In a medium bowl, whisk the egg yolks, egg, and the remaining 3 tablespoons sugar together. Add the salt and flour and whisk until smooth.

Return the saucepan to low heat and bring the walnut milk just to the scalding point. Slowly whisk some of the hot walnut milk into the yolk mixture, then return the mixture to the pan, whisking to combine the tempered yolks with the rest of the walnut milk. Continue to whisk constantly over low heat until the pastry cream becomes thick and mounds slightly, holding its shape for a moment or two, 1 to 2 minutes. Remove from the heat and immediately whisk in the butter and *nocino* or rum.

Strain the pastry cream through a chinois or fine-meshed sieve to remove any lumps of cooked egg. Place it in a bowl, cover by pressing a piece of plastic wrap onto the surface, and chill for at least 2 hours. You can make the pastry cream the night before, if you wish, storing it in an airtight container with plastic wrap pressed on the surface.

To make the *sfinci*: Preheat the oven to 350°F and position a rack in the center. Lightly grease a large baking sheet with nonstick cooking spray or butter or line it with parchment paper.

Place the water, butter, salt, and 1 tablespoon sugar in a small saucepan. Bring the mixture to a full boil over medium heat, then remove the pan from the heat and dump in the flour all at once. Stir the mixture quickly with a heatproof spatula to form a thick pastelike dough. Return the saucepan to medium heat and cook the dough for 2 minutes, constantly spreading it and regathering it over the surface of the pan.

Transfer the dough to the bowl of an electric mixer fitted with a paddle attachment. Beat on medium speed to release some of the heat. When the steam dissipates, beat the cold eggs into the dough, one at a time; do not add another egg until the previous one has been completely beaten into the dough. When the last egg has been added, add the remaining 1 tablespoon sugar and the vanilla extract and baking powder. Continue beating on medium speed until the dough becomes glossy and thick, about 1½ minutes.

Scrape the dough into a piping bag fitted with a large round tip. Pipe 1½-inch mounded circles onto the lined baking sheet, spacing them 1 inch apart. Or spoon the dough onto the baking sheet with a soup spoon to make rounded 1½-inch mounds.

Bake the *sfinci* until nicely golden brown, puffed, and crispy, 17 to 20 minutes. Rotate the baking sheet halfway through the cooking time to ensure even browning. Remove the baking sheet from the oven and quickly prick each puff on the side to release the steam and prevent it from becoming soggy. Allow the puffs to cool completely on the baking sheet.

To assemble the *sfinci*: Whip the heavy cream on high speed until stiff peaks form. Beat the walnut pastry cream by hand or with an electric mixer until smooth and shiny, about 30 seconds. Gently fold the whipped cream into the pastry cream.

Using a sharp knife, cut each cream puff in half horizontally and carefully remove the tops. Fill each puff with a generous amount of pastry cream and replace the tops. Sift confectioners' sugar over the *sfinci* before serving.

EASTER EGG BREAD
pane di pasqua

As a kid, I never received one of those over-the-top Easter baskets filled with all manner of sugar-charged bunnies, chicks, and lambs. I never felt deprived, because my straw basket always contained my own little braided Easter bread, lovingly made by my mom, with a brightly colored egg baked right into it. Although she did concede to giving my siblings and me one chocolate bunny each, it was the bread that I most looked forward to. Every year I bake several round loaves of this sweet, light bread, perfumed with orange zest and vanilla, on the day before Easter Sunday. We display them throughout the restaurant and offer slices to our customers to wish them a happy holiday. The colored eggs cook while the bread is baking, so when you are dyeing your Easter eggs, remember to color some raw eggs for this recipe and set them in a separate corner of the refrigerator to avoid any confusion. I especially love to toast a slice of the leftover bread on Easter Monday morning and spread a little butter on it. Yum. MAKES 1 LARGE BRAIDED LOAF

¼ cup warm water

2¼ teaspoons (1 package) active dry yeast

1 cup whole milk

½ cup granulated sugar

2 teaspoons kosher salt

5¼ cups unbleached all-purpose flour, plus more for kneading

3 large eggs

½ cup (1 stick/4 ounces) unsalted butter, softened

2 teaspoons pure vanilla extract

Freshly grated zest of 1 orange

5 dyed raw eggs, for decoration

1 egg, lightly beaten, for glaze

Place the warm water in the bowl of an electric mixer and sprinkle the yeast over it, whisking to dissolve it. While the yeast is proofing, place the milk in a saucepan and heat over low heat just until it is warm to the touch.

After several minutes the yeast should be creamy and bubbling. Add the milk to the bowl, along with the sugar, salt, and 2½ cups flour. With the paddle attachment on low speed, mix the ingredients to combine them, then increase the speed to medium and beat the dough for 30 seconds. Stop the machine and allow the dough to rest for 10 minutes.

Beat in the eggs, followed by the butter, vanilla, and orange zest. Switch to the dough hook attachment and gradually beat in the remaining 2¾ cups flour on low to medium speed. When all of the flour has been added, continue kneading the dough on medium speed for 3 minutes.

Remove the dough from the mixer and transfer it to a lightly floured board. Knead it by hand a few times to determine its consistency. If it is sticky, knead in a bit more flour until it is smooth and elastic. Transfer the dough to a lightly greased bowl and cover with plastic wrap and a damp towel. Allow the dough to rise in a warm, draft-free spot until it is doubled in bulk, 1½ to 2 hours.

When the dough has doubled, pull it away from the sides of the bowl to collapse it. Transfer it to a large lightly floured surface. Divide the dough into 3 equal pieces. Work with 1 piece at a time, leaving the others covered with the damp towel. Roll each piece into a rope 17 to 18 inches long. Try not to overwork the dough; if it begins to spring back and shrink, stop and allow it to relax before proceeding.

When you have rolled the dough into 3 long ropes, arrange them in front of you vertically, with the tops touching. Braid the bread as you would a pigtail, keeping the tension even through the braid. Join the ends together by tucking them under and over each other to maintain the appearance of the braid.

Transfer the loaf to a large, heavy baking sheet that has been lightly greased. Tuck the dyed eggs into the folds of the braid at even intervals. Cover the loaf with the damp towel and allow it to proof for a final 15 minutes.

Preheat the oven to 350°F. Using a pastry brush, glaze the bread with the lightly beaten egg. Bake the bread until it is evenly golden brown and sounds hollow when thumped with your knuckle, 35 to 45 minutes.

Allow the bread to cool completely on a wire rack. It is best eaten the next day; store overnight in a large plastic bag or wrapped in plastic wrap.

SWEET GRAPE FOCACCIA
schiacciata d'uva

Schiacciata d'Uva *is a treat that celebrates the annual harvest of grapes. It illustrates beautifully the knack that Italians have for finding a use for everything. Leftover grapes from the bottom of the barrel, so to speak, are crushed and spread, seeds and all, over a focaccia-like yeast dough, creating the ultimate snack for an October afternoon.*

At Babbo, I take the traditional form of schiacciata *and put a sweet twist on it by baking crushed Concord grapes from upstate New York onto a sweet dough that resembles brioche. Concord grapes are a bit slimy on the inside, so seeding them can be a colossal pain. You can leave the seeds in if you don't mind a bit of crunch, or spread the grapes out on a baking sheet and partially freeze them, which makes it easy to slice them in half and pop out the seeds with the tip of a small knife.*

This sweet bread works perfectly as a snack or even a breakfast cake, or you can serve it with ice cream for a substantially delicious dessert. It simply would not be autumn at Babbo without this on the menu.

MAKES 1 LARGE FLAT LOAF, 10 TO 12 GENEROUS SERVINGS

½ cup warm water

2 teaspoons (1 package) active dry yeast

¾ cup granulated sugar, plus a pinch

½ cup whole milk

5 cups unbleached all-purpose flour

6 large eggs

2 teaspoons kosher salt

1½ cups (3 sticks/12 ounces) unsalted butter, softened, plus more for greasing

2 cups Concord grapes, seeded

2 tablespoons raw or turbinado sugar, for garnish

Place the warm water in a medium bowl and sprinkle the yeast over it. Add a pinch of sugar and whisk briefly to dissolve the yeast. While the yeast proofs, place the milk in a small saucepan and heat over low heat until it is just warm to the touch.

When the yeast has become bubbly, add the warm milk to the bowl. Whisk in 1½ cups flour to make a thick paste. Cover the bowl with plastic wrap and set the sponge aside to rise in a draft-free spot until it is doubled in bulk, 30 to 35 minutes.

When the sponge has risen, scrape it into the bowl of an electric mixer. Crack the eggs into a separate bowl. With the paddle attachment on medium speed, beat the eggs, 2 at a time, into the sponge, followed by the remaining ¾ cup sugar and the salt. Beat in the remaining 3½ cups flour, then beat the dough for an additional 1½ minutes on medium speed. The dough will be stiff and rough. Beat in the 1½ cups butter, 1 tablespoon at a time, until the dough becomes smooth and creamy, like a very thick batter.

Scrape the dough into a large bowl that has been greased with 1 tablespoon butter. Cover the bowl with plastic wrap and set it in a draft-free place to rise until it is doubled in bulk, 1 to 1½ hours.

When the dough has doubled, preheat the oven to 325°F. Grease a heavy baking sheet with sides or a 13-by-18-inch jelly-roll pan with butter or nonstick cooking spray.

Scrape the dough out of the bowl and onto the pan and, using lightly floured fingers, gently press and spread it evenly across the surface and into the corners of the pan. Cover lightly with plastic wrap and allow the dough to proof for 15 to 20 minutes, until it is slightly puffed. Gently dimple the surface of the dough with your fingertips, then scatter the grapes and their juices evenly over the surface of the dough. Sprinkle the surface with the raw sugar.

Bake the bread until it is golden in color, 18 to 20 minutes, rotating the pan halfway through the baking time to ensure even browning. Allow the *schiacciata* to cool in the pan for 10 minutes, then gently slide it out of the pan and onto a large rack to continue cooling and to prevent it from becoming soggy. It is best enjoyed the day it is made, but it may be stored for up to 2 days in an airtight container.

THE VENDEMMIA

The last weeks of summer and first weeks of autumn are those of fruition for the winemaker. A long season of work, involving many months of tilling and fertilizing, watching and checking, waiting and worrying, comes to an end, culminating in the harvest of grapes, the *vendemmia*. The exact dates vary from region to region and are dependent on local growing conditions and the weather. From the vastest of vineyards to the smallest family arbors, the earth sends the signals, and the harvest is the response. It is a time for hard labor, and for celebration. Despite the presence of modern mechanical aids and the relentless pressure for economic success with the year's vintage, the *vendemmia* remains a time to honor the connection between man and the earth. The Sagra dell'Uva, or celebration of wine and grape, is festive and reflective at the same time.

As with all Italian celebrations, the harvest season is marked with the preparation of special foods. Grapes are harvested at the same time that cheeses from the spring and summer milkings are fully ripened; fresh porcini and wild mushrooms will soon be abundant; chestnuts and walnuts are falling from the trees; truffles are unearthed; wild game is hunted, and fattened pigs are slaughtered.

Though it is a time of abundance, there is the constant reminder of the value of the earth's gifts, and the traditional, sweet Tuscan *schiacciata all'uva* is evidence of that mindset. The last of the grapes are cut from the vine, and those that are perhaps not quite perfect enough for the skills of the vintner are not wasted—they are crushed slightly by hand and baked into bread dough, seeds and all, for a harvesttime treat. Another tradition is to combine newly pressed grape juice with some barely fermented grape must and down it enthusiastically as a restorative tonic. Grapes not destined for the wine bottle may be pressed and cooked for *vincotto* or *saba*. *Mosto*, or grape must, is distilled into grappa or, farther north, layered with turnips in wooden barrels to make the piquant *brovada*, which will be ready to enjoy in the early spring.

The sweets of the *vendemmia* are often made with the other bounties of each region's harvest. In Sicily and Sardinia, traditional cookies, cakes, and pastries of the harvest season often feature almonds, which are also harvested in the fall; in Piedmont, the famous hazelnuts are used. The orchards of Friuli–Venezia Giulia and Trentino–Alto Adige are bursting with red and golden apples, ready to be rolled into strudels and stuffed

into omelets, which are part of the Slavic- and Austrian-influenced cuisine of those regions. And no table of an autumn harvest celebration would be complete without heaping piles of huge, juicy table grapes, in shades of deepest purple to palest green, ripe and plump with flavor and sweetness.

The olive harvest follows the grape harvest in mid- to late November, bringing the green and spicy new oil, or *olio nuovo*, to the table for an all-too-fleeting time. Soon afterward the earth goes still as the cold of winter sets in and the growth cycle steps into slumber mode. The bounty of the grape harvest resonates vividly in the hearts and minds of Italians season after season, year after year.

CHOCOLATE SALAMI
salame di cioccolato

Whoever heard of chocolate salami? Every kid in Italy, that's who. Chocolate salami is a treat beloved by children, as well as by children who have grown into adults. It is a staple in many Italian homes around the holidays, or whenever Mama wants to turn an ordinary day into a special occasion. Easy to make and quick to put together, it never fails to elicit smiles and cries of delight; if you don't believe me, you will just have to make it yourself to find out. I think my version is especially flavorful, thanks to the orange zest and a splash of grappa or rum. Since the main ingredient is chocolate, try to use the best bittersweet chocolate you can find. Also be sure to use a neutral, not-too-sweet Italian cookie; I like to use the crisp version of anisette toast or plain butter cookies from Stella D'Oro. Rolling the salami in a bit of confectioners' sugar to coat it lightly gives the finishing touch, truly making it look like a real, cured salami. MAKES 1 CHOCOLATE SALAMI*

8 ounces bittersweet chocolate

4 tablespoons (½ stick/2 ounces) unsalted butter

2 tablespoons Dutch-processed cocoa powder

¼ cup boiling water

¼ cup whole shelled unsalted pistachios

½ cup whole hazelnuts, skinned or unskinned (see page 53)

½ cup sliced almonds, toasted and finely chopped

Approximately 2 ounces plain cookies, such as *biscotti* or butter cookies, crushed into coarse chunks (¾ cup)

4 large egg yolks

1 cup granulated sugar

1 tablespoon grappa or dark rum

Freshly grated zest of 1 small orange

Confectioners' sugar, for dusting

Melt the chocolate and butter together in a large bowl set over a pan of simmering water, whisking to combine them; set aside in a warm spot. In a small bowl, whisk together the cocoa powder and boiling water and set aside. Coarsely chop the pistachios and hazelnuts with a sharp knife and combine them with the chopped almonds and crumbled cookies in a medium bowl.

In the bowl of an electric mixer, use the paddle attachment on medium speed to beat the egg yolks and sugar together until pale yellow and thick, about 1 minute. Beat in the grappa and orange zest. Whisk the cocoa mixture into the melted chocolate and butter, then add that mixture to the egg mixture and beat to combine. Add the nut mixture and beat briefly to incorporate the ingredients. Cover the bowl with plastic wrap and chill the mixture until it is firm enough to handle, about 1 hour.

Lightly dust your rolling surface with confectioners' sugar. Using your hands, roll the mixture into a plump log about 2 inches in diameter, to resemble a salami. Lightly dust the surface with a bit more confectioners' sugar. Wrap the chocolate salami in a sheet of parchment paper and twist the ends. Chill the salami for 2 or more hours before serving.

To serve, cut thin slices, either straight or on the bias. Wrap any leftovers in plastic wrap. The salami may be kept, wrapped and chilled, for up to 3 days.

PANFORTE DI SIENA

When I visited Tuscany for the first time, I fell completely under the spell of pan-forte. I bought five of them, and wound up having to ship home some of my clothes to accommodate the panforte stuffed into my suitcase. I couldn't help it. Panforte di Siena overtakes my senses as well as my good judgment. More of a confection than a cake, it is made with a copious amount of honey, studded with nuts and dried fruit, redolent with spices—just one slice is never enough. It makes a wonderful gift, especially when wrapped in some exquisite handmade Italian paper.

The tradition of panforte dates back to the Middle Ages, when a Sienese nun baked it to fortify her fellow citizens after they survived a brazen attack from invad-ers and an outbreak of the plague. The original version contained black pepper, otherwise known as pan pepato. In later years, it was made lighter and less spicy to appeal to the visiting Queen Margaret of Savoy. Legend says that panforte di Siena has the power to unite families and keep husbands from fighting with their wives. I believe it. MAKES 1 PANFORTE, 16 SERVINGS

3 cups whole blanched almonds

1¾ cups whole hazelnuts, skinned or unskinned (see page 53)

2 cups diced candied orange peel

6 ounces dried apricots, diced

5 ounces dried figs, diced

1 cup unbleached all-purpose flour

2 tablespoons ground cinnamon

1 tablespoon Dutch-processed cocoa powder

1 teaspoon salt

1 teaspoon ground nutmeg

½ teaspoon ground cloves

¼ teaspoon freshly ground black pepper

1¾ cups granulated sugar

1¾ cups honey

6 tablespoons (¾ stick/3 ounces) unsalted butter

Confectioners' sugar, for dusting

Preheat the oven to 325°F and position a rack in the center. Generously grease a 9-by-2-inch round cake pan with nonstick cooking spray (a heavy nonstick pan works best). Line the bottom of the pan with a circle of parchment paper, then grease the parchment paper as well. Dust the paper and the sides of the pan with flour, tapping out the excess.

Using a sharp knife, roughly chop the nuts and place them in a large, wide bowl. Add the orange peel, apricots, and figs and toss them to combine.

In a medium bowl, stir together the flour, cinnamon, cocoa powder, salt, nutmeg, cloves, and pepper, taking care to combine them thoroughly. Add them to the bowl with the nuts and fruits and, using your hands or a large wooden spoon, combine the two mixtures thoroughly.

Place the granulated sugar, honey, and butter in a medium saucepan. Clip a candy thermometer to the side of the pan and place it over medium heat. Cook the mixture until it reaches 217°F. Remove the pan from the heat, remove the candy thermometer, and quickly pour the sugar mixture over the dry ingredients. Using a heatproof spatula, stir to combine the two mixtures thoroughly. Quickly transfer the contents of the bowl to the cake pan, smoothing and evening out the surface with the spatula.

Bake the *panforte* for 15 to 20 minutes, or until the entire surface is bubbling. Remove the pan from the oven and allow the cake to cool completely in the pan on a wire rack. When it is completely cool, remove it from the pan and wrap it well in parchment paper and then in plastic wrap. Store it in a cool, dry place for up to 3 weeks.

To serve, dust the *panforte* with confectioners' sugar and cut into thin wedges with a chef's knife.

STRUFOLI

Every Italian mother from Naples southward has a recipe for strufoli, *honey-coated fried balls of doughy love enjoyed at many a Christmas celebration. I adore* strufoli *and have worked on my recipe year after year to get it just right. I think the secret is to heat the honey in a large sauté pan and then add the fried* strufoli; *allowing them to really soak up the honey prevents them from drying out. Adding a bit of* vin santo *to the pot is a trick I learned from my grandmother; it prevents the honey from reducing too much and making the* strufoli *too sticky. Multicolored sprinkles, of course, are a must.* MAKES 45 TO 50 *STRUFOLI*

1½ cups unbleached all-purpose flour, plus more for kneading

2 teaspoons baking powder

½ teaspoon kosher salt

3 large eggs

4 tablespoons (½ stick/2 ounces) unsalted butter, softened

2 tablespoons confectioners' sugar

1 tablespoon granulated sugar

2 teaspoons pure vanilla extract

Olive oil, for frying

2 cups honey

½ cup *vin santo* or other sweet dessert wine

Multicolored or Christmas-colored sprinkles

In a medium bowl, whisk together the 1½ cups flour, baking powder, and salt.

In the bowl of an electric mixer fitted with the paddle attachment, beat the eggs on medium speed with the butter, confectioners' sugar, granulated sugar, and vanilla extract until combined; the mixture will appear somewhat curdled. Add the dry ingredients and beat on low speed, to form a soft dough, about 1 minute. Turn the mixture onto a floured board and, using the remaining flour as needed, knead until the dough is smooth and firm enough to handle, about 1 minute.

Divide the dough into 3 pieces. Work with 1 piece at a time, keeping the other 2 pieces wrapped in plastic in the refrigerator. Have ready a parchment- or wax-paper-lined baking sheet, lightly dusted with flour.

Lightly dust your rolling surface and the piece of dough with flour. Using your hands, roll the dough into a long rope about ½-inch in diameter. Cut the rope into ½-inch pieces and roll each piece in your palms to form a ball. Place each ball on the flour-dusted baking sheet; as you make the *strufoli*, keep them covered with a sheet of plastic wrap to prevent them from drying and forming a skin. Repeat with the other 2 pieces of dough, keeping the *strufoli* covered with plastic wrap as you continue to roll and shape the dough.

When all of the dough has been rolled, heat 6 inches (4 to 6 cups) of olive oil to 360°F in a heavy-bottomed stockpot or countertop fryer. Fry the *strufoli* in batches of 10 to 12, taking care not to overcrowd the pot. The *strufoli* should be puffed and golden brown on all sides. Drain them on a baking sheet lined with paper towels.

After you have fried all the dough, place the honey and *vin santo* in a large sauté pan with high sides and heat it slowly over medium heat until it just comes to a boil. Add the *strufoli* in batches, coating them completely with honey. Remove the *strufoli* with a slotted spoon and pile them on a serving plate. Drizzle any leftover honey over the pile of *strufoli* and decorate them with the colored sprinkles.

When the *strufoli* have cooled, cover the pile with plastic wrap to prevent them from drying out.

Strufoli are best served on the same day they are fried; any leftovers should be wrapped in plastic and stored at room temperature for 1 additional day.

PANDORO

Since our first Christmas at Babbo in 1998, I have baked over 5,400 mini Christmas breads to give to our customers to wish them buone feste, *or happy holidays. My favorite of the various Christmas breads of Italy is* pandoro, *or "bread of gold," which gets its rich yellow color from egg yolks. A holiday bread that originated in the city of Verona in the Veneto,* pandoro *is soft and cakey, sweet, luxuriously textured, and elegant, with a hint of lemon zest and a vanilla-scented sugar glaze on top.*

Pandoro is traditionally baked in a tall, star-shaped pan, which you can order from the King Arthur Flour Company (see Sources, pages 285–87). I recommend getting one, because the result is so very pretty, but if you decide not to, try using a 7-inch round panettone *pan. A pan of last resort would be a large, #10-size can. You can create the traditional Christmas star on top of the loaf by cutting a star stencil out of a piece of parchment, placing it over the glazed loaf, then dusting with additional confectioners' sugar.*

Don't be intimidated by the various stages of this recipe! It is really quite easy and well worth the effort; the slow, multiple risings make for the lightest and most heavenly texture. **MAKES 1 LARGE LOAF, 12 TO 16 SERVINGS**

FOR THE SPONGE
2¼ teaspoons (1 package) active dry yeast
½ cup whole milk, warm
1 tablespoon granulated sugar
1 large egg yolk
½ cup unbleached all-purpose flour

FOR THE FIRST RISE
3 cups unbleached all-purpose flour
4 large egg yolks
¾ cup granulated sugar
4 tablespoons (½ stick/2 ounces) unsalted
   butter, softened
½ cup water
¼ cup heavy cream
2 teaspoons kosher salt

FOR THE SECOND RISE
4 large egg yolks
1 large egg

½ cup granulated sugar
Freshly grated zest of 2 lemons
1 tablespoons grappa or brandy
2 tablespoons pure vanilla extract
2 cups unbleached all-purpose flour
1 teaspoon kosher salt

FOR THE GLAZE
1 egg yolk
1 tablespoon water

FOR THE ICING
1½ cup confectioners' sugar
3 tablespoons whole milk
½ teaspoon pure vanilla extract

Confectioners' sugar, for garnish

To make the sponge: In a medium bowl, sprinkle the yeast over the warm milk and whisk to dissolve it. Allow the yeast to proof until it is creamy and bubbling, about 2 minutes. Whisk in the sugar, egg yolk, and flour until smooth. Cover the bowl with plastic wrap and set it in a warm, draft-free spot for 30 minutes or until the sponge has become very foamy and tripled in volume.

To prepare the first rise: Remove the plastic wrap, stir down the sponge and scrape it into the bowl of an electric mixer. Using the paddle attachment on low speed, beat in the flour, followed by the egg yolks, sugar, butter, water, heavy cream, and salt, increasing the speed to medium as you add the ingredients. Continue to beat the dough for about 1 minute until it is smooth and appears stringy as it comes away from the beater. Scrape the dough into a large greased bowl, cover with plastic wrap, and place the bowl in a warm, draft-free spot. Allow the dough to rise for 45 minutes to 1 hour, or until it has doubled in bulk.

To prepare the second rise: Shake the bowl gently to deflate the dough and scrape it into the bowl of an electric mixer. Begin with the paddle attachment, beating in the egg yolks, egg, sugar, lemon zest, grappa, vanilla extract, flour, and salt. Beat until the ingredients are well incorporated and the dough is smooth, then switch to the dough hook. Knead on medium speed for 3 minutes, adding a bit more flour if the dough appears too sticky. It should be smooth, soft, and glossy, but it will not form a ball.

Place the dough in a large greased bowl, cover with plastic wrap, and allow it to rise in a warm, draft-free spot for 1½ to 2 hours, or until doubled in bulk. The dough can also be placed in the refrigerator to rise overnight, 8 to 10 hours.

To shape, glaze, and bake: Prepare the pan by greasing it with softened unsalted butter or nonstick cooking spray. If you are using a #10 can, grease the can well and make a "collar" by taping a double-thickness of aluminum foil evenly around the top to extend the can's height by 2 inches; this will accommodate any additional rising of the bread dough during baking.

Gently deflate the dough by turning it out onto a lightly floured board. Shape it into a ball and place it in the center of the prepared pan or can, ensuring that the top of the loaf is smooth. Cover the pan with plastic wrap and allow the dough to rise until it has proofed enough to bake and has nearly doubled in bulk, about 25 to 30 minutes.

In the meantime, preheat the oven to 375°F and position a rack in the center.

(continued on next page)

To glaze the loaf, lightly beat the egg yolk and water with a fork and brush it over the top of the loaf with a small pastry brush. Bake the *pandoro* for 10 minutes, then reduce the temperature to 325°F and continue to bake, rotating the pan to ensure even browning, for 50 to 60 additional minutes. The loaf will be done when it is golden brown on top and sounds hollow when tapped. Cool the *pandoro* in the pan for 10 minutes, then remove it and place on a wire rack to cool completely.

To prepare the icing: Sift the confectioners' sugar into a bowl to remove any lumps and then whisk in the milk and vanilla extract. When the loaf is completely cool, brush the icing on top, allowing it to run down the sides. When the icing has set, decorate the *pandoro* by sifting more confectioners' sugar on top. The *pandoro* will keep, wrapped in plastic wrap, for 2 or 3 days at room temperature.

CASSATA ALLA SICILIANA

Cassata alla Siciliana *is the unofficial dessert of Sicily, and more often than not, it is more of a feast for the eyes and imagination than it is for the palate. One of the main reasons why is its traditional elaborate decoration, which usually consists of an outer shell of rolled sugar fondant tinted a minty shade of pale green, as well as an assortment of whimsical fruits, either candied or formed from marzipan.* Cassata alla Siciliana, *presented in full regalia, is completely and wonderfully over the top.*

My version is more understated, but filled with the flavors of Sicily itself: creamy ricotta combined with orange, pistachio, and a hint of chocolate, spread between layers of rum-soaked sponge cake. A thin veil of icing and a shower of toasted almonds provides a light finishing touch. Be forewarned: this is not the quickest cake to make, and it is almost heartbreakingly easy to devour. I promise that every bite will be well worth the effort. MAKES ONE 9-INCH CAKE, 10 SERVINGS

FOR THE SPONGE CAKES

2 cups bleached cake flour, sifted

2 teaspoons baking powder

1 teaspoon kosher salt, plus a pinch

8 large eggs, separated

1½ cups granulated sugar

2 teaspoons pure vanilla extract

½ cup (1 stick/4 ounces) unsalted butter, melted and cooled

FOR THE RUM SYRUP

2 cups granulated sugar

¾ cup cold water

½ cup rum

FOR THE FILLING

3 ounces bittersweet chocolate

¾ cup shelled whole unsalted pistachios

3 cups fresh, whole-milk ricotta

1 cup confectioners' sugar, sifted

½ teaspoon ground cinnamon

Freshly grated zest of 2 medium oranges

FOR THE ICING

2 cups confectioners' sugar, sifted

1 large egg white

2 tablespoons water

¼ teaspoon pure almond extract

½ cup sliced blanched almonds, toasted and cooled, for garnish

Maraschino or amarena cherries, for garnish (optional)

Candied orange zest, for garnish (optional)

Preheat the oven to 350°F and position a rack in the center. Lightly grease two 9-by-2-inch round cake pans with butter or nonstick cooking spray, line them with parchment paper, then grease the parchment.

(continued on next page)

To make the sponge cakes: Sift together the cake flour, baking powder, and 1 teaspoon salt into a medium bowl and set aside.

In the bowl of an electric mixer, use the whisk attachment to beat the egg yolks with the sugar on medium speed until very light and pale yellow in color and doubled in volume, about 3 minutes. Beat in the vanilla extract, followed by the melted butter. Transfer the egg mixture to a large, clean mixing bowl. Fold in the dry ingredients quickly and lightly, using a rubber spatula, stopping just before they are fully incorporated. Clean the whisk attachment and mixing bowl.

Place the egg whites and the pinch of salt in the cleaned bowl of the electric mixer. Using the whisk attachment on medium-high speed, beat the egg whites until they form firm peaks. Fold the egg whites into the batter quickly and lightly; this will also incorporate any streaks of dry ingredients that remain.

Evenly divide the batter between the prepared pans, smoothing the tops with a spatula. Bake the cakes for 35 to 40 minutes, or until they are golden brown, a cake tester inserted in the center comes out clean, and the cakes have begun to pull away from the sides of the pan. Allow the cakes to cool for 5 minutes in the pan, then carefully turn them out onto a wire rack to cool completely.

While the cakes are cooling, prepare the rum syrup: In a medium saucepan, stir together the sugar, water, and rum. Place the saucepan over medium heat and bring the contents to a boil, then lower the heat slightly and allow the syrup to simmer for 5 minutes. Remove the pan from the heat and allow the syrup to cool.

Next, prepare the filling: Using a microplane or box grater, grate the chocolate into fine, feathery shreds. Using a sharp knife, finely chop the pistachios. Place the ricotta, confectioners' sugar, and cinnamon in the bowl of an electric mixer and, using the paddle attachment, beat until the ricotta is creamy and soft. Add the grated chocolate, chopped pistachios, and orange zest and beat just until combined.

To assemble the *cassata*: Have ready a 9-inch springform pan. Using a serrated knife, carefully split each cake layer in half horizontally to make four layers. Place one of the layers in the bottom of the pan and, using a pastry brush, moisten it generously and evenly with some of the rum syrup. Spread the cake layer evenly with one third of the ricotta mixture. Repeat twice with another cake layer, more of the rum syrup, and another third of the ricotta mixture. Place the final cake layer on top and generously brush with the rum syrup. Wrap the springform pan tightly in plastic wrap; this helps the layers fit snugly on top of each other. Chill the cake in the refrigerator for at least 4 hours or overnight.

To prepare the icing: Place the sifted confectioners' sugar in the bowl of an electric mixer. Add the egg white and water and beat the ingredients together with the paddle attachment on medium speed until the mixture is smooth. Beat in the almond extract.

To finish the *cassata:* Remove the *cassata* from the refrigerator and carefully remove the sides of the pan. You may need to run a hot knife around the sides first. You may leave the cake on the bottom of the springform pan, or carefully transfer it to a cardboard cake circle with an offset spatula. Place the cake on a wire rack to ice it; you can place some parchment or wax paper underneath to catch any drips.

Spread the icing over the top and sides of the cake, spreading it evenly with a spatula. Scatter the toasted almonds over the top and let the cake sit until the icing sets. Return the cake to the refrigerator to chill until you are ready to serve it, at least 3 hours.

Before serving, carefully transfer the cake to a platter or cake stand, and, if desired, decorate the *cassata* with maraschino or amarena cherries and some strips of candied orange zest.

Leftovers should be wrapped and stored in the refrigerator for up to 1 additional day.

GUBANA

Gubana is a specialty of Friuli–Venezia Giulia, and what a treat it is. Essentially it is a pasta sfogliata, or yeasted, layered dough, similar to a Danish or croissant. The buttery dough is filled with a luscious mixture of fruit, nuts, and spices and rolled into a spiral before baking. The effect is dramatic when you slice into it. Gubana originated as a celebration cake, especially at Christmas and Easter, but over time has become more of a year-round pleasure. For a real kick, do as the Friulians do and sprinkle a slice of gubana *with some droplets of grappa.*

MAKES 1 *GUBANA*, 10 TO 12 SERVINGS

FOR THE DOUGH

1½ cups (3 sticks/12 ounces) unsalted butter, cold

3¾ cups unbleached all-purpose flour, plus more for kneading

1 tablespoon (2 packages) active dry yeast

⅓ cup warm water

⅓ cup granulated sugar, plus a pinch

1½ teaspoons kosher salt

1 large egg

1 cup whole milk, at room temperature

FOR THE FILLING

½ cup golden raisins

½ cup walnut pieces

½ cup sliced blanched almonds

¼ cup pine nuts

¼ cup granulated sugar

1 tablespoon unsweetened Dutch-processed cocoa powder

2 teaspoons ground cinnamon

½ teaspoon ground cloves

½ teaspoon ground nutmeg

Freshly grated zest of 1 orange

3 tablespoons grappa

2 tablespoons unsalted butter, melted

To make the dough: Cut the butter into small pieces and place it in a bowl. Sprinkle ¼ cup flour over it and, using your fingers, work the butter and flour together to make a uniform mixture. The butter should remain malleable. Shape the mixture into a 4-inch square, wrap it in plastic, and set it aside in a cool place but not in the refrigerator.

In a small bowl, whisk together the yeast and warm water to dissolve the yeast. Add the pinch of sugar and let the mixture sit until it is foamy, about 5 minutes.

In the bowl of an electric mixer, combine 2 cups flour with the salt. Add the yeast mixture, the remaining ⅓ cup sugar, and the egg and milk. Using the paddle attachment, beat the ingredients together until smooth. Switch to the dough hook and knead in the remaining 1½ cups of flour until you have a smooth, elastic dough, 3 to 5 minutes. Place the dough in a greased bowl, cover it with plastic wrap or a damp towel, and let it relax for 30 to 45 minutes.

Turn out the dough onto a well-floured board and roll it into a large square, about 16 by 16 inches. Sprinkle the surface with some flour and place the square of butter and flour in the middle of the dough. Fold the left and right sides over the middle, then fold the top and bottom sides over that; the goal is to make a package of dough.

Generously sprinkle the work surface and the top of the dough, as well as your rolling pin, with flour. Roll the dough from the middle toward the top and bottom, making a long rectangle, maintaining the width but increasing the length. Fold the bottom to the center, making a flap, and then fold the top over that, making an envelope. Turn the dough counterclockwise so that the top flap faces right. Once again, flour the work surface, the dough, and the rolling pin and repeat the rolling and folding process. You will end up with another envelope. Wrap the dough tightly in plastic and refrigerate it for at least 4 hours, or overnight.

To make the filling and assemble the *gubana*: Remove the dough from the refrigerator. If you stored it overnight, allow it to come to room temperature, about 1 hour, before attempting to roll it.

Place the filling ingredients in the bowl of a food processor. Process to chop the nuts finely and thoroughly combine the mixture. On a lightly floured board, roll the dough into a rectangle about 18 by 8 inches. Brush the surface of the rectangle with some of the melted butter and spread the filling across the dough, leaving a ½-inch border.

Roll the dough jelly-roll style, starting from the bottom (wide) side; you will wind up with a long snake. Grease a 10-inch round springform pan. Roll the snake into a tight coil and lay it in the pan. Brush the dough with the remaining melted butter. Cover the dough with a towel and allow it to rise until doubled, about 1 hour.

Preheat the oven to 350°F and position a rack in the center.

Bake the *gubana* for 45 to 50 minutes, or until it is golden brown. Rotate the pan halfway through the cooking period to ensure that it browns evenly. Allow the *gubana* to cool for 20 minutes in the pan on a wire rack, then carefully remove the sides of the pan to cool it completely.

To serve, slice the *gubana* in wedges. The *gubana* will keep wrapped in plastic for 2 days.

SAVORY
BITES

bocconi saporiti

VERY PASTRY CHEF SHOULD HAVE A FEW SAVORY TREATS IN HER BAG of tricks, if only to spice things up a bit every so often. If you are famous for your skills with cakes and cookies, try surprising the guests at your next dinner party with something warm from the oven to enjoy before dinner with a glass of wine. As with sweet baking, the quality of the ingredients is an important factor in achieving the best possible results. It is hard to resist the lure of crispy *grissini*, fragrant with extra-virgin olive oil, or home-baked crackers savory and rich with real Parmigiano-Reggiano. The purity and excellence of such ingredients can elevate a predinner nosh or afternoon snack from the basic to the sublime.

Some sentimental favorites appear in the pages that follow, such as the unusual and delicious crescent pastries known as *calcioni,* which remind me of the historical link between sweet and savory baking. The savory baker and the sweet baker in Italy, once one and the same, parted company professionally and went their separate ways around the turn of the sixteenth century, but the flavor combination of both elements has an enduring appeal.

Cheese is major player in most of the recipes in this chapter, as an ingredient or a suggested accompaniment. I have included a primer on some of my favorite Italian cheeses that are becoming more widely available in the United States. My hope is that it will inspire you to sample, seek out, and request the wonderful, unforgettable cheeses of Italy from your cheesemongers and market managers. The small-scale Italian cheesemaker faces a frustrating paradox: Italy is a major producer but a relatively minor consumer of its own artisanal cheeses. There are nearly four hundred varieties of Italian cheese in existence, a large percentage of which are facing extinction because of increasingly modernized methods of production. An easing of U.S. regulations regarding the importation of unpasteurized milk products would open a door for small cheese producers to an American marketplace that is clamoring for more authentic, artisanal products from Italy.

So forge ahead, perhaps with a bit of wine nearby and the sugar canister on the shelf for the time being, and enjoy your walk on the savory side of the street.

PUGLIA, THE BREADBASKET OF ITALY

Puglia, a narrow region with a long coastline along the Adriatic Sea, forms the heel of Italy's boot. Unlike the historically poverty-stricken neighboring regions of southern Italy, Puglia is agriculturally bountiful, an abundant producer of the three dominant crops of the Mediterranean: grains, olives, and grapes. The northernmost province of Puglia is Foggia, with the Gargano Peninsula sitting at the top and jutting out into the Adriatic, forming the spur of the boot. A mountain as well as a peninsula, the Gargano is an entirely separate land formation, and within its plains is an expanse of land that has been devoted to the cultivation of wheat and other grains for centuries. The harvest of the Gargano plains is a source for the many flour mills and pasta factories throughout Puglia, especially in the neighboring province of Bari.

It is no surprise that the Pugliese are fantastic bakers, as evidenced by their excellent flat, focaccia-type breads, plump round loaves, and crunchy, hard biscuits perfect for dunking in local wines. There are plenty of pastries to keep the sweet tooth satisfied as well, including doughy fritters soaked in honey, crispy shells filled with fresh, sweet ricotta and candied fruits, and *carteddate*, a sweet version of *taralli*. Puglia even has its own DOP bread, *Pane di Altamura*, a very large loaf almost burned black on the outside but with a soft interior, created centuries ago to nourish a working family for several days. Anyone on one of those trendy low-carbohydrate diets be warned: a visit to Puglia will set you delightfully far off course.

BABBO BREADSTICKS
grissini

We serve these spicy, cheesy breadsticks every night at the Babbo bar. I like to flavor them with cayenne pepper, but you can add or substitute fresh or dried herbs; you can even skip the Parmigiano-Reggiano on the outside if you prefer a subtler flavor. The dough comes together quickly and easily, and if you are making these for a special occasion, allowing the dough to rise overnight in the refrigerator is a time-saver. I prefer the rough appearance of homemade, hand-rolled grissini *to the packaged, machine-cut variety; wrap them in a pretty napkin and stand them up in a tall glass for an easy and dramatic presentation.* **MAKES ABOUT 30 BREADSTICKS**

⅓ cup warm water

1½ teaspoons (1 package) active dry yeast

Pinch of granulated sugar

2 cups unbleached all-purpose flour, plus more for kneading

1 cup "oo" flour (see page 84)

1 teaspoon kosher salt

½ teaspoon cayenne pepper

1 cup cold water

2 tablespoons extra-virgin olive oil, plus more for greasing the pans and brushing the breadsticks

½ cup grated Parmigiano-Reggiano or Grana Padano, plus more for garnish (optional)

1 tablespoon unsalted butter, softened

Kosher salt, for garnish

Place the warm water in a small bowl and sprinkle the dry yeast over it. Add the pinch of sugar and stir the yeast to dissolve it. Set the yeast aside to proof for 5 to 7 minutes.

Place the two flours in the bowl of an electric mixer with the salt and cayenne pepper and stir to combine them. Check the yeast to make sure it has proofed; it will be appear foamy, with bubbles forming on the surface. Make a well in the center of the dry ingredients and pour in the yeast mixture and the cold water. Attach the dough hook and knead the ingredients together on medium speed for 2 minutes; the dough will start out rough and gradually become smooth. Stop the machine and add the 2 tablespoons olive oil, ½ cup cheese, and butter; then continue kneading on medium speed for an additional 2 to 3 minutes. The dough should be relatively smooth and beginning to pull away from the sides of the bowl.

Remove the dough from the bowl and, on a lightly floured board, knead it by hand until it is velvety smooth and elastic, about 1 minute. Place the dough in a clean mixing bowl greased with olive oil, turning it once to coat it. Cover the bowl with plastic wrap and set it in a warm, draft-free area to rise until doubled in volume, about 2 hours. If you want it to rise overnight in the refrigerator, place it in an airtight plastic container, also greased with olive oil, that is large enough to accommodate the dough when it has doubled in volume. The following day, remove the dough from the refrigerator and allow it to come to room temperature before rolling and forming the breadsticks.

Preheat the oven to 375°F and place racks in the center and lower positions. Prepare three baking sheets by brushing them lightly with olive oil, lining them with parchment paper, and then brushing the parchment with oil as well.

Turn out the dough onto a lightly floured board and divide it into 4 pieces. Return 3 of the pieces to the bowl and cover with a damp towel or plastic wrap to prevent them from drying out while you work with the fourth piece. Cut the dough into ten or eleven 1-inch pieces. Using your hands, form the breadsticks by rolling each piece into a long strand, about 14 to 15 inches in length and ⅛ inch in width. Keep your fingers spread apart, gently stretching the dough as you roll. Repeat with the remaining 3 pieces of dough.

Place the breadsticks on an oiled baking sheet, ½ inch apart. You should be able to fit 10 or 11 breadsticks on each sheet. Use a pastry brush to gently brush them with olive oil, and, sprinkle them lightly with additional kosher salt, or, if desired, grated cheese.

Bake the breadsticks for 12 to 14 minutes, rotating the baking sheet halfway through the baking time to ensure even browning. The breadsticks are done when they are an even golden brown. Allow them to cool for a few moments on the baking sheet before removing them to a rack to cool completely.

The breadsticks may be served while still warm, reheated on a lightly oiled baking sheet, or when completely cooled. Store any leftover *grissini* in an airtight container for up to 2 days.

TARALLI WITH RED PEPPER AND OREGANO
taralli con peperoncino e herbe

Taralli *are best described as an Italian version of a pretzel. These crunchy, curly biscuits are boiled and then baked, and the lingering flavor of extra-virgin olive oil makes them truly unique. The process may look difficult, but it isn't. It's a good idea to make the dough the night before; then you can easily roll the* taralli, *boil them, and bake them as an afternoon project. Or get a group together and form an assembly line of rolling, boiling, and baking. Either way, the best moment will be when you take them out of the oven, shiny and golden brown, and fill your ears with that first deafening crunch.*

On a floured board, the taralli *will roll out easily with a light touch. "oo" flour gives them a fine texture, but you may substitute all-purpose flour if that is all you have on hand. I like to season my* taralli *with crushed red pepper flakes and finely chopped fresh oregano; you may also experiment with 1 tablespoon crushed fennel seed or 1 tablespoon cracked black peppercorns and 2 tablespoons grated Grana Padano.* MAKES 16 TO 20 *TARALLI*

4½ cups "oo" flour (see page 84)

2 tablespoons kosher salt

1 tablespoon granulated sugar

2 tablespoons finely chopped fresh oregano or
    1 tablespoon dried oregano

2 teaspoons crushed red pepper flakes

1 cup plus 2 tablespoons dry white wine

1 cup extra-virgin olive oil

All-purpose or "oo" flour, for dusting the bowl
    and kneading

Place the flour, 1 tablespoon salt, sugar, oregano, and red pepper flakes in the bowl of an electric mixer. Add the wine and oil and use the paddle attachment on medium speed to form a smooth dough. Continue beating for 3 minutes; the dough should be firm and velvety.

Lightly brush the inside of another bowl with olive oil and sprinkle it generously with additional flour. Place the dough in the bowl and dust the top with flour. Cover with plastic wrap or a towel and allow the dough to rest for 2 hours. You can also refrigerator the dough overnight in an airtight container; bring it to room temperature before proceeding with the recipe.

Preheat the oven to 375°F and position a rack in the center.

In a stockpot or Dutch oven, bring about 4 quarts water to a boil over high heat, then reduce the heat to a simmer. Season the water with the remaining 1 tablespoon salt.

Cover the pot to prevent the water from evaporating. Prepare two baking sheets by lightly brushing them with olive oil. Have ready some paper towels to drain the *taralli* as they come out of the water.

Turn the dough out onto a floured board and knead it lightly. Divide the dough into 4 pieces; return 3 of the pieces to the bowl and cover with a damp towel or plastic wrap while you work with the fourth piece. Roll the piece of the dough into a long rope about ¾ inch in diameter and 18 inches long. Cut the rope into 4 or 5 pieces and shape each piece into a ring, making a small knot at the top. Repeat with the remaining pieces of dough.

Working in batches of 4 or 5, drop the rings, one at a time, into the simmering water. The *taralli* will sink and then rise to the surface. Increase the heat under the pot as needed to maintain an even simmer. Allow them to float on the surface for 30 to 45 seconds, then gently scoop them out of the water with a slotted spoon or a Chinese skimmer. Drain for a moment in the spoon before placing them on the paper towels for a few moments more to remove any excess water. Transfer the *taralli* to the baking sheets; you do not have to space them too far apart, as they will not expand while they bake. Repeat until all the *taralli* are boiled.

Bake the *taralli* for about 25 minutes, rotating the baking sheets 180° halfway through to ensure even browning. When they are evenly golden brown, remove them from the oven and transfer to a rack to cool completely before serving. Store them in an airtight container for up to 2 weeks.

SEMOLINA AND SESAME CRACKERS

The notion of cheese with crackers is more American than Italian, but I like to have a crisp morsel with a hunk of cheese now and then. These sesame-sprinkled gems fit the bill perfectly, and they are also yummy with honey or a dab of jam. I love anything with sesame seeds, so I make these often to have on hand for snacking or an impromptu get-together.

Crackers are as easy and quick to make as cookies—just make the dough, roll it out, cut, and bake. The tender, flaky nature of this dough means that it benefits from the least amount of handling. If you roll the dough out and then cut it in a grid pattern with a knife, there is no waste, and the dough remains tender.

MAKES ABOUT 32 CRACKERS

1½ cups unbleached all-purpose flour, plus more for kneading

½ cup semolina

½ teaspoon baking powder

1½ teaspoons sugar

1 teaspoon kosher salt

1 large egg, separated

½ cup heavy cream, plus more if needed

¼ cup sesame seeds

Preheat the oven to 350°F and position a rack in the center. Prepare two baking sheets by brushing them lightly with olive oil or coating them lightly with nonstick cooking spray.

In a medium bowl, place the flour, semolina, baking powder, sugar, and salt, whisking to combine them completely.

In a small bowl, whisk together the egg yolk and the heavy cream. Add this mixture to the dry ingredients and stir them together with a fork to form a flaky dough. Add a few more drops of cream if necessary to make the dough come together.

On a lightly floured work surface, pat the dough to form a small square. Using a rolling pin dusted with flour, roll the dough into a thin square, about ⅛-inch thick. With a sharp knife, cut the dough into a grid, forming 1¼- to 1½-inch squares. Transfer the squares to the prepared baking sheets, spacing them ¼ inch apart. Prick each cracker with a fork two times.

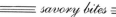

Place the egg white in a small bowl and beat it lightly with a fork until it is foamy. With a small pastry brush, lightly brush each cracker with the egg white, then sprinkle with the sesame seeds.

Bake the crackers for 12 to 14 minutes, or until light golden in color, rotating the sheets halfway through to ensure even browning. Allow the crackers to cool completely on a wire rack, then transfer to an airtight container, layering them with parchment or wax paper. They will keep for 2 or 3 days.

PARMIGIANO-REGGIANO CRACKERS

The cheese contained in these morsels and sprinkled on top before baking makes them an irresistible nibble, paired with a fine Italian red wine. The dough comes together quickly, and you can serve them at an impromptu party or take them along as a hostess gift. I use only real Parmigiano-Reggiano; it makes a difference in the flavor. Every time I make these, I barely get to taste one before they all disappear. Since they are made with real cheese and no preservatives, it is best to serve them on the day you bake them. Stored in an airtight container, they will keep for an additional day. MAKES 30 TO 36 CRACKERS

2 cups unbleached all-purpose flour, plus more for rolling

1¼ teaspoons baking powder

½ teaspoon kosher salt

¾ cup grated Parmigiano-Reggiano, plus more for sprinkling

3 tablespoons unsalted butter, cold and cut into small cubes

2 tablespoons extra-virgin olive oil

¼ cup whole milk

1 egg yolk beaten with 2 teaspoons water, for glaze

Prehead the oven to 350°F and position a rack in the center. Prepare two baking sheets by brushing them lightly with olive oil or coating them lightly with nonstick cooking spray.

Place the flour, baking powder, salt, and Parmigiano-Reggiano in the bowl of a food processor and pulse just to combine them.

Scatter the cubes of butter on top of the dry ingredients, then pour the olive oil evenly over them. Put the cover back on and pulse until the butter cubes are finely combined with the dry ingredients. Add the milk, pulsing to form a crumbly dough that comes together in your hands.

Gather the dough into a ball on a lightly floured work surface and pat it down to form a circle. With a lightly floured rolling pin, roll the dough out to a thickness of ⅛ inch. With a 1½-inch round cutter, cut the dough into circles. Gather the scraps together and reroll them, cutting more circles until all the dough has been used.

Transfer the circles to the prepared baking sheets, spacing them ½ inch apart. With a small pastry brush, lightly brush each cracker with the egg glaze, then sprinkle generously with Parmigiano-Reggiano.

Bake the crackers for 12 to 14 minutes, or until they are golden brown; rotate the sheets halfway through to ensure even browning. Remove the crackers to a wire rack and allow them to cool completely. Transfer to an airtight container, layering them with parchment or wax paper. They will keep for up to 3 days.

CALCIONI

*These just may be my favorite baked pastry ever. Sweet pastry dough encases a fill-
ing of beaten egg and aged grated cheese; the contrast between the salty and the
sweet is sublime. My good friend Lisa Ainbinder graciously shared her mother's
recipe with me after I told her I was having dreams about them.*

*Lisa's mother, Maria, is from Abruzzo, the region of Italy that is directly east of
Lazio and south of Le Marche. Both regions produce wonderful pecorino cheeses
from local sheep, and it is traditional to combine a sweet pastry dough with a
savory pecorino filling. Every year Lisa and her mother make these crescent pastries
for family celebrations, and I am eternally grateful to share this part of her family
history.* **MAKES 24 TO 28 CALCIONI**

FOR THE DOUGH

3 large eggs

½ cup granulated sugar

¼ teaspoon kosher salt

4 tablespoons (½ stick/2 ounces) unsalted
    butter, melted and cooled

½ teaspoon pure vanilla extract

2–2¼ cups unbleached all-purpose flour, plus
    more for rolling

FOR THE FILLING

2 large eggs

1 cup grated Pecorino Romano, or any hard,
    aged sheep's-milk cheese

Freshly grated black pepper

1 egg, lightly beaten, for glaze

To make the dough: In the bowl of an electric mixer, use the paddle attachment on
medium speed to beat the eggs, sugar, and salt together until combined. Add the melted
butter and vanilla extract and beat for a few more seconds. Add 2 cups flour and beat
on low speed to form a soft, smooth dough that does not stick to your fingers; if necessary, add 1 to 2 tablespoons more flour, but take care not to make the dough too stiff.
Cover the bowl with plastic wrap and chill the dough in the refrigerator for 1 hour.

To make the filling: Just before taking the dough out of the refrigerator to roll, beat the
eggs together well with a fork in a small bowl and then stir in the grated cheese and a
few grinds of black pepper. The filling should be moist but not runny; you are basically
moistening the cheese with the eggs.

Preheat the oven to 350°F and position a rack in the center. Prepare two baking sheets
by brushing them lightly with olive oil or spraying them with nonstick cooking spray.

Remove the dough from the refrigerator. On a well-floured work surface, roll the dough to a thickness of about ⅛ inch. Using a 3½- to 4-inch round cutter, cut circles as close together as possible; discard the scraps. (If your work surface is small, divide the dough into 2 pieces and cut the circles in 2 batches.)

Place a heaping teaspoon of the filling slightly off-center on each circle and fold the dough over to form a half-moon shape, pressing the dough together at the edges to seal. Bend the ends toward each other to form a crescent. Using a toothpick, poke 2 tiny holes at the base of the filling mound; this will allow air to escape and prevent the crescents from exploding. For a decorative effect, press the tines of a fork around the border to create a pattern. Place the *calcioni* on the baking sheets, ½ inch apart. Use a small pastry brush to glaze each one with the beaten egg.

Bake the *calcioni* for 12 to 14 minutes, or until they are lightly golden brown; rotate the baking sheets after 7 or 8 minutes to ensure even browning. Using a spatula, transfer the *calcioni* from the baking sheets to a cooling rack.

The *calcioni* are delicious served warm or may be cooled and stored in an airtight container for up to 3 days.

CHEESE PUFFS
bigne con fontina

Gougères are a classic French hors d'oeuvre: puffs of pâte à choux made with Gruyère cheese. Give this concept the Italian treatment and you have bigne, *which are the same kind of dough with a different name, baked with Fontina, a nutty, firm cheese made in the Alpine valleys of Val d'Aosta, in the northwesternmost corner of Italy. Imagine sophisticated ladies in black cocktail dresses nibbling on these from a polished silver tray. Or conjure your neighbors popping them into their mouths on movie night. They will work for either occasion.* MAKES 24 TO 30 CHEESE PUFFS

¾ cup water

4 tablespoons (½ stick/2 ounces) unsalted
   butter, cut into pieces

1 teaspoon kosher salt

Freshly ground black pepper to taste

1 cup unbleached all-purpose flour

4 large eggs, cold

½ teaspoon baking powder

2 cups finely grated Fontina

Preheat the oven to 400°F and position a rack in the center. Prepare two baking sheets by brushing them lightly with olive oil or spraying them with nonstick cooking spray.

In a large saucepan, heat the water, butter, salt, and pepper over medium heat until the butter is melted and the water is simmering. Add the flour all at once and use a heatproof spatula to combine the flour and water into a thick paste. Lower the heat and cook the paste, spreading it along the bottom of the pan and gathering it up into a ball with the spatula. Repeat this procedure for 1 minute, until the paste appears dull and dry and has begun to stick to the bottom of the pan.

Immediately transfer the paste to the bowl of an electric mixer and, using the paddle attachment on medium speed, beat the cold eggs in, one at a time. Be sure each egg is fully incorporated into the dough before adding the next. Scrape down the sides of the bowl after each addition. Add the baking powder and continue to beat the dough until it is completely cool and stiff, about 1 minute, then beat in 1 cup of the Fontina.

Drop the mixture by teaspoonfuls onto the greased baking sheets, 1 inch apart. The batter can also be put into a pastry bag and piped onto the baking sheets in ¾-inch rounds. Place a generous pinch of the remaining grated Fontina on top of each cheese puff. Bake the puffs until they are puffed and golden brown, 12 to 15 minutes, rotating the baking sheets 180° halfway through the baking time to ensure even browning. Remove them from the oven and serve immediately.

MY FAVORITE ITALIAN CHEESES

It has been thrilling to witness the steady arrival of Italian cheeses that were nearly impossible to get in America a decade ago. The influx is the result of basic supply and demand—as interest in and exportation of Italian wines have increased sharply, as more Americans have visited Italy as tourists, and as the concept of authentic Italian cuisine has expanded beyond spaghetti and meatballs, so too has the demand for a wider and more exciting selection of fine cheeses from Italy increased. Like wine, cheese must be tasted and experienced in order for us to understand it fully. The more you know about where the cheese is from, who makes it, and how it is produced, the more pleasure you will take in eating it.

Cheese is enjoying a vogue these days, which has resulted in the appearance of specialty cheese shops in many cities and towns across the United States, and vast cheese departments are popular features of modern, upscale markets. There are also a number of Internet retailers that can deliver an impressive selection of imported cheeses to your doorstep with a few clicks of the mouse (see Sources, pages 285–87).

My experience with Italian cheeses has convinced me that they are absolutely unequaled in terms of variety, quality, and flavor. Some of my very favorite Italian cheeses are ready to step into the spotlight and take their place among Parmigiano-Reggiano, Taleggio, and *mozzarella di bufala*. All of them are being imported into the United States on a wider basis, though some of them may be harder to find than others. Keep in mind that some cheeses are produced seasonally and are therefore available only at certain times of the year. Make friends with your local cheesemonger, and if he or she does not already carry some of my favorites listed here, ask for them!

I like to think of *burrata* as a bundle of creamy, milky heaven. Shaped like a beggar's purse and knotted at the top, it will remind you at first glance of traditional *mozzarella di bufala*. The method for making *burrata* is similar to that for mozzarella; the outer layer is formed of stretched mozzarella-like cheese curd. It is the contents of the pouch that will make you swoon. Give the *burrata* a gentle poke and it will reveal a mound of soft, loose curd oozing with cream, with a rich, melting texture and mild, buttery flavor. *Burrata* is originally from Puglia, but producers in Campania and Basilicata are joining the ranks and answering the demand for this ever-popular cheese. I have sampled *burrata* made from both cow's milk and buffalo's milk; both are wonderful, but the buffalo variety has the edge on creaminess. *Burrata* has a very limited shelf life, and it reaches the United States only by air; the best purveyors offer it for sale only within two or three days of its production. You may find the pouches wrapped in a green leaf of *asfodelo*, a plant native to Puglia that is similar to the leek. If the leaf remains green, the *burrata* inside will still be fresh. My favorite way to enjoy *burrata* is with a drizzle

(continued on next page)

of the finest extra-virgin olive oil, but it is also delicious with fresh plums or peaches or a few drops of *vincotto*.

I love the story behind *Stracchino Crescenza*, a delightfully soft and creamy fresh cow's-milk cheese from Lombardy. *Stracchino* was once a term associated with an entire family of Italian cheeses, including Taleggio, with a history that reaches as far back as the twelfth century. The original *stracchino* was made from the milk of cows that spent their summers grazing on Alpine mountainsides and then migrated down to the valleys to pass the brutal winter. Their twice-yearly journey made the cows justifiably tired, or *stracca*, and the milk they produced at the end of each trip was supposedly distinctively different. Today's *Stracchino Crescenza* is made from cows that lead a far less strenuous life; although it still has a noticeable tang, the texture is incredibly rich and buttery. *Crescenza* is a perfect breakfast cheese when partnered with a dollop of jam or preserves, and for dessert it is wonderful with ripe summer berries. My favorite accompaniment, however, is either fresh or poached pears and few whisper-thin slices of prosciutto. *Stracchino Crescenza* is a delicate fresh cheese with a very short shelf life, so buy it and enjoy it right away.

A vast number of small, soft-ripened cheeses with blooming rinds are classified as *robiola*. They are produced almost exclusively in Piedmont and Lombardy and can be made from all or a combination of cow's, sheep's, and goat's milk. The best *robiole* are still traditionally made from unpasturized milk; regarded as contraband here in the United States, they do not easily or often make it out of Italy. To my delight, I discovered a selection of *robiole* from a small producer from the Langhe area of Piedmont that has been producing and exporting some excellent pasteurized versions. Caseificio dell'Alta Langa is located in a small town south of Alba, and its cheeses are about as good as pasteurized *robiola* can get—rich and creamy, with subtle notes of soil, grass, mushrooms, vanilla, and spice. I am particularly fond of its Rochetta, which is made from cow's and goat's milk; it has a gorgeous, rippled, blooming rind and a creamy white interior. La Tur is another favorite, made with cow's, sheep's, and goat's milk in the shape of a plump cupcake, with a texture that is oozing and runny just under the rind, firm and chalky in the center. Bosina is shaped into a flattish square, with a straw-colored interior that is satiny-smooth and has the penetrating flavor of the damp, grassy earth. *Robiola* is best enjoyed with the red wines of Piedmont, some crusty bread, and thinly sliced apples.

Fresh goat cheeses are made in a number of regions of Italy, including Friuli–Venezia Giulia, Abruzzo, Sardinia, and Lombardy, all bearing the general name of *caprino fresco*. Italian goat cheeses are anything but ordinary, rivaling the best *chèvres* of France—dense and creamy, with that unmistakable goaty tang and bright, grassy flavor. My favorites are shaped into plump little disks and rolled in herbs or red pepper or marinated in extra-virgin olive oil. I can make an entire meal from *caprino fresco*, a selection of cured olives, sliced salami, and crusty bread. Pair it with some fresh strawberries or cherries and some *aceto balsamico tradizionale* and you have an instant and perfect no-fuss dessert on a balmy summer night. I also love to toss fresh Italian goat cheese with hot pasta or crumble it into omelets. As with the finest *robiole*, the greatest Italian goat cheeses are made with unpasteurized milk and rarely travel beyond the local shops and markets. Luckily, the exported, pasteurized versions that you can find in the United States are pretty special too. Aged goat cheeses from Italy may be labeled *caprino stagionato*; they are a bit harder to find but equally delicious.

The word *pecorino* can be used to describe any aged cheese made entirely from sheep's milk, and many fine varieties of pecorino are made in a number of Italian regions, including Tuscany, Umbria, Le Marche, Abruzzo, Lazio, and Sardinia. Most Americans first become acquainted with Pecorino Toscano, but another fine pecorino is now available here and ready to capture your heart as it did mine—Pecorino Dolce Sardo. The word *dolce* refers to the grassy sweetness of the milk it is made from. *Sardo* refers to its region of origin, the rugged island of Sardinia, where seven million sheep graze the rough terrain. Pecorino Dolce Sardo has a brighter, fruitier flavor than its Tuscan cousin and less of the rich nuttiness. A youthful, semisoft cheese is aged for two months, while an older cheese may be up to six months old, with a firmer texture and a slightly salty edge. This is another great cheese for serving with ripe pears, a pile of crisp green grapes, or a glass of the glorious white wine of Sardinia, Vermentino di Sardegna.

The Piave River rises in the Carnic Alps, which line the border between Italy and Austria, flows through the Italian region of the Veneto, and eventually empties into the Gulf of Venice. Along the way it passes through a pristine Alpine valley and into the plains of Treviso. In these areas, herds of cows graze to produce the milk for an absolutely fabulous cheese that takes its name from that very same river, Piave. The cheese is made in the town of Belluno, which lies between the Piave River and the other great river of the Veneto, the Ardo. Tradition dictates that the milk must be obtained from both the morning and evening milkings, which contributes to its huge and distinctive flavor profile. Piave is shaped into large, shallow wheels and salted in a bath of brine. After maturing for two months, it is still considered young; after six months, it reaches my favorite age, known as *mezzo*. The texture resembles that of a great cheddar, soft but chewy, filling your mouth with a melting, nutty creaminess. After one year, the cheese becomes known as Piave Vecchio (aged); the flavor transitions from big to enormous and the texture takes on the firm, slightly granular nature of Parmigiano-Reggiano. Piave is one of those sturdy cheeses that can stand up to the crunch of an apple, a substantial cracker,

(continued on next page)

or thick-crusted bread. Once I start eating it, I can't seem to stop.

When you spot *Castelmagno DOP* at your local cheese shop, it will most likely be a milky white color. In actuality, *Castelmagno* is a cow's-milk cheese that develops a character-istic blue mold when it is allowed to mature to its full potential. At whatever age you come across it, do give it a try; it will reveal its spe-cial qualities right away. *Castelmagno* is one of the greatest DOP cheeses produced within the region of Piedmont, in the southwestern prov-ince of Cuneo. The super-crumbly texture is achieved by a specific method of finely cutting, pressing, and recutting the curds to remove all the whey. The curds are then pressed into a tall, fat cylinder; the cheese is dry-rubbed with salt and aged in a damp cave. The result is a cheese with a unique, slightly sour flavor that develops from the small amount of goat's milk that is added. *Castelmagno* is often crumbled onto pasta with fresh truffles or stirred into a steaming pot of risotto or polenta. When it is eaten as a table cheese, the perfume creeps from your nose directly into your throat, beg-ging you to pop a huge, juicy purple grape into your mouth.

If you are afraid even to try a stinky blue-veined cheese, I say to you now, give *gorgonzola cremificato* a chance. Also known as *gorgonzola dolce*, it is a very mild, entirely approachable blue cheese that truly deserves a place of honor on your next cheese board. Although the blue vein-ing comes from *Penicillium roqueforti*, the strain of bacteria that is present in the spicy *gorgonzola picante*, it is gentler and subtler in *gorgonzola cremificato*, delicately weaving its way through the rich, creamy, ivory-col-ored interior of the cheese. "Creamy" is the operative word here, and with good reason; *gorgonzola cremificato* is rich, rich, rich, with an almost reflective sheen that glistens in the light. Made from cow's milk, the curds are barely cut and then molded while they are still wet and heavy with whey. As with all blue varieties, the cheeses are punctured with long copper needles that introduce the air that is necessary to spur the growth of the mold. In the case of *cremificato*, the soft, moist, dense texture allows only a minimal amount of air to penetrate, which results in the light and feathery tangle of blue veining. *Gorgonzola cremificato* is easier to spread than it is to cut, and my favorite way to enjoy it is to slather it on a slice of dense wheat bread and drizzle it with honey. It is also a perfect match with sweet and heady Muscat grapes, juicy red cherries, and warm toasted walnuts. All gorgonzolas are DOP cheeses; the area of production encompasses portions of both Piedmont and Lombardy.

DiPalo Dairy
200 Grand St. (at Mott St.)
New York, NY 10013
212-226-1033

Lou DiPalo and his family sell their own fresh ricotta, along with an impressive array of imported Italian cheeses, including mascarpone. You can also find Italian honey, olive oil, jams, jellies, *amaretti*, and a wealth of other treasures. I especially love the Italian candy bars! In the heart of Little Italy, this is a must-stop for anyone visiting New York.

Murray's Cheese
254 Bleecker St. (between 6th and 7th Ave.)
New York, NY 10014
212-243-3289
1-888-MY-CHEEZ (692–4339)
www.murrayscheese.com

Murray's has an unbelievable selection of domestic and imported cheeses, including Calabro ricotta, Vermont Butter & Cheese Co. mascarpone, and lots of Italian specialty products. They can process orders the same day for overnight shipment and will ship to the continental United States, Hawaii, Alaska, and Puerto Rico.

Accademia Barilla
http://shop.us.academiabarilla.com

Based in Parma, Accademia Barilla's mission is to protect, develop, and promote Italian gastronomy and culture around the world. Its online store offers a wealth of Italian products that are unique and fulfill its mission. It offers a wide array of cheeses, olive oils, *aceto balsamico* (both *tradizionale* and *condimento*), and a limited selection of cured meats.

The Rogers Collection
10 Dana St.
Portland, ME 04101
207-828-2000
www.rogersintl.com

Rogers International specializes in unique and exclusive products from Italy and Spain, including the finest cheeses, vinegars, oils, honey, and condiments from small farmers and artisans.

Calabro Cheese Corporation
580 Coe Ave.
P.O. Box 120186
East Haven, CT 06512
203-469-1311
www.calabrocheese.com

Calabro makes fresh, creamy ricotta that is near and dear to my heart. Call to find retailers of its cheese near you.

Vermont Butter & Cheese Company
P.O. Box 95, 40 Pitman Rd.
Websterville, VT 05678
1-800-884-6287
www.vtbutterandcheeseco.com

A line of fresh cheese products truly worthy of seeking out, especially the incredible mascarpone. Call to find retailers of its cheeses in your area.

Manicaretti Italian Food Importers
1-800-799-9830
www.manicaretti.com

This San Fransisco–based company imports olive oils, honey, and other specialty items from Italy for the sweet pantry. The website will guide you to a number of retail sources for in-person or online purchase of the products.

(continued on next page)

Formaggio Kitchen
244 Huron Ave.
Cambridge, MA 02138
617-354-4750
1-888-212-3224
http://formaggio-kitchen.com
Formaggio Essex Market
Essex Street Market
120 Essex St.
New York, NY 10002
212-982-8200

An institution in Cambridge for over 20 years, Formaggio Kitchen is one of the best sources of unique European specialty products. Their selection of Italian cheeses comes only from small, artisan producers, and they have an impressive array of Italian honey, jams, marmalades, and other delectable accompaniments. Their newest store, in the Essex Street Market on the Lower East Side of Manhattan, is sure to become a regular haunt for New York foodies.

Zingerman's
620 Phoenix Dr.
Ann Arbor, MI 48108
1-888-636-8162
www.zingermans.com

If you find yourself in Ann Arbor, do not leave without visiting this company's deli, bakehouse, creamery, and all-around heavenly food emporium on Detroit St. The owners search the globe for the finest products and deliver them to your doorstep, and aim to educate as well as delight their customers. You can find some of the finest Italian olive oils, honeys, cheeses, polenta, Arborio rice, and other assorted delicacies in their mail-order catalog or on their excellent website.

Mike's Deli
Arthur Avenue Retail Market
2344 Arthur Avenue
Bronx, NY 10458
718-295-5033
1-866-2-SALAMI (725264)

Ask me where the real Little Italy is in New York, and I will tell you it is on Arthur Avenue in the Bronx. Tucked inside the Arthur Avenue Market is Mike's Deli, the heart and soul of Arthur Avenue for over 50 years. This place is so much more than the name implies. It also happens to be a family affair, tended by my beloved cousin David Greco alongside his father, the namesake and family patriarch, Michele. What will you find here? Just about any Italian product you can think of. They make a mean sandwich, too.

The Baker's Catalogue, King Arthur Flour
58 Billings Farm Rd.
White River Junction, VT 05001
1-800-827-6836
www.bakerscatalogue.com
www.kingarthurflour.com

This is the ultimate source for baking and dessert enthusiasts. You can find not only every kind of flour and baking ingredient you'll ever need but also a great selection of cookware, appliances, and tableware.

L'Epicerie
1-866-350-7575
www.lepicerie.com

I am a big fan of this company, which offers a treasure trove of items for the enthusiastic cook and baker. Hard-to-find pastry items, many imported and previously available only for professionals, are found here, including fine chocolates, nuts, fruit purees, olive oils, and jams and jellies. Specialty bakeware is also available. Hint: You'll find Piedmontese hazelnuts here too.

Kalustyan's
123 Lexington Ave.
New York, NY 10016
212-685-3451
www.kalustyans.com

Another destination that belongs on any passionate cook's or gourmand's list of places to visit, in person or online. If it is hard to find, exotic, or unusual, you will find it at Kalustyan's, the New York emporium of flavor.

Bazzini
200 Food Center Dr.
Bronx, NY 10474
1-800-228-0172
www.bazzininuts.com

Every nut imaginable is here, as well as dried fruits. Everything is packed fresh and shipped quickly. You can even buy in bulk, which is especially handy during the holidays!

DaVero
1195 Westside Rd.
Healdsburg, CA 95448
1-888-431-8008
www.davero.com

DaVero's Dry Creek Estate Extra Virgin Olive Oil is superlative. The company has an excellent website that offers a wealth of information about olive oil production, and you can order its oils online, as well as other fine products such as jams, preserves, marmalades, and dipping dishes for oils.

Italian Wine Merchants
108 East 16th St.
New York, NY10003
212-473-2323
www.italianwinemerchant.com

It's all in the family. My esteemed employers, Joe Bastianich and Mario Batali, share ownership of this fantastic Italian wine shop with managing partner Sergio Esposito. Just off of Union Square, Italian Wine Merchants is for the collector and enthusiast alike. Its selection of Italian wines includes fine grappa and Italian dessert wines.

Vino Italian Wine and Spirits
121 East 27th St.
New York, NY 10016
212-725-6516
1-800-965-VINO (8466)
www.vinosite.com

You will find an incredibly large and informed list of fine grappa and sweet wines at this shop and website, to accommodate every budget and occasion. You may contact the company directly about shipment arrangements or visit in person when in New York.

ABOUT THE AUTHOR

Gina DePalma grew up in a close-knit Italian family, and learned to cook alongside her mother and grandmother. She worked in several top New York restaurants, including the Gramercy Tavern and the Cub Room, before being hired as the opening pastry chef at Babbo in 1998. She has been nominated for the James Beard Foundation's Outstanding Pastry Chef Award. This is her first book. DePalma lives in New York City.

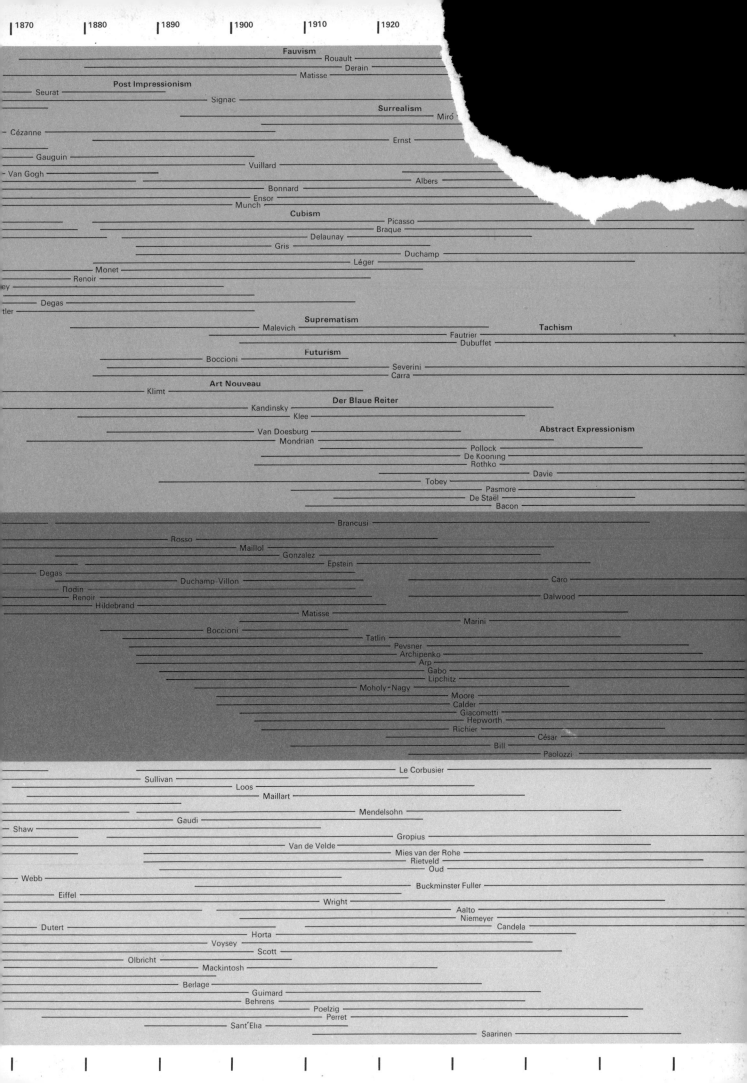